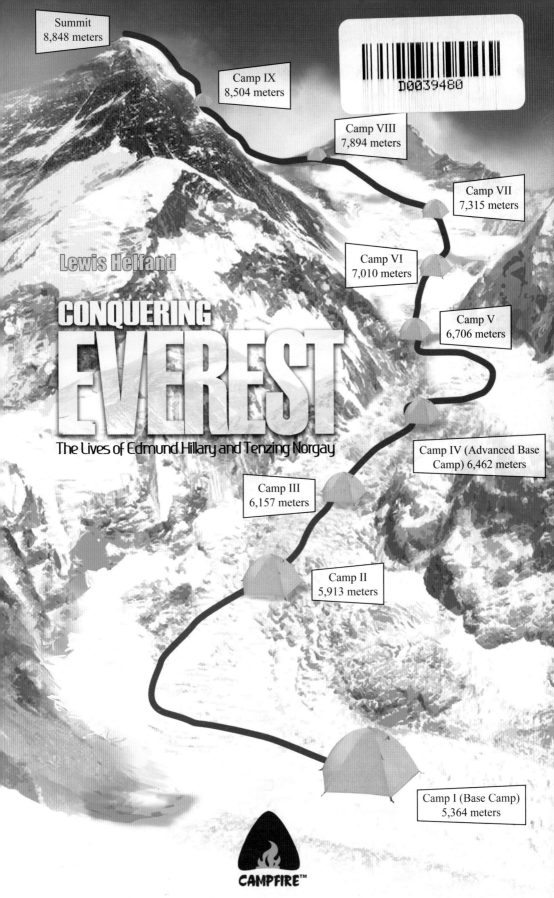

Summit
8,848 meters

Camp IX
8,504 meters

Camp VIII
7,894 meters

Camp VII
7,315 meters

Camp VI
7,010 meters

Camp V
6,706 meters

Camp IV (Advanced Base
Camp) 6,462 meters

Camp III
6,157 meters

Camp II
5,913 meters

Camp I (Base Camp)
5,364 meters

Lewis Helfand

CONQUERING
EVEREST
The Lives of Edmund Hillary and Tenzing Norgay

CAMPFIRE™

KALYANI NAVYUG MEDIA PVT LTD
New Delhi

CONQUERING EVEREST

The Lives of Edmund Hillary and Tenzing Norgay

Sitting around the Campfire, telling the story, were:

AUTHOR **LEWIS HELFAND**

ILLUSTRATOR **AMIT TAYAL**

COLORIST **AJO KURIAN**

LETTERER **BHAVANATH CHAUDHARY**

EDITORS **SUPARNA DEB & ADITI RAY**

EDITOR (INFORMATIVE CONTENT) **RASHMI MENON**

PRODUCTION CONTROLLER **VISHAL SHARMA**

ART DIRECTOR **RAJESH NAGULAKONDA**

COVER ART **AMIT TAYAL & JAYAKRISHNAN K. P.**

DESIGNERS **VIJAY SHARMA**

CAMPFIRE™

www.campfire.co.in

Published by Kalyani Navyug Media Pvt. Ltd.
101 C, Shiv House, Hari Nagar Ashram, New Delhi 110014, India

ISBN: 978-93-80741-24-6

Printed in India at Rave India

ABOUT THE AUTHOR

Lewis Helfand was born on April 27, 1978 in Philadelphia, and grew up in nearby Narberth, Pennsylvania. Although interested in cartoons and animation from a young age, by the time he was twelve, Lewis's focus had turned to writing. After completing high school, he remained in the Philadelphia area with the intention of pursuing a degree in English.

Four years later, with a degree in Political Science and a passion for comic books, Lewis began working for local publishers, proofreading books and newspaper articles. At the age of twenty-four, Lewis had been editing phone books for a year and a half, and felt no closer to his lifelong goal of writing comic books. So, one day, he decided to quit his job.

Lewis then spent the next two months working day and night to write and draw his first comic book, *Wasted Minute*. It tells the story of a world without crime where superheroes are forced to work regular jobs. To cover the cost of self-publishing, he began working odd jobs in offices and restaurants, and started exhibiting his book at local comic-book conventions. With the first issue received well, he was soon collaborating with other artists, and released four more issues over the next few years.

Outside the field of comic books, Lewis works as a freelance writer and reporter for a number of national print and online publications. He has covered everything from sports and travel to politics and culture for magazines such as *Renaissance*, *American Health and Fitness*, and *Computer Bits*.

Lewis is one of Campfire's most prolific writers, having adapted many Western classics, written several biographies, and scripted the original titles *400 BC* and *Photo Booth*.

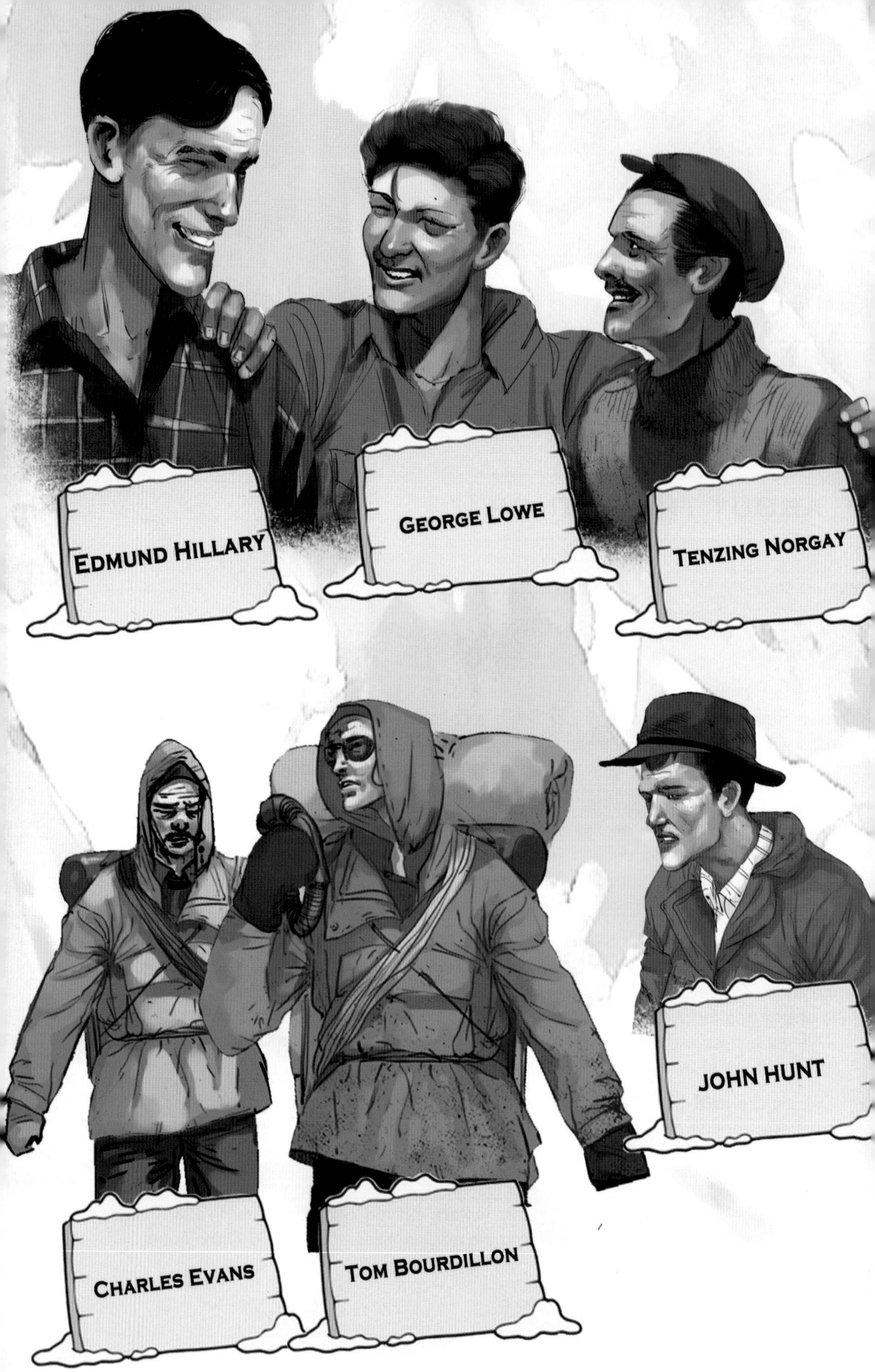
EDMUND HILLARY
GEORGE LOWE
TENZING NORGAY
CHARLES EVANS
TOM BOURDILLON
JOHN HUNT

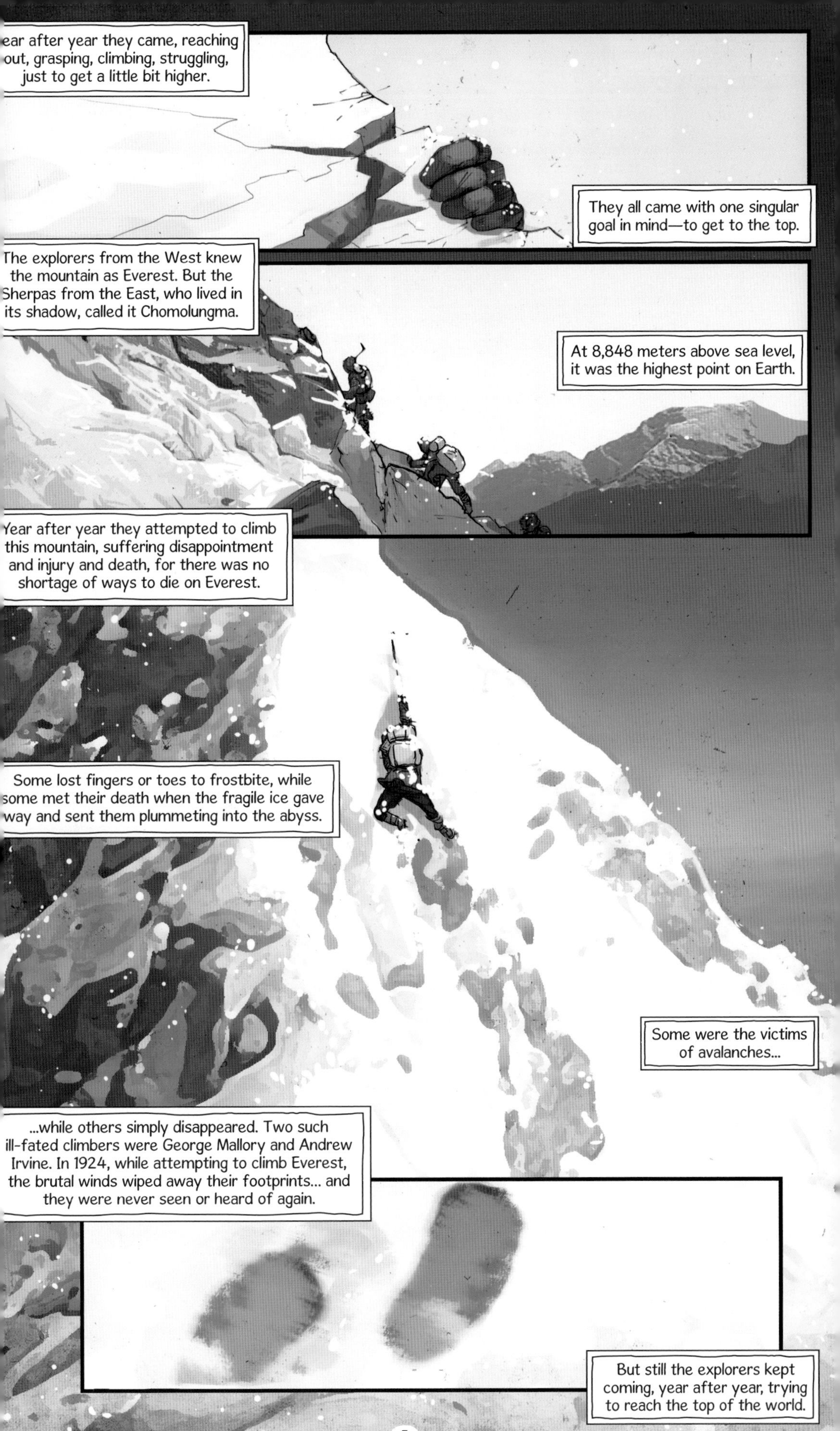
ear after year they came, reaching out, grasping, climbing, struggling, just to get a little bit higher.
They all came with one singular goal in mind—to get to the top.
The explorers from the West knew the mountain as Everest. But the Sherpas from the East, who lived in its shadow, called it Chomolungma.
At 8,848 meters above sea level, it was the highest point on Earth.
Year after year they attempted to climb this mountain, suffering disappointment and injury and death, for there was no shortage of ways to die on Everest.
Some lost fingers or toes to frostbite, while some met their death when the fragile ice gave way and sent them plummeting into the abyss.
Some were the victims of avalanches...
...while others simply disappeared. Two such ill-fated climbers were George Mallory and Andrew Irvine. In 1924, while attempting to climb Everest, the brutal winds wiped away their footprints... and they were never seen or heard of again.
But still the explorers kept coming, year after year, trying to reach the top of the world.

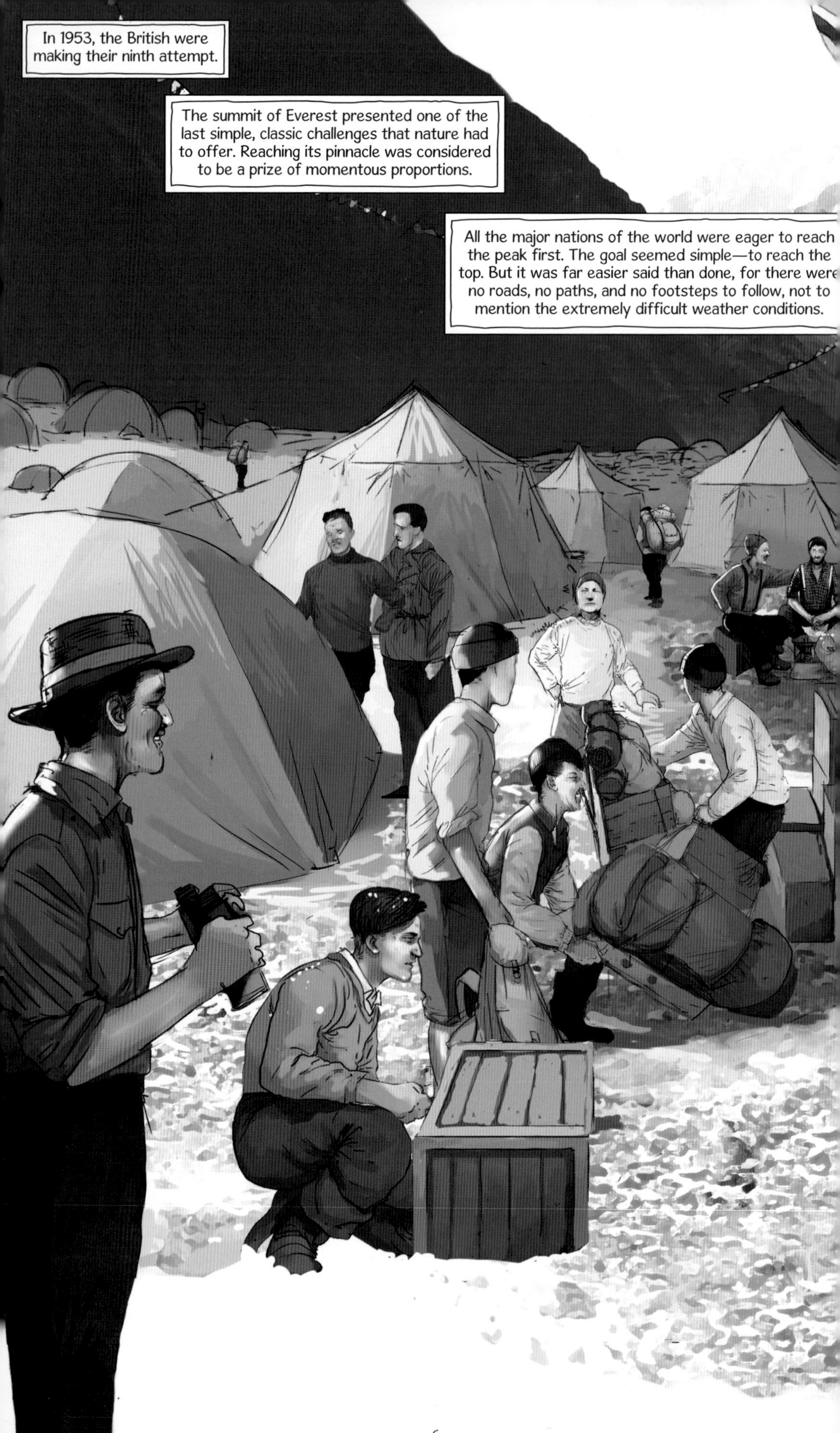
In 1953, the British were making their ninth attempt.
The summit of Everest presented one of the last simple, classic challenges that nature had to offer. Reaching its pinnacle was considered to be a prize of momentous proportions.
All the major nations of the world were eager to reach the peak first. The goal seemed simple—to reach the top. But it was far easier said than done, for there were no roads, no paths, and no footsteps to follow, not to mention the extremely difficult weather conditions.

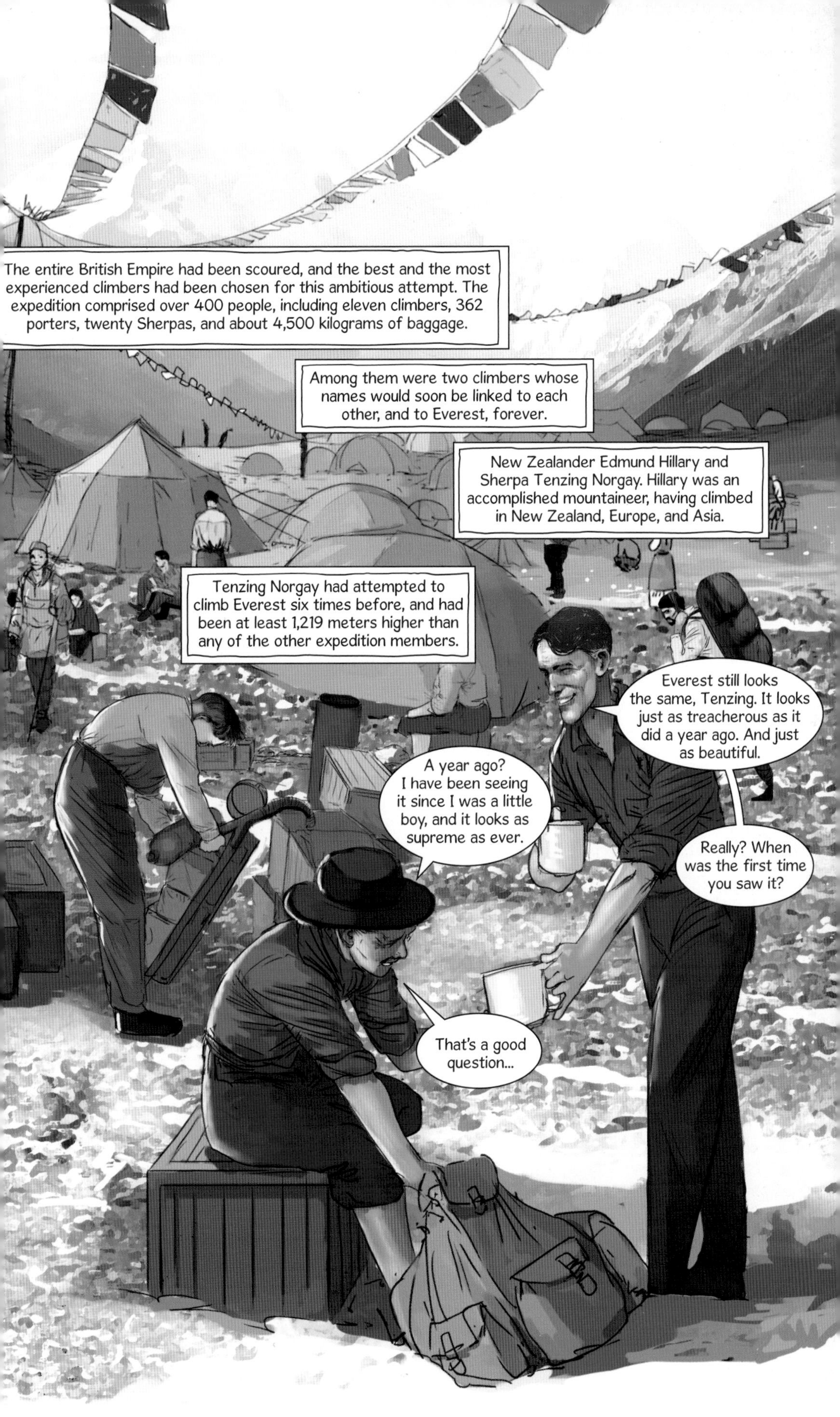
The entire British Empire had been scoured, and the best and the most experienced climbers had been chosen for this ambitious attempt. The expedition comprised over 400 people, including eleven climbers, 362 porters, twenty Sherpas, and about 4,500 kilograms of baggage.
Among them were two climbers whose names would soon be linked to each other, and to Everest, forever.
New Zealander Edmund Hillary and Sherpa Tenzing Norgay. Hillary was an accomplished mountaineer, having climbed in New Zealand, Europe, and Asia.
Tenzing Norgay had attempted to climb Everest six times before, and had been at least 1,219 meters higher than any of the other expedition members.
Everest still looks the same, Tenzing. It looks just as treacherous as it did a year ago. And just as beautiful.
A year ago? I have been seeing it since I was a little boy, and it looks as supreme as ever.
Really? When was the first time you saw it?
That's a good question...

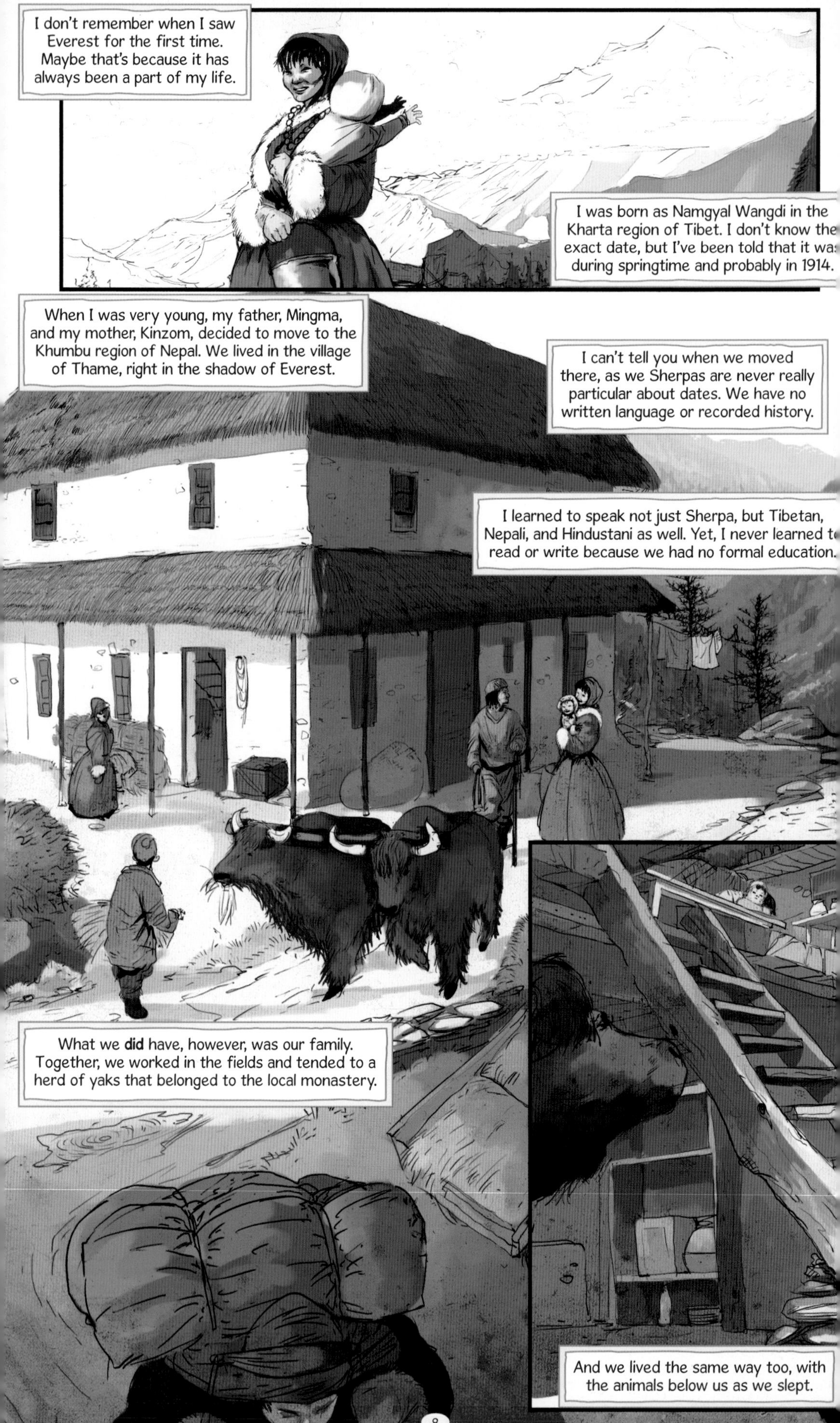
I don't remember when I saw Everest for the first time. Maybe that's because it has always been a part of my life.
I was born as Namgyal Wangdi in the Kharta region of Tibet. I don't know the exact date, but I've been told that it was during springtime and probably in 1914.
When I was very young, my father, Mingma, and my mother, Kinzom, decided to move to the Khumbu region of Nepal. We lived in the village of Thame, right in the shadow of Everest.
I can't tell you when we moved there, as we Sherpas are never really particular about dates. We have no written language or recorded history.
I learned to speak not just Sherpa, but Tibetan, Nepali, and Hindustani as well. Yet, I never learned to read or write because we had no formal education.
What we **did** have, however, was our family. Together, we worked in the fields and tended to a herd of yaks that belonged to the local monastery.
And we lived the same way too, with the animals below us as we slept.

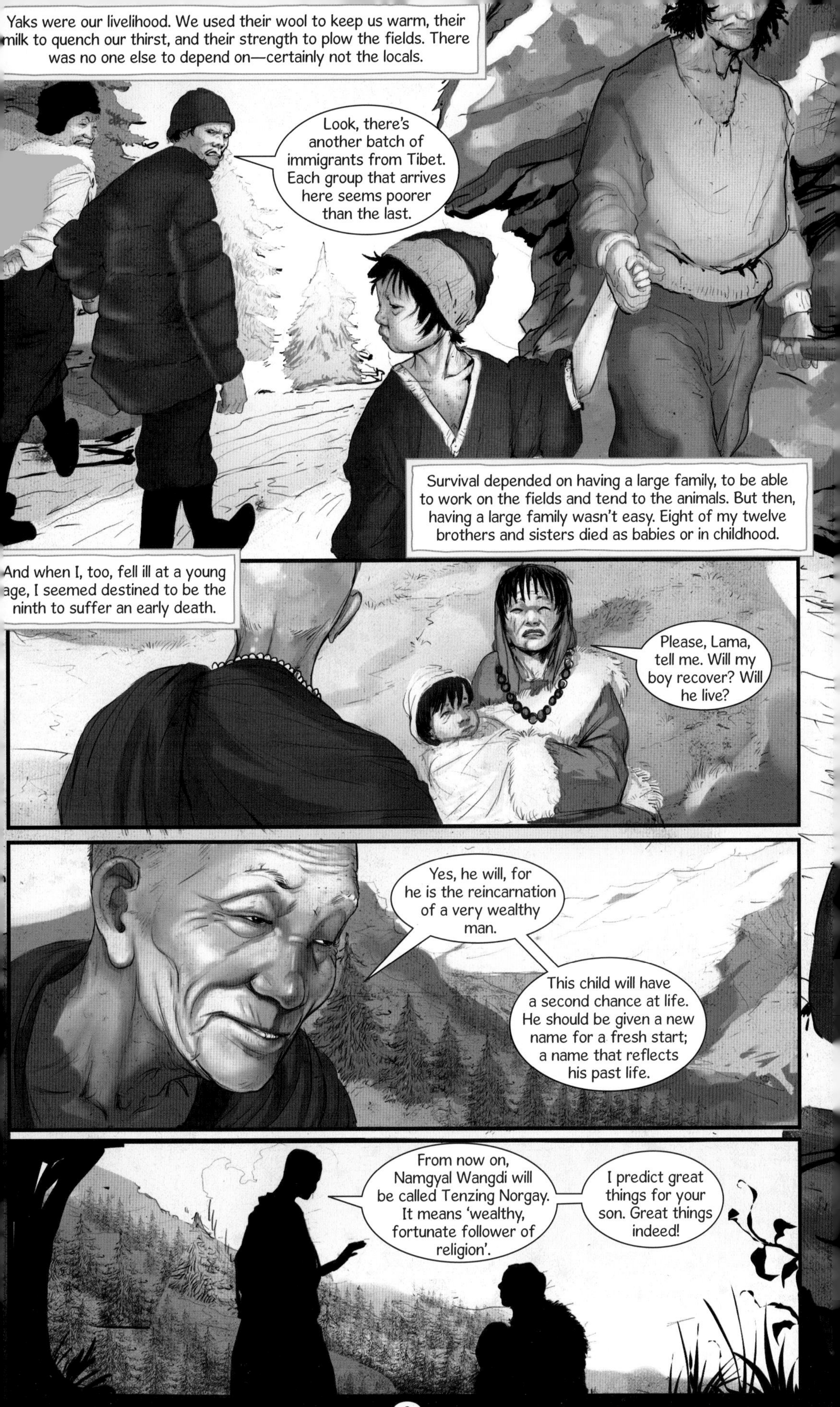
Yaks were our livelihood. We used their wool to keep us warm, their milk to quench our thirst, and their strength to plow the fields. There was no one else to depend on—certainly not the locals.
Look, there's another batch of immigrants from Tibet. Each group that arrives here seems poorer than the last.
Survival depended on having a large family, to be able to work on the fields and tend to the animals. But then, having a large family wasn't easy. Eight of my twelve brothers and sisters died as babies or in childhood.
And when I, too, fell ill at a young age, I seemed destined to be the ninth to suffer an early death.
Please, Lama, tell me. Will my boy recover? Will he live?
Yes, he will, for he is the reincarnation of a very wealthy man.
This child will have a second chance at life. He should be given a new name for a fresh start; a name that reflects his past life.
From now on, Namgyal Wangdi will be called Tenzing Norgay. It means 'wealthy, fortunate follower of religion'.
I predict great things for your son. Great things indeed!

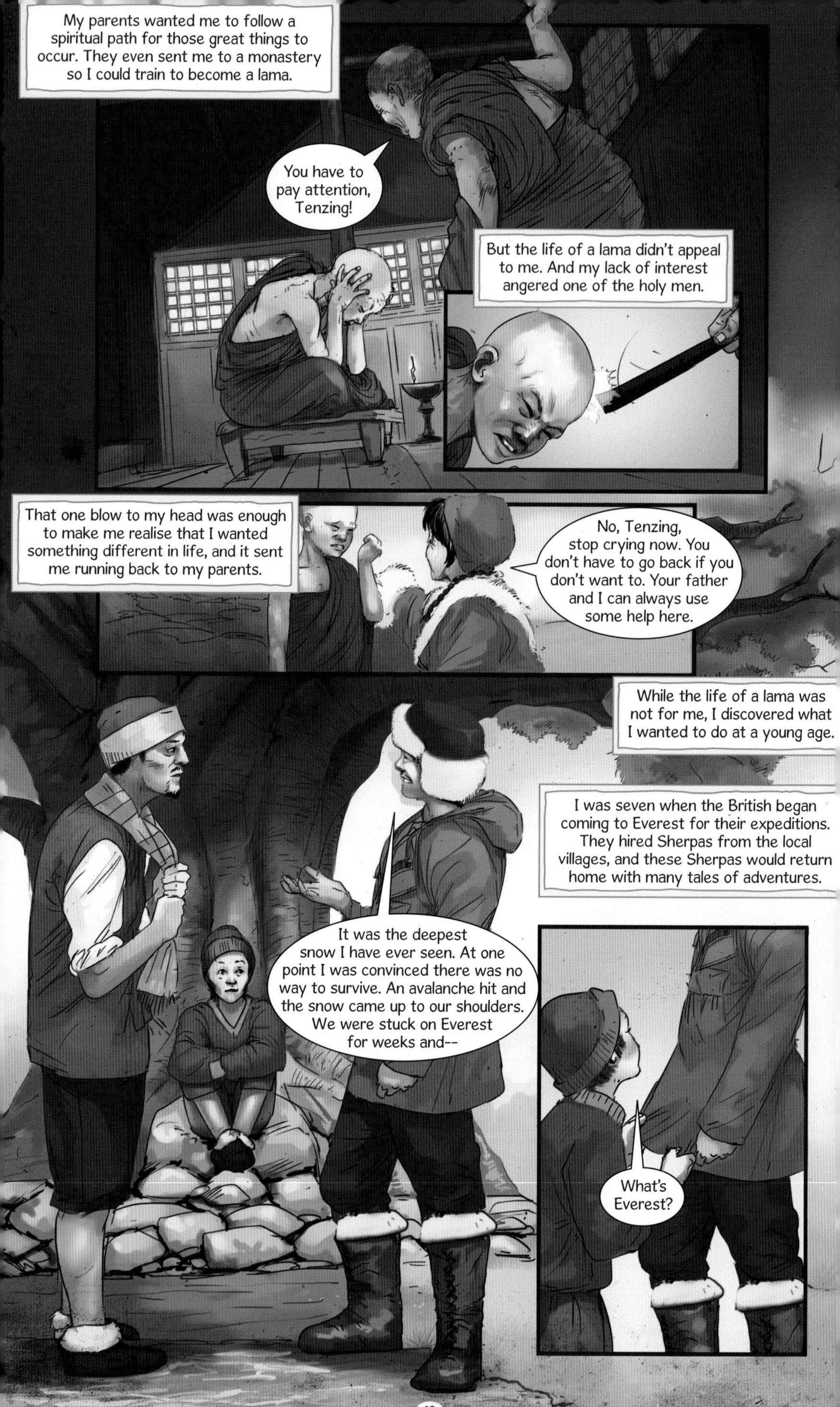

My parents wanted me to follow a spiritual path for those great things to occur. They even sent me to a monastery so I could train to become a lama.
You have to pay attention, Tenzing!
But the life of a lama didn't appeal to me. And my lack of interest angered one of the holy men.
That one blow to my head was enough to make me realise that I wanted something different in life, and it sent me running back to my parents.
No, Tenzing, stop crying now. You don't have to go back if you don't want to. Your father and I can always use some help here.
While the life of a lama was not for me, I discovered what I wanted to do at a young age.
I was seven when the British began coming to Everest for their expeditions. They hired Sherpas from the local villages, and these Sherpas would return home with many tales of adventures.
It was the deepest snow I have ever seen. At one point I was convinced there was no way to survive. An avalanche hit and the snow came up to our shoulders. We were stuck on Everest for weeks and--
What's Everest?

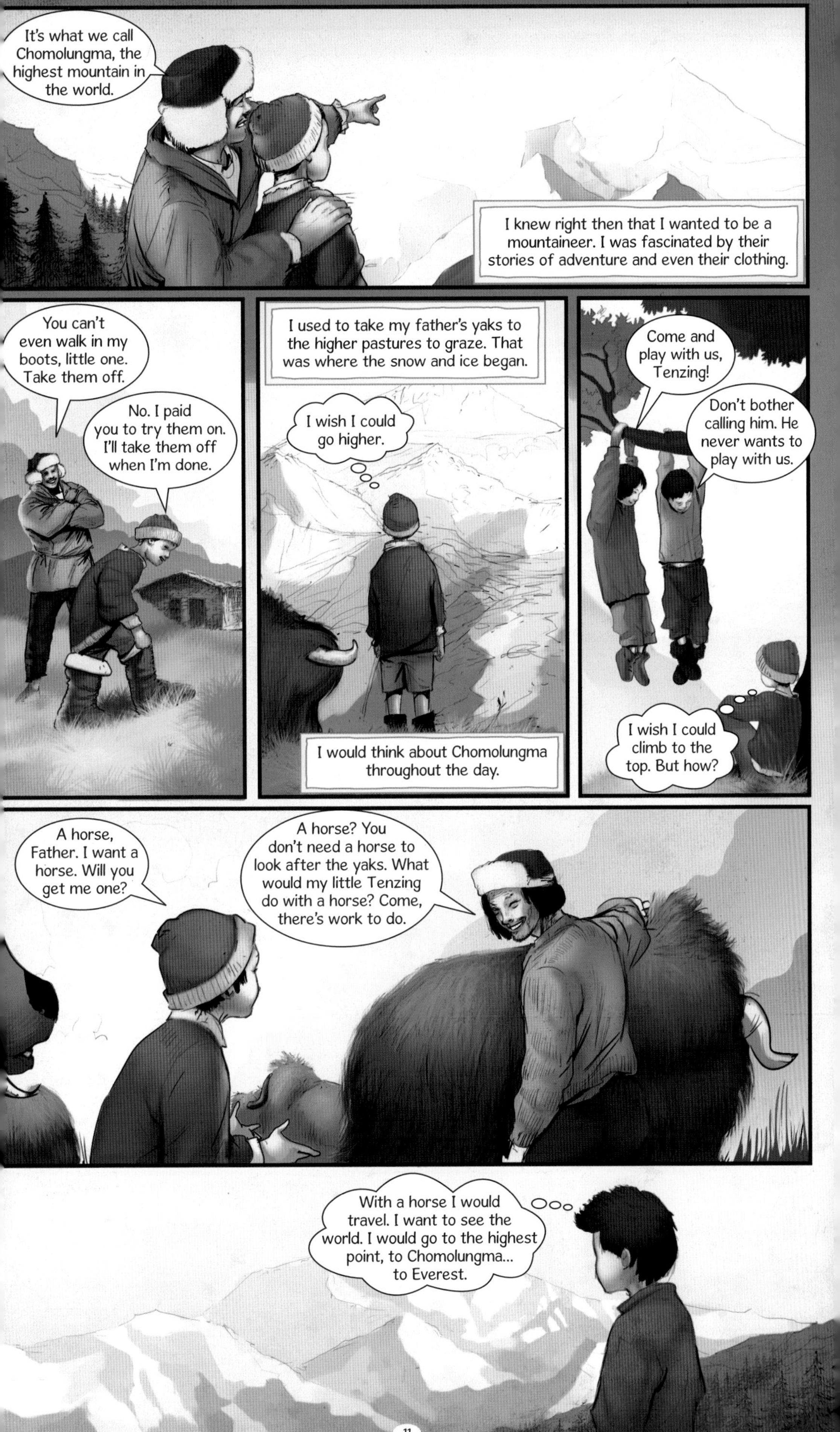
It's what we call Chomolungma, the highest mountain in the world.
I knew right then that I wanted to be a mountaineer. I was fascinated by their stories of adventure and even their clothing.
You can't even walk in my boots, little one. Take them off.
No. I paid you to try them on. I'll take them off when I'm done.
I used to take my father's yaks to the higher pastures to graze. That was where the snow and ice began.
I wish I could go higher.
I would think about Chomolungma throughout the day.
Come and play with us, Tenzing!
Don't bother calling him. He never wants to play with us.
I wish I could climb to the top. But how?
A horse, Father. I want a horse. Will you get me one?
A horse? You don't need a horse to look after the yaks. What would my little Tenzing do with a horse? Come, there's work to do.
With a horse I would travel. I want to see the world. I would go to the highest point, to Chomolungma... to Everest.

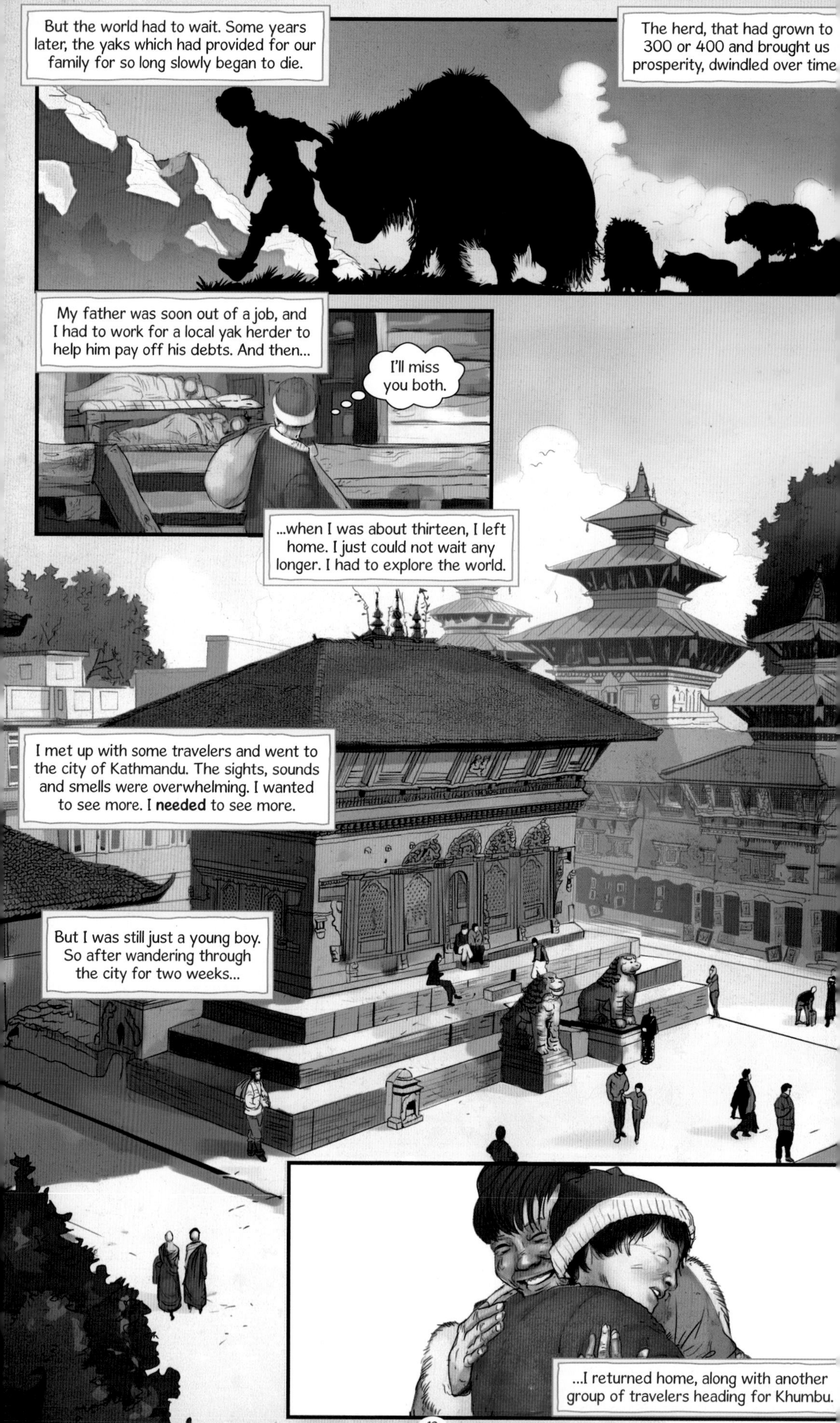
But the world had to wait. Some years later, the yaks which had provided for our family for so long slowly began to die.
The herd, that had grown to 300 or 400 and brought us prosperity, dwindled over time
My father was soon out of a job, and I had to work for a local yak herder to help him pay off his debts. And then...
I'll miss you both.
...when I was about thirteen, I left home. I just could not wait any longer. I had to explore the world.
I met up with some travelers and went to the city of Kathmandu. The sights, sounds and smells were overwhelming. I wanted to see more. I **needed** to see more.
But I was still just a young boy. So after wandering through the city for two weeks...
...I returned home, along with another group of travelers heading for Khumbu.

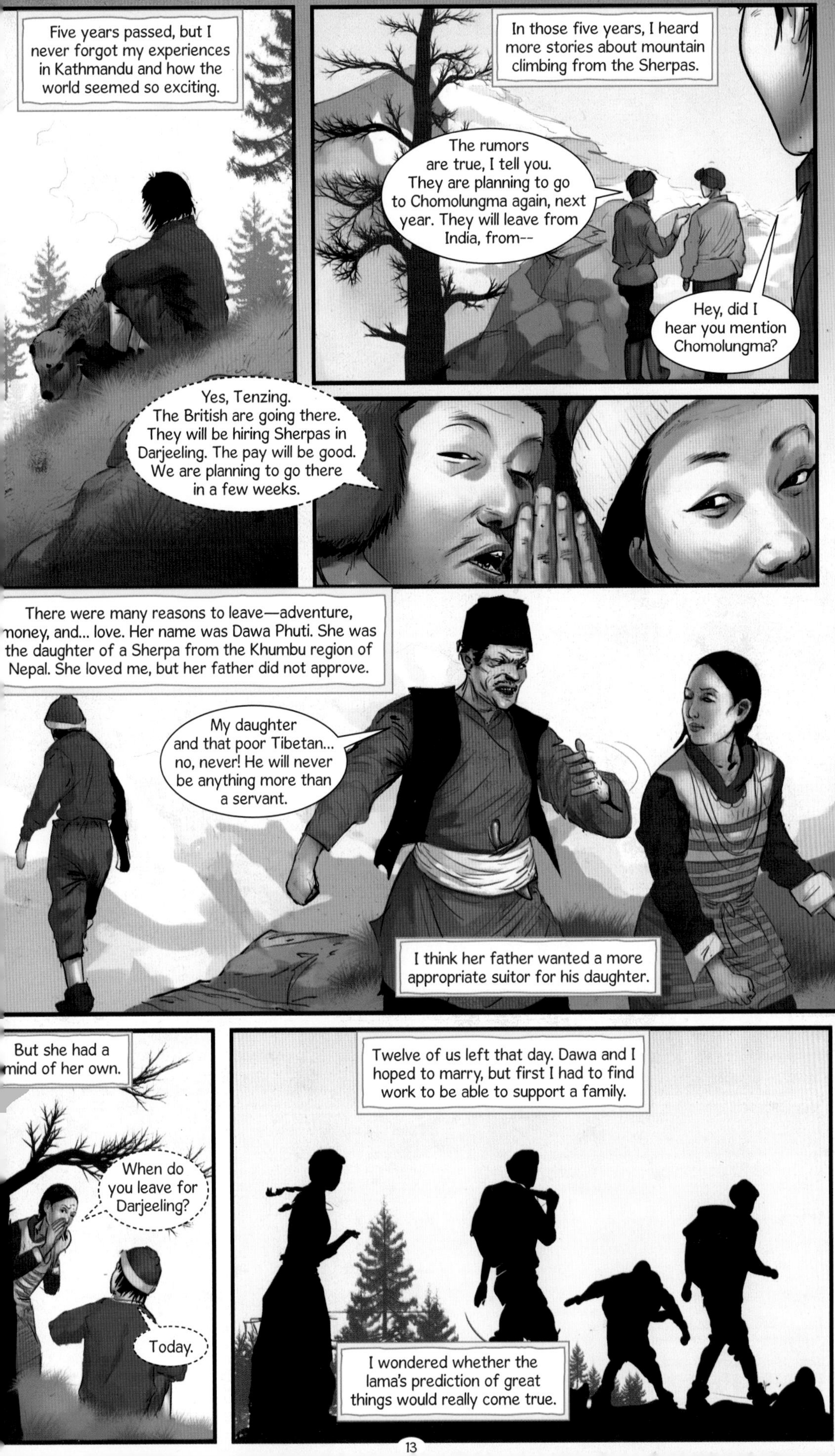

Five years passed, but I never forgot my experiences in Kathmandu and how the world seemed so exciting.
In those five years, I heard more stories about mountain climbing from the Sherpas.
The rumors are true, I tell you. They are planning to go to Chomolungma again, next year. They will leave from India, from--
Hey, did I hear you mention Chomolungma?
Yes, Tenzing. The British are going there. They will be hiring Sherpas in Darjeeling. The pay will be good. We are planning to go there in a few weeks.
There were many reasons to leave—adventure, money, and... love. Her name was Dawa Phuti. She was the daughter of a Sherpa from the Khumbu region of Nepal. She loved me, but her father did not approve.
My daughter and that poor Tibetan... no, never! He will never be anything more than a servant.
I think her father wanted a more appropriate suitor for his daughter.
But she had a mind of her own.
When do you leave for Darjeeling?
Today.
Twelve of us left that day. Dawa and I hoped to marry, but first I had to find work to be able to support a family.
I wondered whether the lama's prediction of great things would really come true.

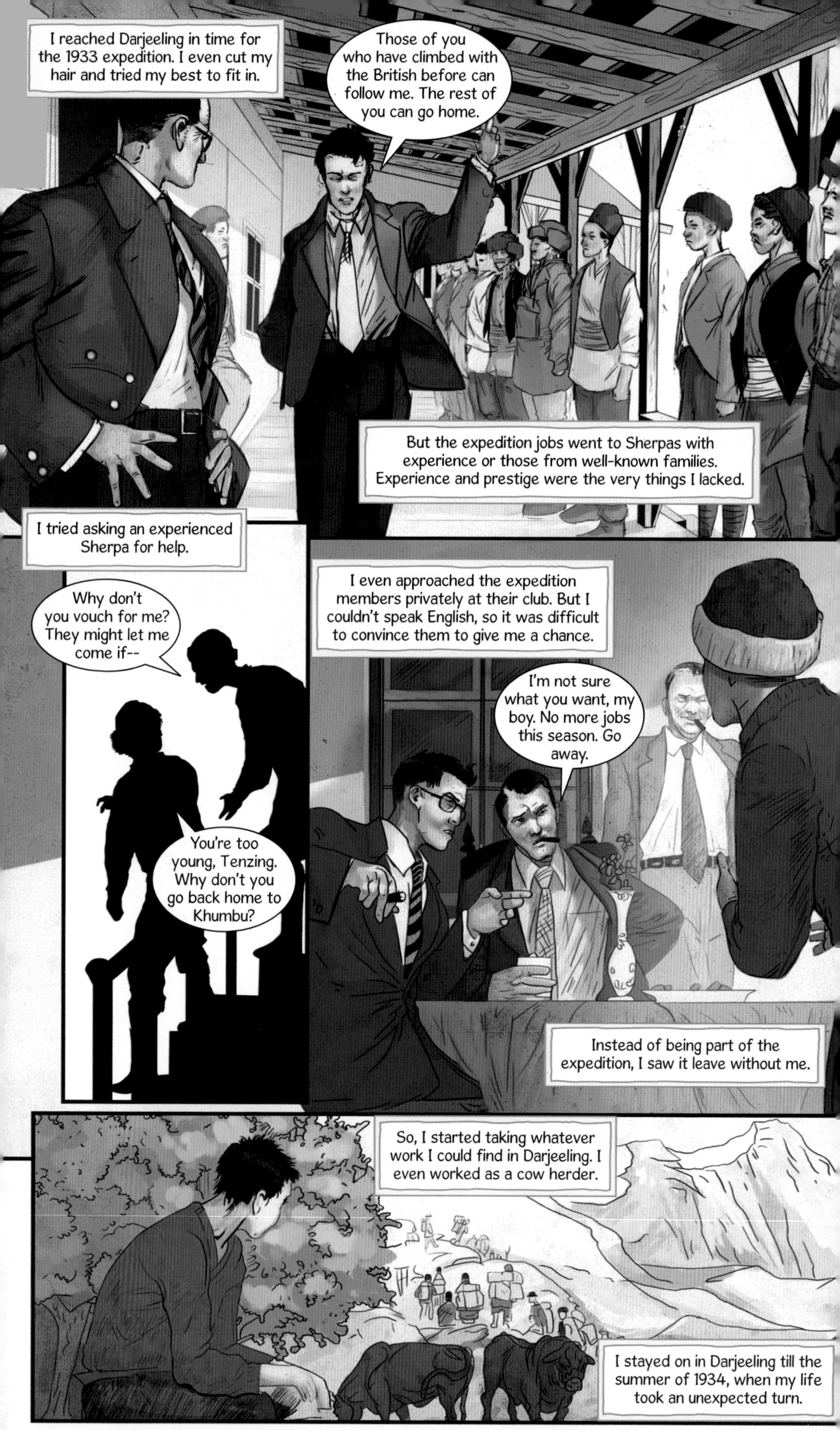
I reached Darjeeling in time for the 1933 expedition. I even cut my hair and tried my best to fit in.
Those of you who have climbed with the British before can follow me. The rest of you can go home.
But the expedition jobs went to Sherpas with experience or those from well-known families. Experience and prestige were the very things I lacked.
I tried asking an experienced Sherpa for help.
Why don't you vouch for me? They might let me come if--
You're too young, Tenzing. Why don't you go back home to Khumbu?
I even approached the expedition members privately at their club. But I couldn't speak English, so it was difficult to convince them to give me a chance.
I'm not sure what you want, my boy. No more jobs this season. Go away.
Instead of being part of the expedition, I saw it leave without me.
So, I started taking whatever work I could find in Darjeeling. I even worked as a cow herder.
I stayed on in Darjeeling till the summer of 1934, when my life took an unexpected turn.

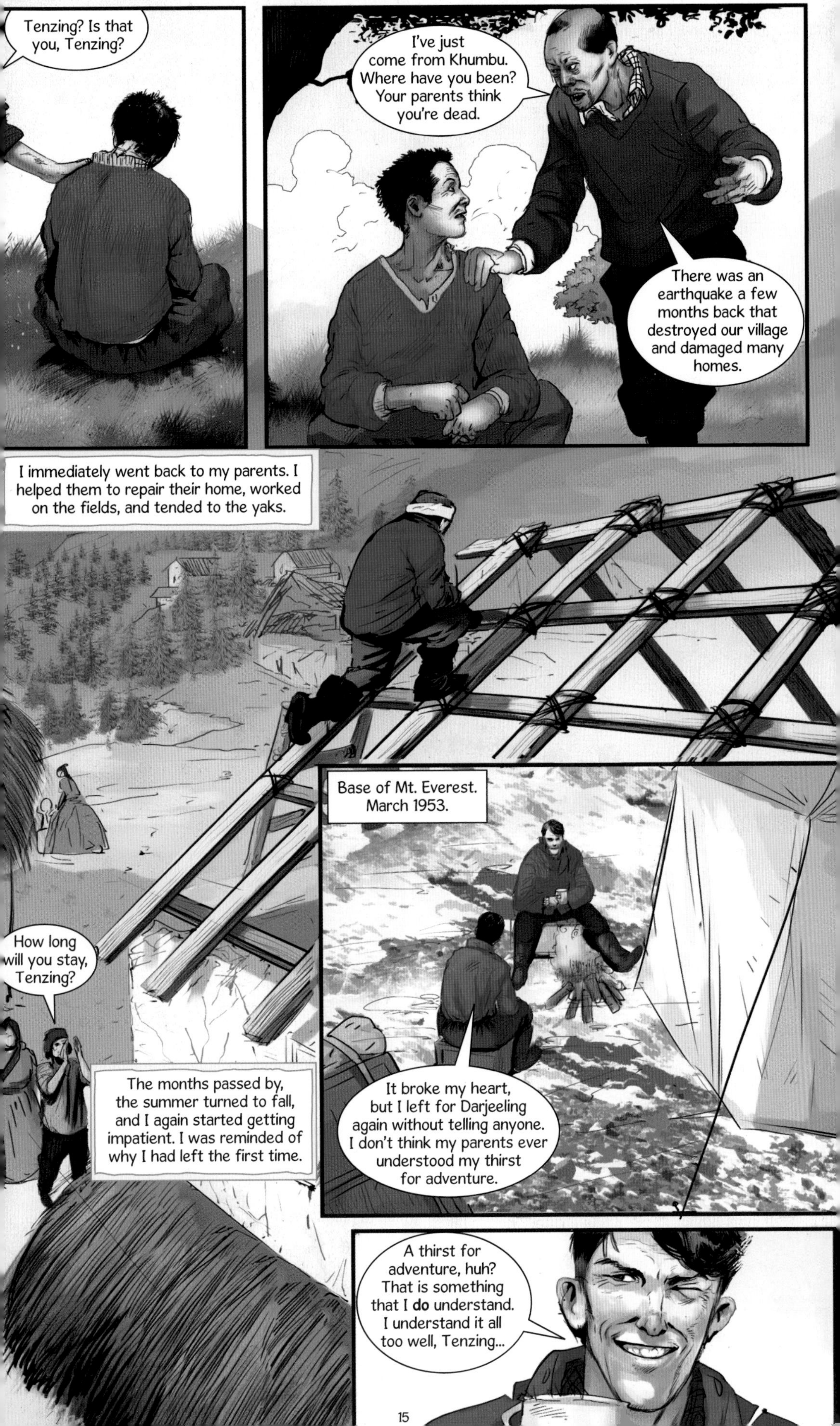

Tenzing? Is that you, Tenzing?
I've just come from Khumbu. Where have you been? Your parents think you're dead.
There was an earthquake a few months back that destroyed our village and damaged many homes.
I immediately went back to my parents. I helped them to repair their home, worked on the fields, and tended to the yaks.
How long will you stay, Tenzing?
The months passed by, the summer turned to fall, and I again started getting impatient. I was reminded of why I had left the first time.
Base of Mt. Everest. March 1953.
It broke my heart, but I left for Darjeeling again without telling anyone. I don't think my parents ever understood my thirst for adventure.
A thirst for adventure, huh? That is something that I **do** understand. I understand it all too well, Tenzing...

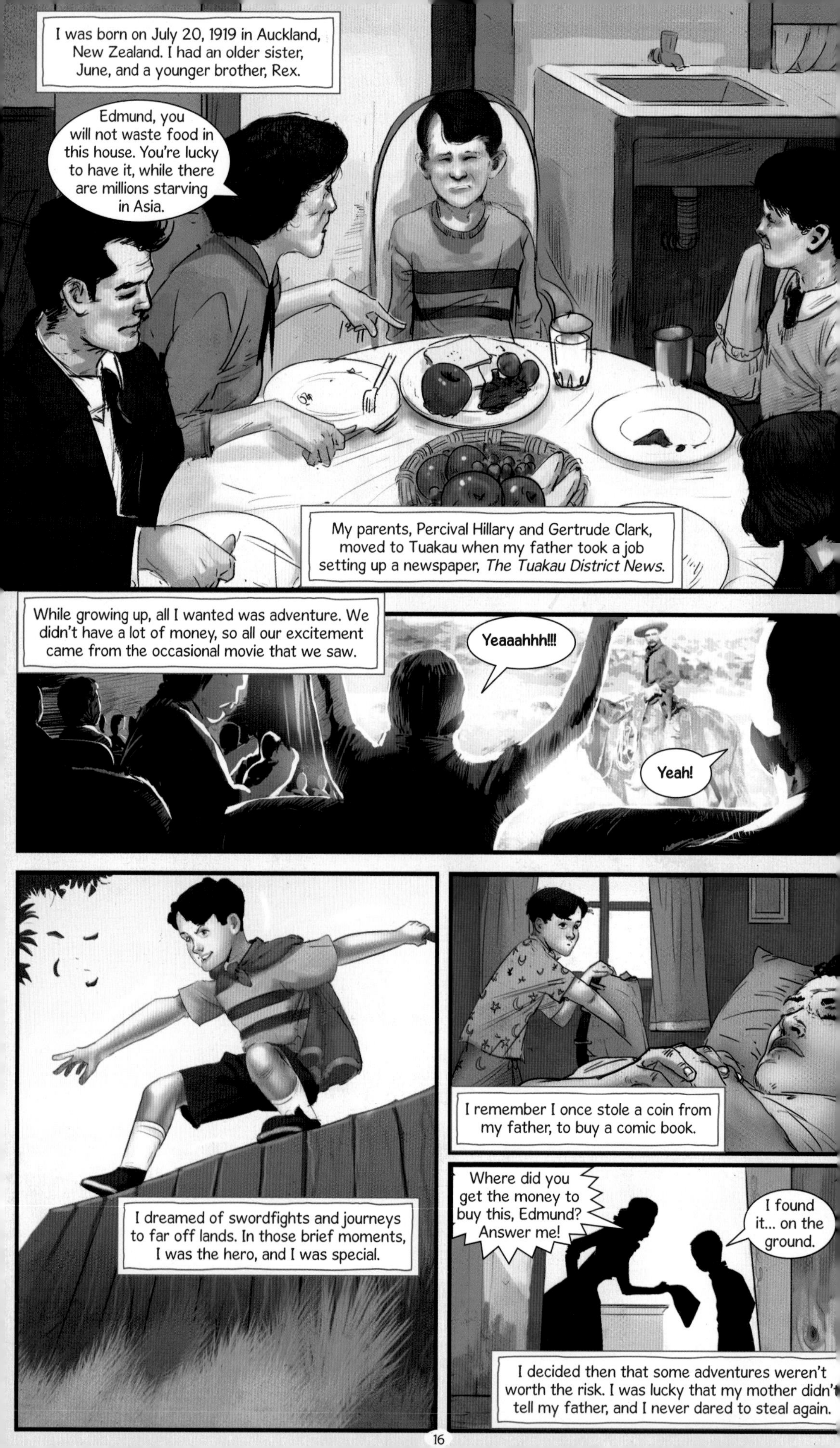
I was born on July 20, 1919 in Auckland, New Zealand. I had an older sister, June, and a younger brother, Rex.
Edmund, you will not waste food in this house. You're lucky to have it, while there are millions starving in Asia.
My parents, Percival Hillary and Gertrude Clark, moved to Tuakau when my father took a job setting up a newspaper, *The Tuakau District News*.
While growing up, all I wanted was adventure. We didn't have a lot of money, so all our excitement came from the occasional movie that we saw.
Yeaaahhh!!!
Yeah!
I dreamed of swordfights and journeys to far off lands. In those brief moments, I was the hero, and I was special.
I remember I once stole a coin from my father, to buy a comic book.
Where did you get the money to buy this, Edmund? Answer me!
I found it... on the ground.
I decided then that some adventures weren't worth the risk. I was lucky that my mother didn't tell my father, and I never dared to steal again.

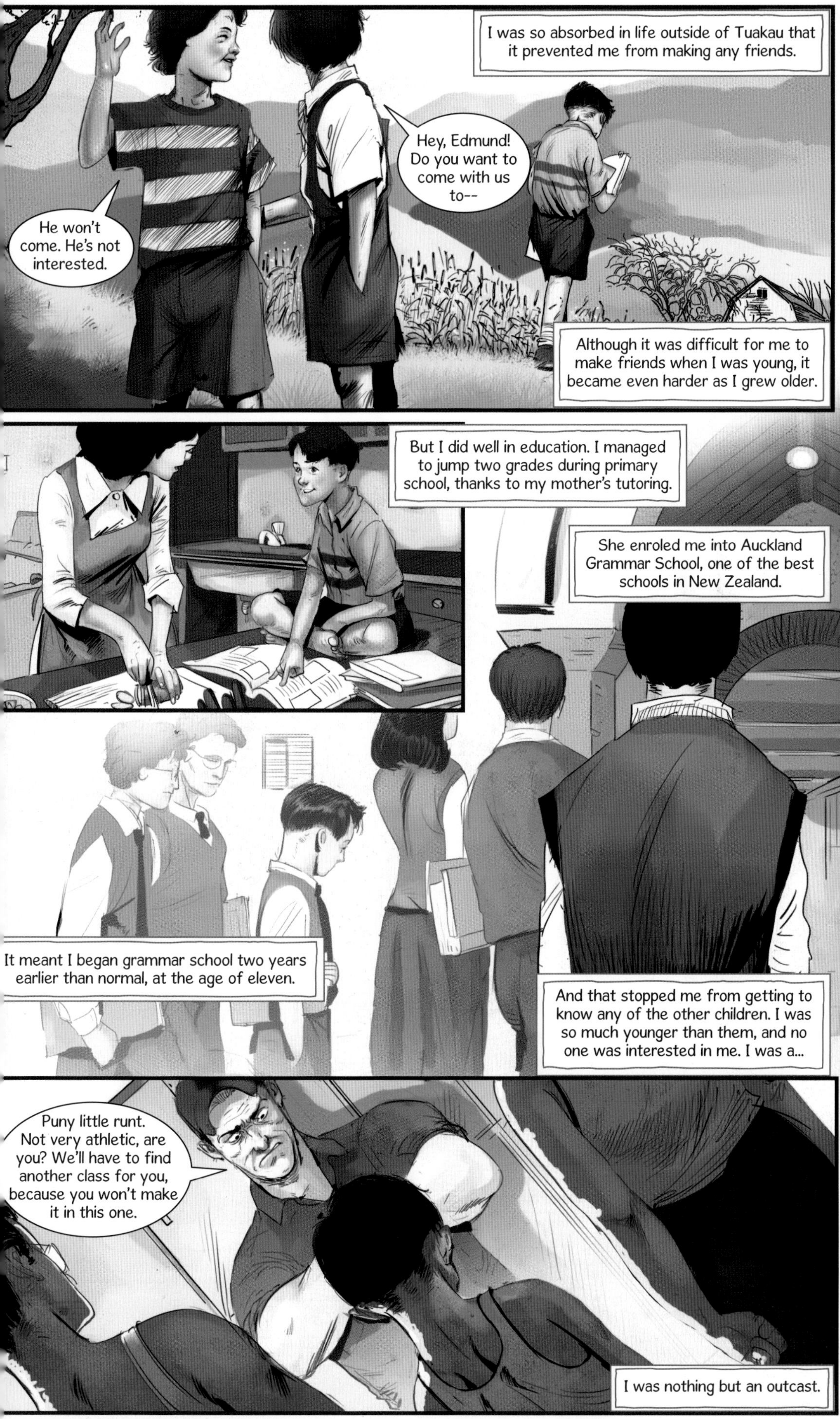

I was so absorbed in life outside of Tuakau that it prevented me from making any friends.
Hey, Edmund! Do you want to come with us to--
He won't come. He's not interested.
Although it was difficult for me to make friends when I was young, it became even harder as I grew older.
But I did well in education. I managed to jump two grades during primary school, thanks to my mother's tutoring.
She enroled me into Auckland Grammar School, one of the best schools in New Zealand.
It meant I began grammar school two years earlier than normal, at the age of eleven.
And that stopped me from getting to know any of the other children. I was so much younger than them, and no one was interested in me. I was a...
Puny little runt. Not very athletic, are you? We'll have to find another class for you, because you won't make it in this one.
I was nothing but an outcast.

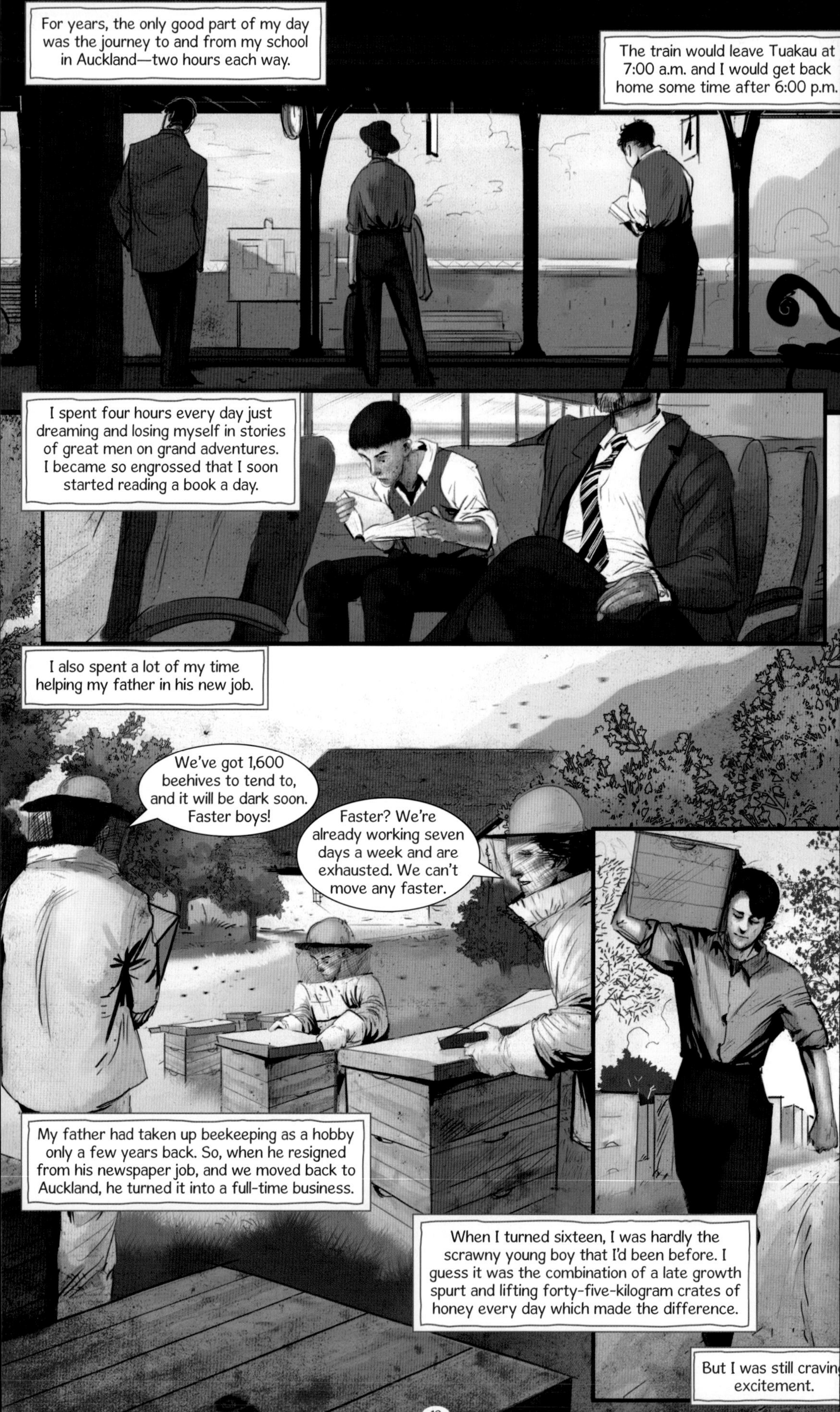
For years, the only good part of my day was the journey to and from my school in Auckland—two hours each way.
The train would leave Tuakau at 7:00 a.m. and I would get back home some time after 6:00 p.m.
I spent four hours every day just dreaming and losing myself in stories of great men on grand adventures. I became so engrossed that I soon started reading a book a day.
I also spent a lot of my time helping my father in his new job.
We've got 1,600 beehives to tend to, and it will be dark soon. Faster boys!
Faster? We're already working seven days a week and are exhausted. We can't move any faster.
My father had taken up beekeeping as a hobby only a few years back. So, when he resigned from his newspaper job, and we moved back to Auckland, he turned it into a full-time business.
When I turned sixteen, I was hardly the scrawny young boy that I'd been before. I guess it was the combination of a late growth spurt and lifting forty-five-kilogram crates of honey every day which made the difference.
But I was still craving excitement.

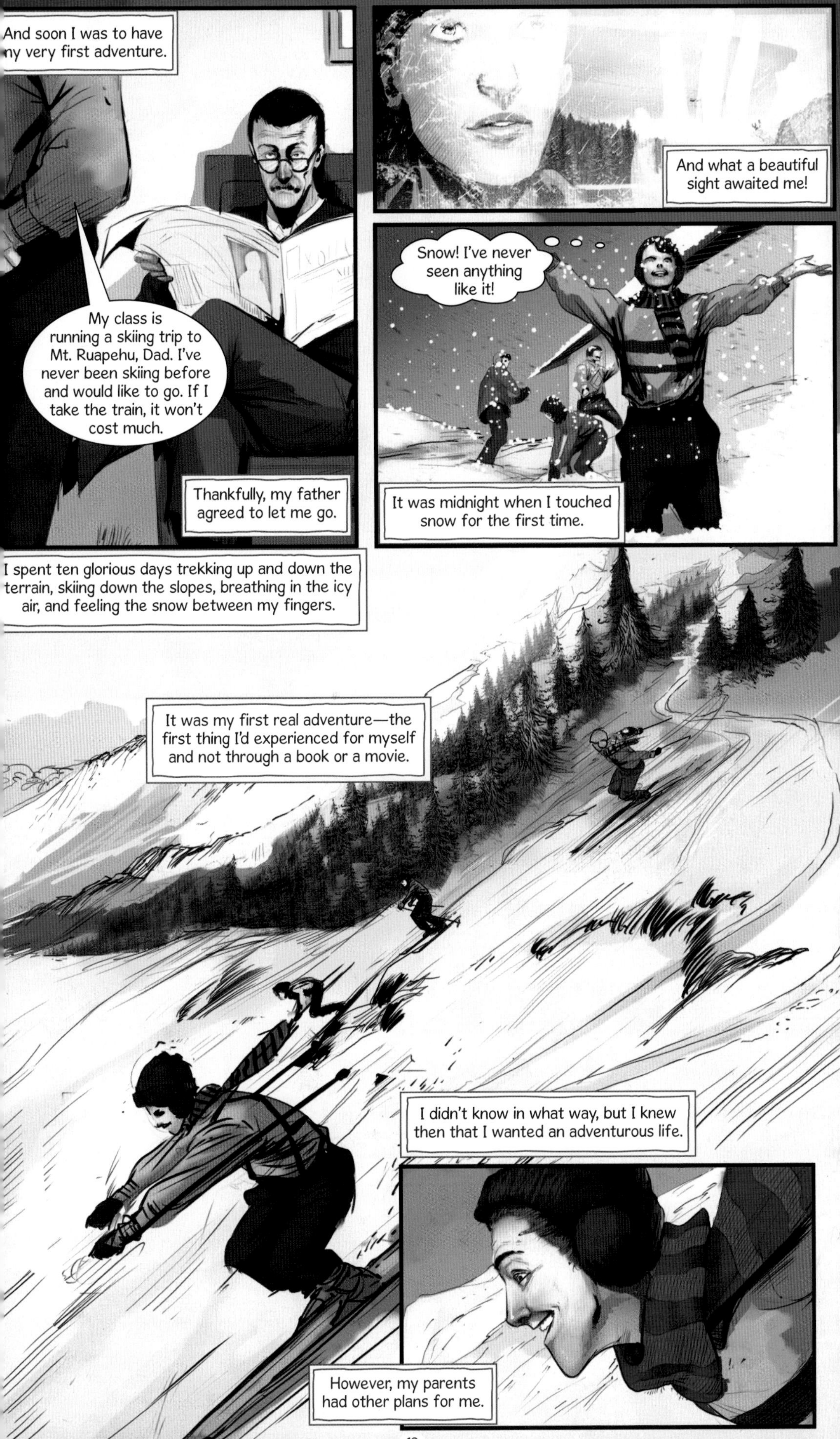
And soon I was to have my very first adventure.
My class is running a skiing trip to Mt. Ruapehu, Dad. I've never been skiing before and would like to go. If I take the train, it won't cost much.
Thankfully, my father agreed to let me go.
And what a beautiful sight awaited me!
Snow! I've never seen anything like it!
It was midnight when I touched snow for the first time.
I spent ten glorious days trekking up and down the terrain, skiing down the slopes, breathing in the icy air, and feeling the snow between my fingers.
It was my first real adventure—the first thing I'd experienced for myself and not through a book or a movie.
I didn't know in what way, but I knew then that I wanted an adventurous life.
However, my parents had other plans for me.

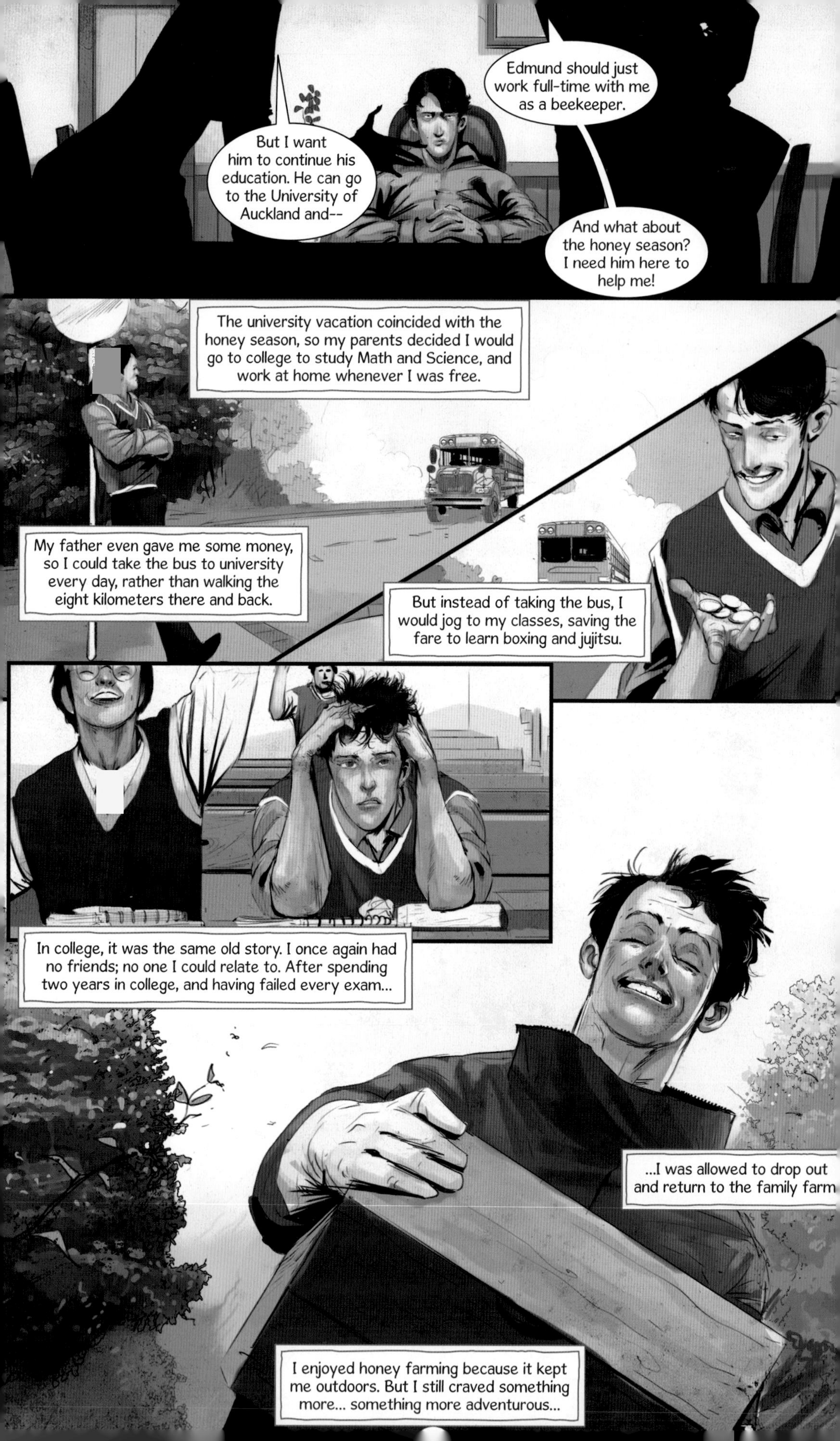

Edmund should just work full-time with me as a beekeeper.
But I want him to continue his education. He can go to the University of Auckland and--
And what about the honey season? I need him here to help me!
The university vacation coincided with the honey season, so my parents decided I would go to college to study Math and Science, and work at home whenever I was free.
My father even gave me some money, so I could take the bus to university every day, rather than walking the eight kilometers there and back.
But instead of taking the bus, I would jog to my classes, saving the fare to learn boxing and jujitsu.
In college, it was the same old story. I once again had no friends; no one I could relate to. After spending two years in college, and having failed every exam...
...I was allowed to drop out and return to the family farm
I enjoyed honey farming because it kept me outdoors. But I still craved something more... something more adventurous...

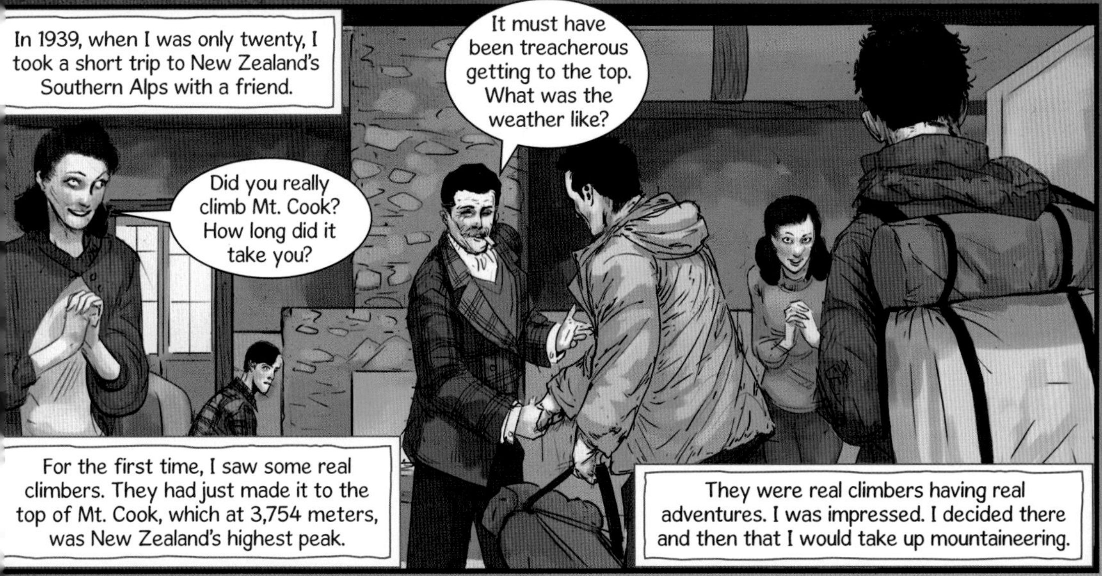
In 1939, when I was only twenty, I took a short trip to New Zealand's Southern Alps with a friend.
Did you really climb Mt. Cook? How long did it take you?
It must have been treacherous getting to the top. What was the weather like?
For the first time, I saw some real climbers. They had just made it to the top of Mt. Cook, which at 3,754 meters, was New Zealand's highest peak.
They were real climbers having real adventures. I was impressed. I decided there and then that I would take up mountaineering.

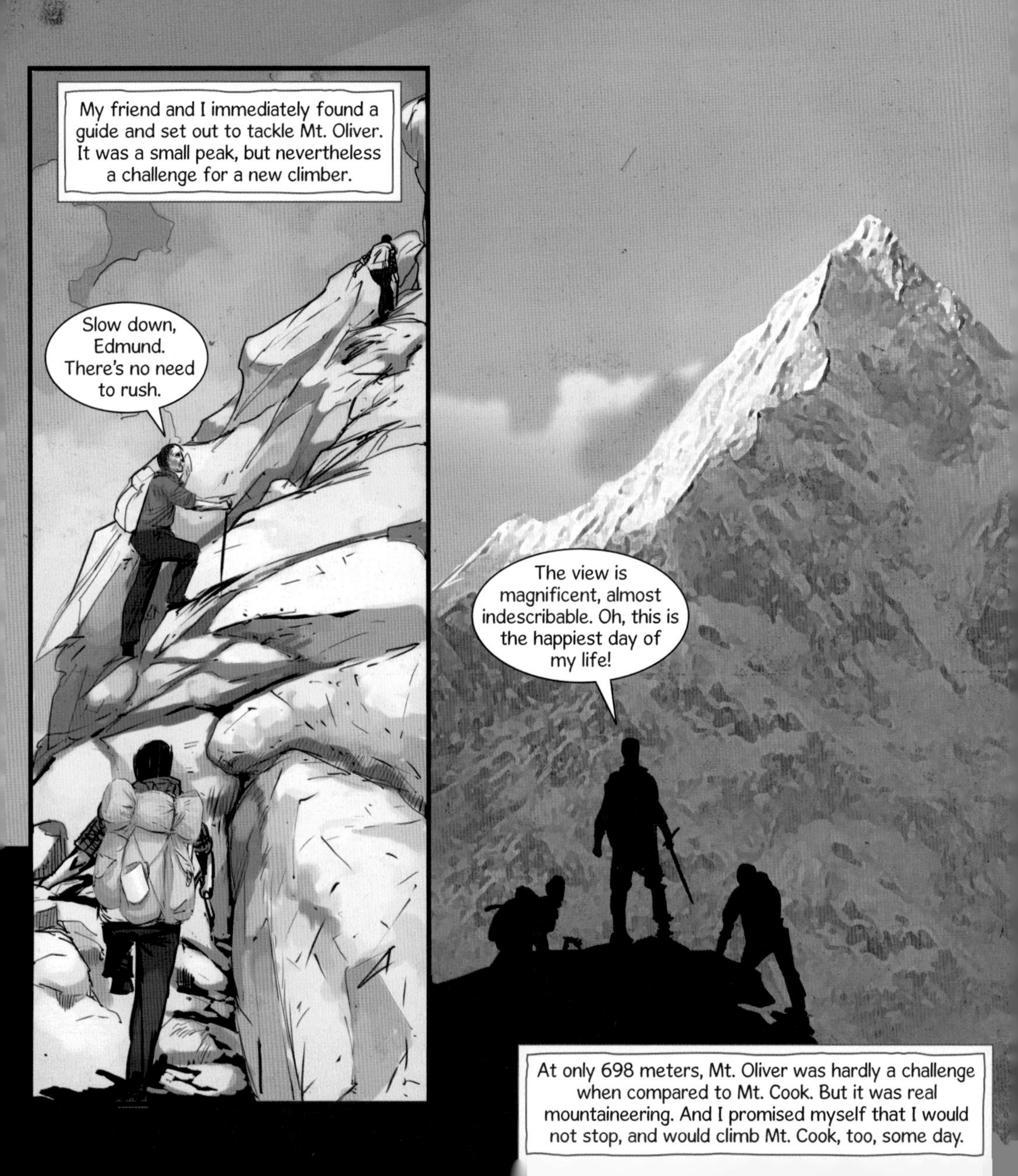
My friend and I immediately found a guide and set out to tackle Mt. Oliver. It was a small peak, but nevertheless a challenge for a new climber.
Slow down, Edmund. There's no need to rush.
The view is magnificent, almost indescribable. Oh, this is the happiest day of my life!
At only 698 meters, Mt. Oliver was hardly a challenge when compared to Mt. Cook. But it was real mountaineering. And I promised myself that I would not stop, and would climb Mt. Cook, too, some day.

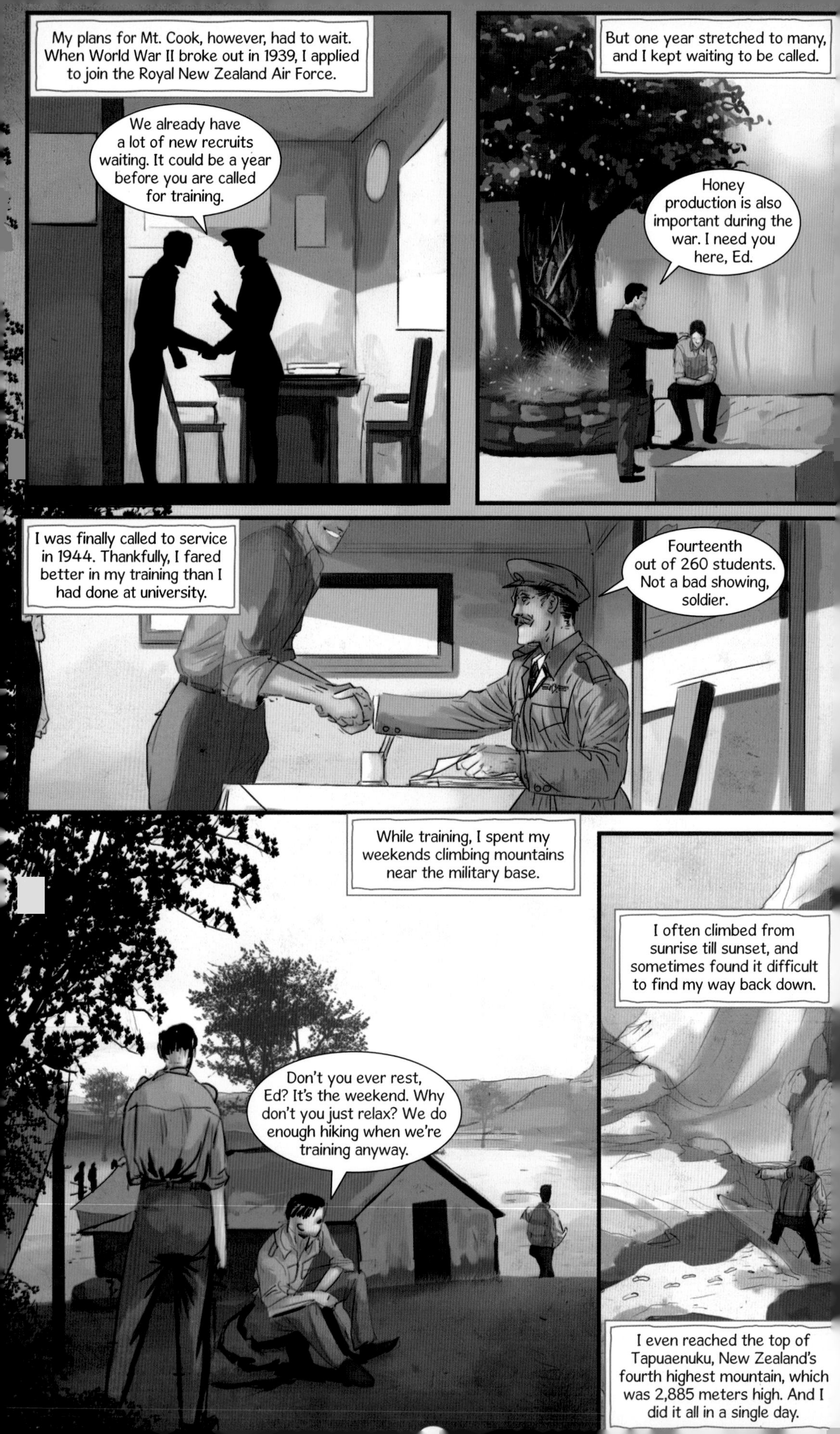
My plans for Mt. Cook, however, had to wait. When World War II broke out in 1939, I applied to join the Royal New Zealand Air Force.
We already have a lot of new recruits waiting. It could be a year before you are called for training.
But one year stretched to many, and I kept waiting to be called.
Honey production is also important during the war. I need you here, Ed.
I was finally called to service in 1944. Thankfully, I fared better in my training than I had done at university.
Fourteenth out of 260 students. Not a bad showing, soldier.
While training, I spent my weekends climbing mountains near the military base.
Don't you ever rest, Ed? It's the weekend. Why don't you just relax? We do enough hiking when we're training anyway.
I often climbed from sunrise till sunset, and sometimes found it difficult to find my way back down.
I even reached the top of Tapuaenuku, New Zealand's fourth highest mountain, which was 2,885 meters high. And I did it all in a single day.

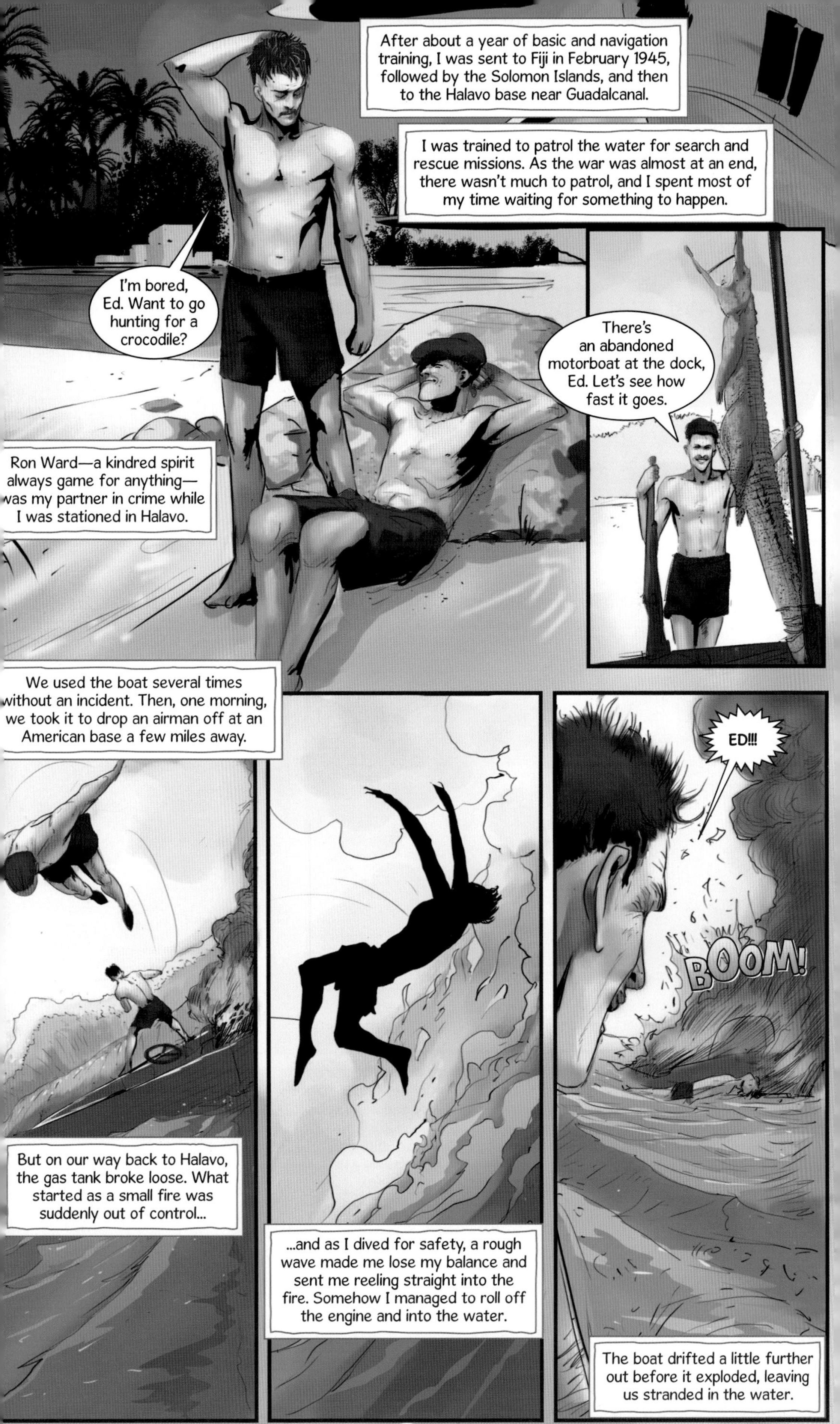

After about a year of basic and navigation training, I was sent to Fiji in February 1945, followed by the Solomon Islands, and then to the Halavo base near Guadalcanal.
I was trained to patrol the water for search and rescue missions. As the war was almost at an end, there wasn't much to patrol, and I spent most of my time waiting for something to happen.
I'm bored, Ed. Want to go hunting for a crocodile?
Ron Ward—a kindred spirit always game for anything—was my partner in crime while I was stationed in Halavo.
There's an abandoned motorboat at the dock, Ed. Let's see how fast it goes.
We used the boat several times without an incident. Then, one morning, we took it to drop an airman off at an American base a few miles away.
But on our way back to Halavo, the gas tank broke loose. What started as a small fire was suddenly out of control...
...and as I dived for safety, a rough wave made me lose my balance and sent me reeling straight into the fire. Somehow I managed to roll off the engine and into the water.
ED!!!
BOOM!
The boat drifted a little further out before it exploded, leaving us stranded in the water.

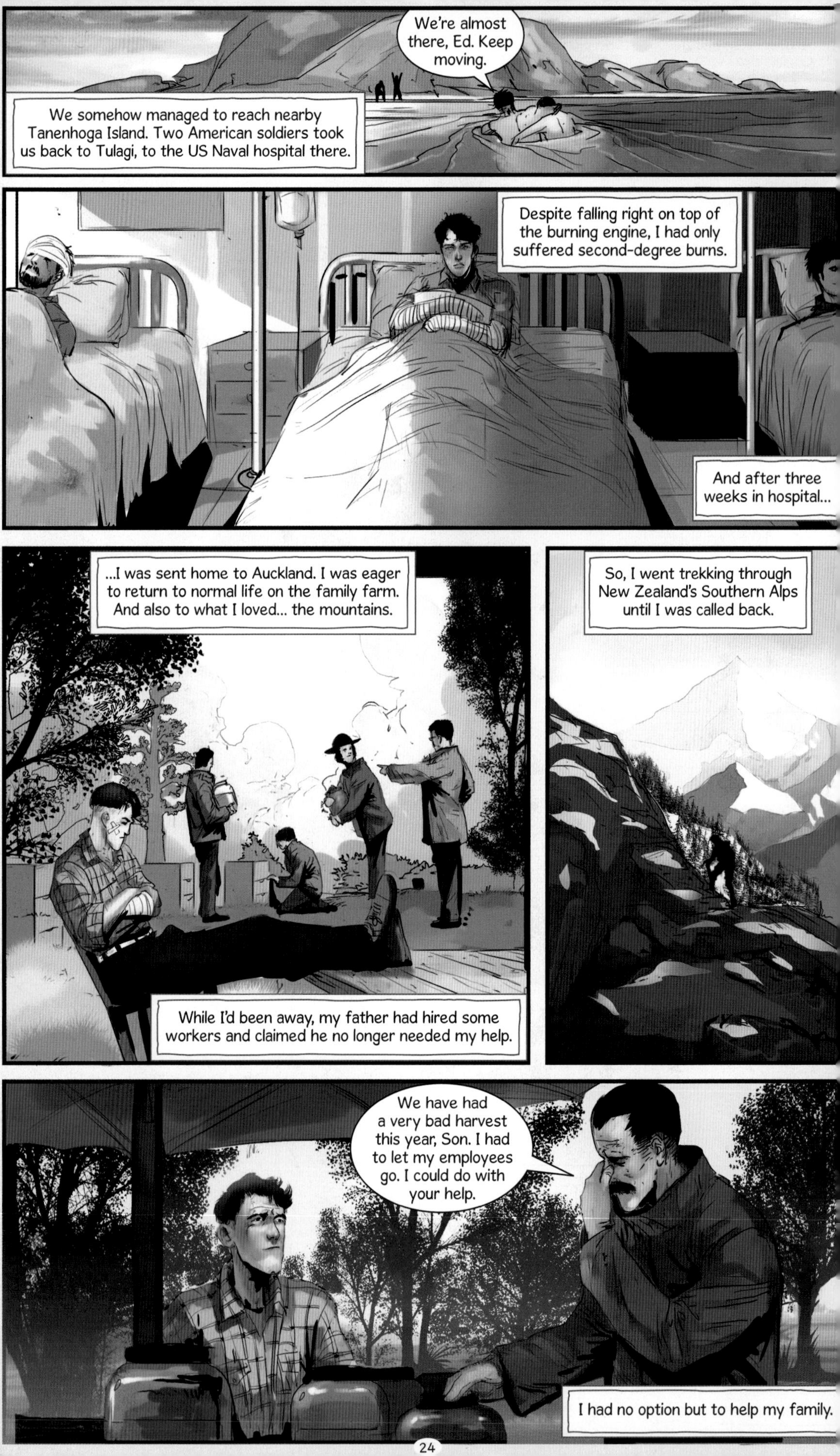
We're almost there, Ed. Keep moving.
We somehow managed to reach nearby Tanenhoga Island. Two American soldiers took us back to Tulagi, to the US Naval hospital there.
Despite falling right on top of the burning engine, I had only suffered second-degree burns.
And after three weeks in hospital...
...I was sent home to Auckland. I was eager to return to normal life on the family farm. And also to what I loved... the mountains.
While I'd been away, my father had hired some workers and claimed he no longer needed my help.
So, I went trekking through New Zealand's Southern Alps until I was called back.
We have had a very bad harvest this year, Son. I had to let my employees go. I could do with your help.
I had no option but to help my family.

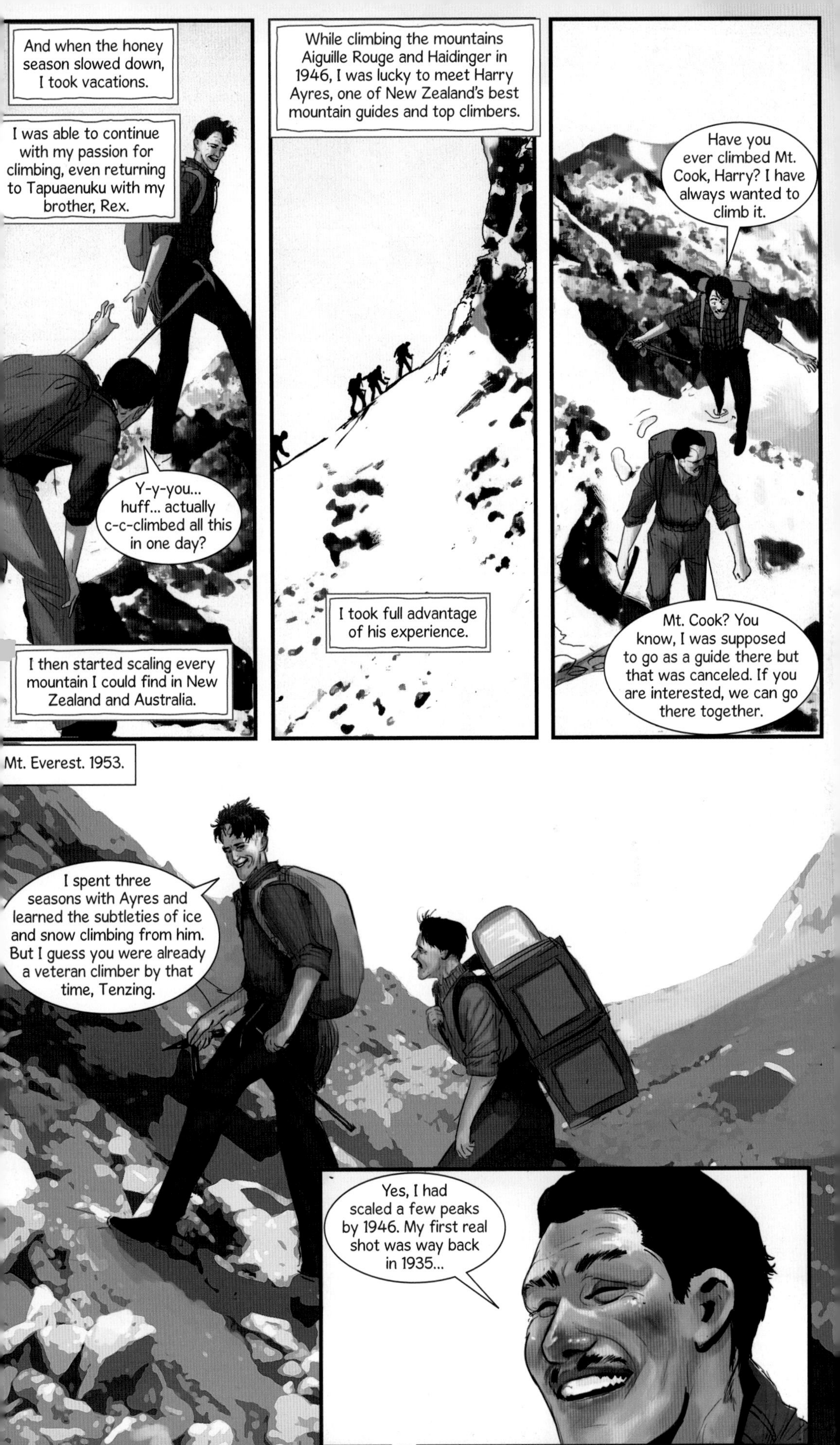
And when the honey season slowed down, I took vacations.
I was able to continue with my passion for climbing, even returning to Tapuaenuku with my brother, Rex.
Y-y-you... huff... actually c-c-climbed all this in one day?
I then started scaling every mountain I could find in New Zealand and Australia.
While climbing the mountains Aiguille Rouge and Haidinger in 1946, I was lucky to meet Harry Ayres, one of New Zealand's best mountain guides and top climbers.
I took full advantage of his experience.
Have you ever climbed Mt. Cook, Harry? I have always wanted to climb it.
Mt. Cook? You know, I was supposed to go as a guide there but that was canceled. If you are interested, we can go there together.
Mt. Everest. 1953.
I spent three seasons with Ayres and learned the subtleties of ice and snow climbing from him. But I guess you were already a veteran climber by that time, Tenzing.
Yes, I had scaled a few peaks by 1946. My first real shot was way back in 1935...

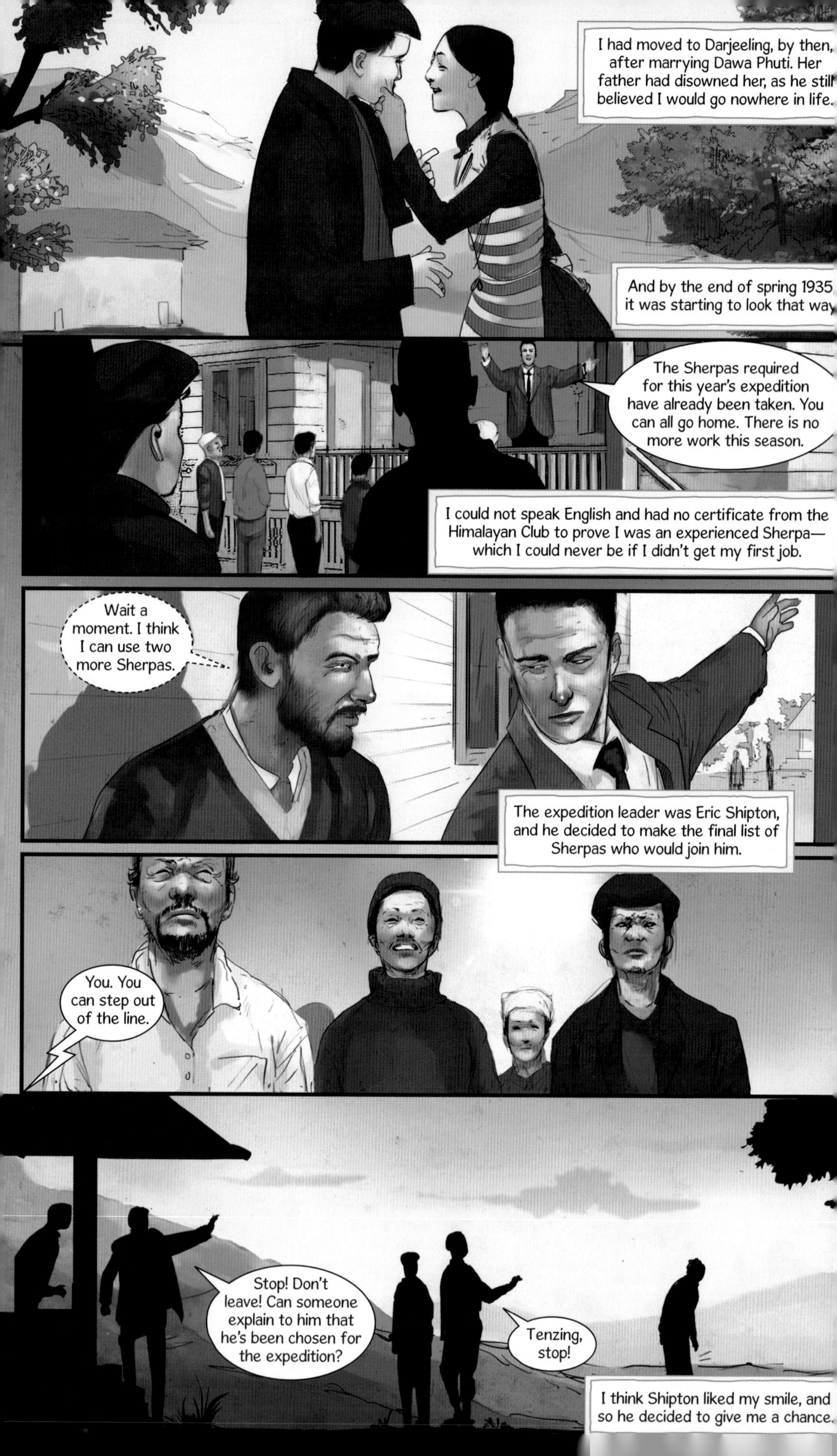
I had moved to Darjeeling, by then, after marrying Dawa Phuti. Her father had disowned her, as he still believed I would go nowhere in life.
And by the end of spring 1935 it was starting to look that way
The Sherpas required for this year's expedition have already been taken. You can all go home. There is no more work this season.
I could not speak English and had no certificate from the Himalayan Club to prove I was an experienced Sherpa—which I could never be if I didn't get my first job.
Wait a moment. I think I can use two more Sherpas.
The expedition leader was Eric Shipton, and he decided to make the final list of Sherpas who would join him.
You. You can step out of the line.
Stop! Don't leave! Can someone explain to him that he's been chosen for the expedition?
Tenzing, stop!
I think Shipton liked my smile, and so he decided to give me a chance.

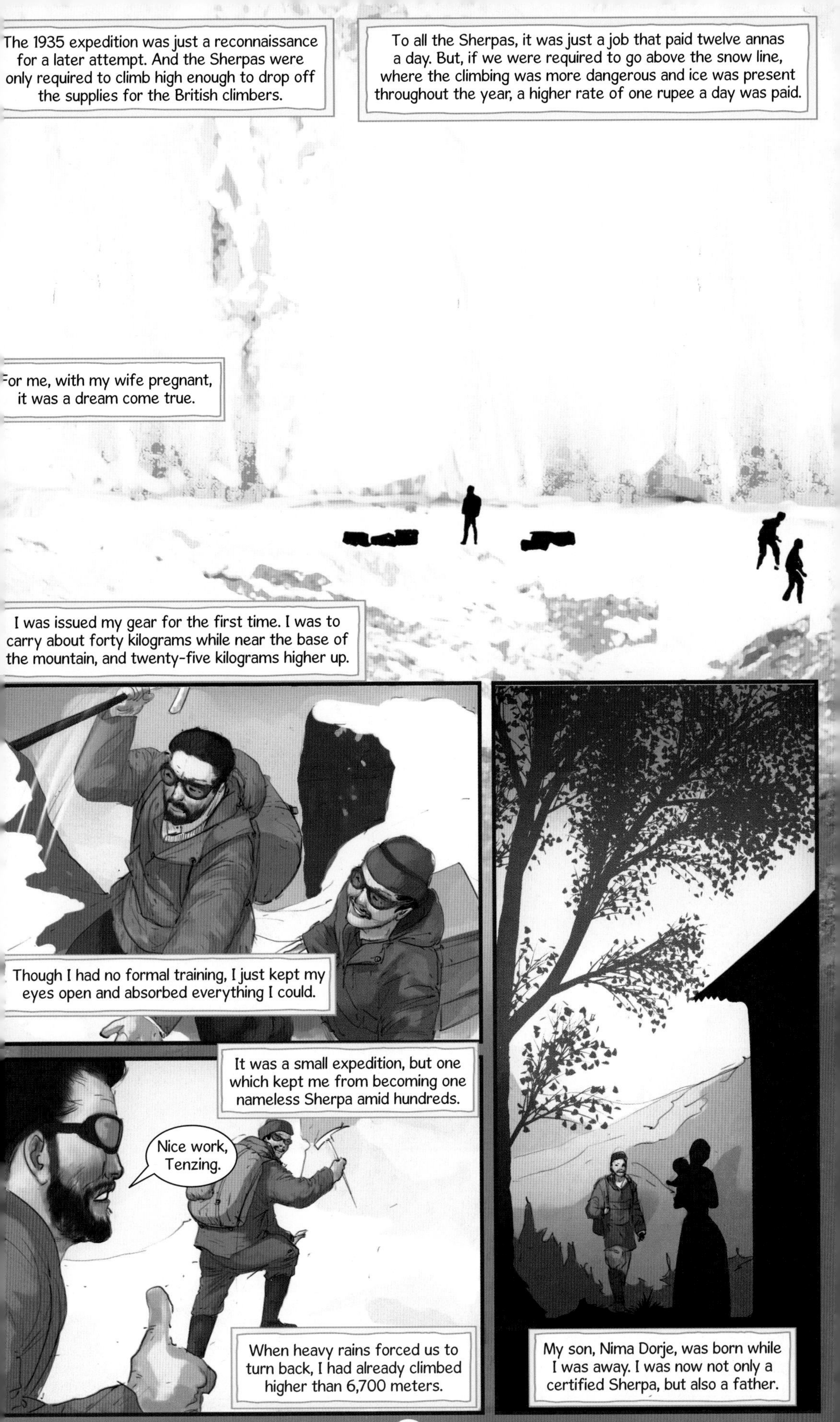
The 1935 expedition was just a reconnaissance for a later attempt. And the Sherpas were only required to climb high enough to drop off the supplies for the British climbers.
To all the Sherpas, it was just a job that paid twelve annas a day. But, if we were required to go above the snow line, where the climbing was more dangerous and ice was present throughout the year, a higher rate of one rupee a day was paid.
For me, with my wife pregnant, it was a dream come true.
I was issued my gear for the first time. I was to carry about forty kilograms while near the base of the mountain, and twenty-five kilograms higher up.
Though I had no formal training, I just kept my eyes open and absorbed everything I could.
It was a small expedition, but one which kept me from becoming one nameless Sherpa amid hundreds.
Nice work, Tenzing.
When heavy rains forced us to turn back, I had already climbed higher than 6,700 meters.
My son, Nima Dorje, was born while I was away. I was now not only a certified Sherpa, but also a father.

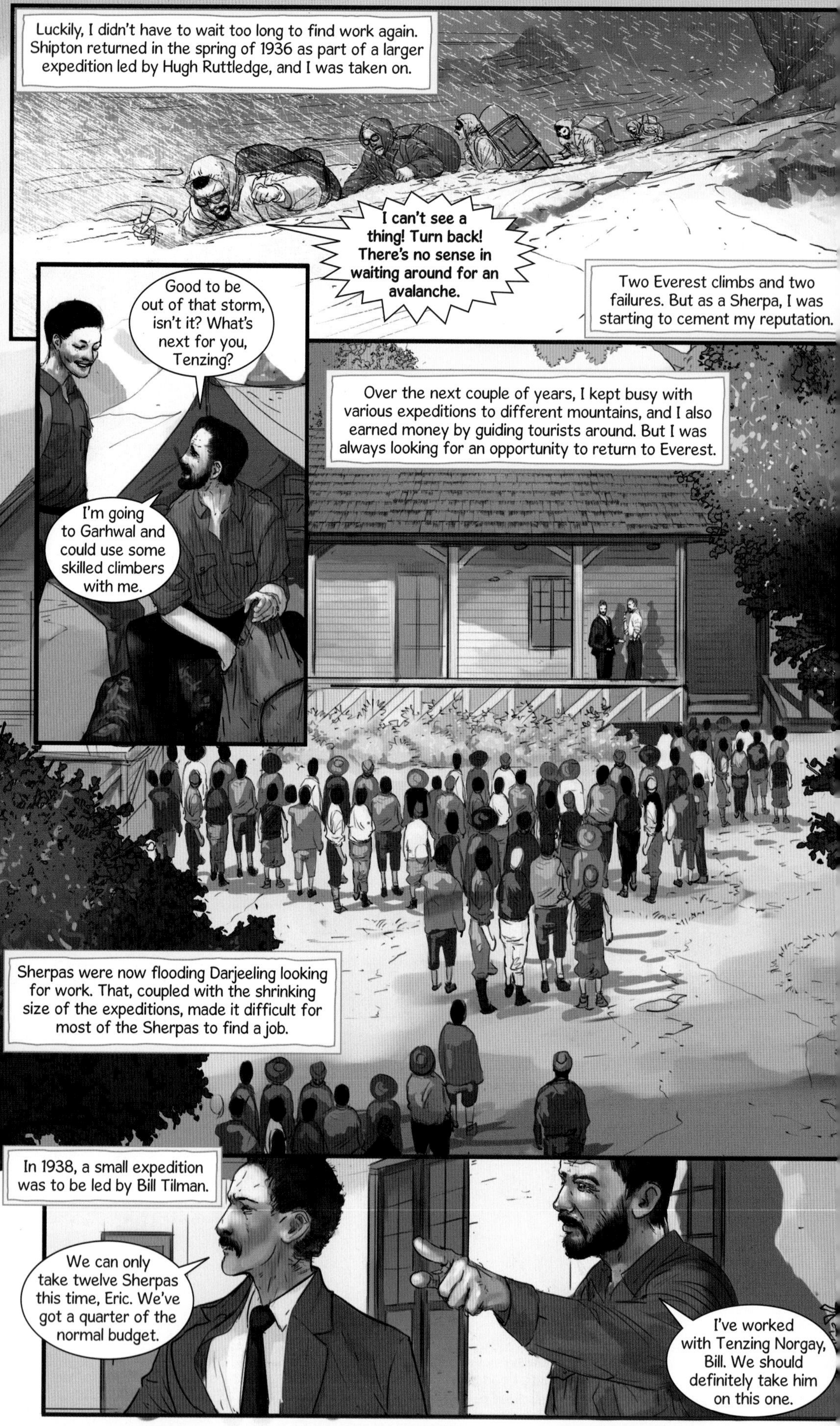
Luckily, I didn't have to wait too long to find work again. Shipton returned in the spring of 1936 as part of a larger expedition led by Hugh Ruttledge, and I was taken on.
I can't see a thing! Turn back! There's no sense in waiting around for an avalanche.
Two Everest climbs and two failures. But as a Sherpa, I was starting to cement my reputation.
Good to be out of that storm, isn't it? What's next for you, Tenzing?
I'm going to Garhwal and could use some skilled climbers with me.
Over the next couple of years, I kept busy with various expeditions to different mountains, and I also earned money by guiding tourists around. But I was always looking for an opportunity to return to Everest.
Sherpas were now flooding Darjeeling looking for work. That, coupled with the shrinking size of the expeditions, made it difficult for most of the Sherpas to find a job.
In 1938, a small expedition was to be led by Bill Tilman.
We can only take twelve Sherpas this time, Eric. We've got a quarter of the normal budget.
I've worked with Tenzing Norgay, Bill. We should definitely take him on this one.

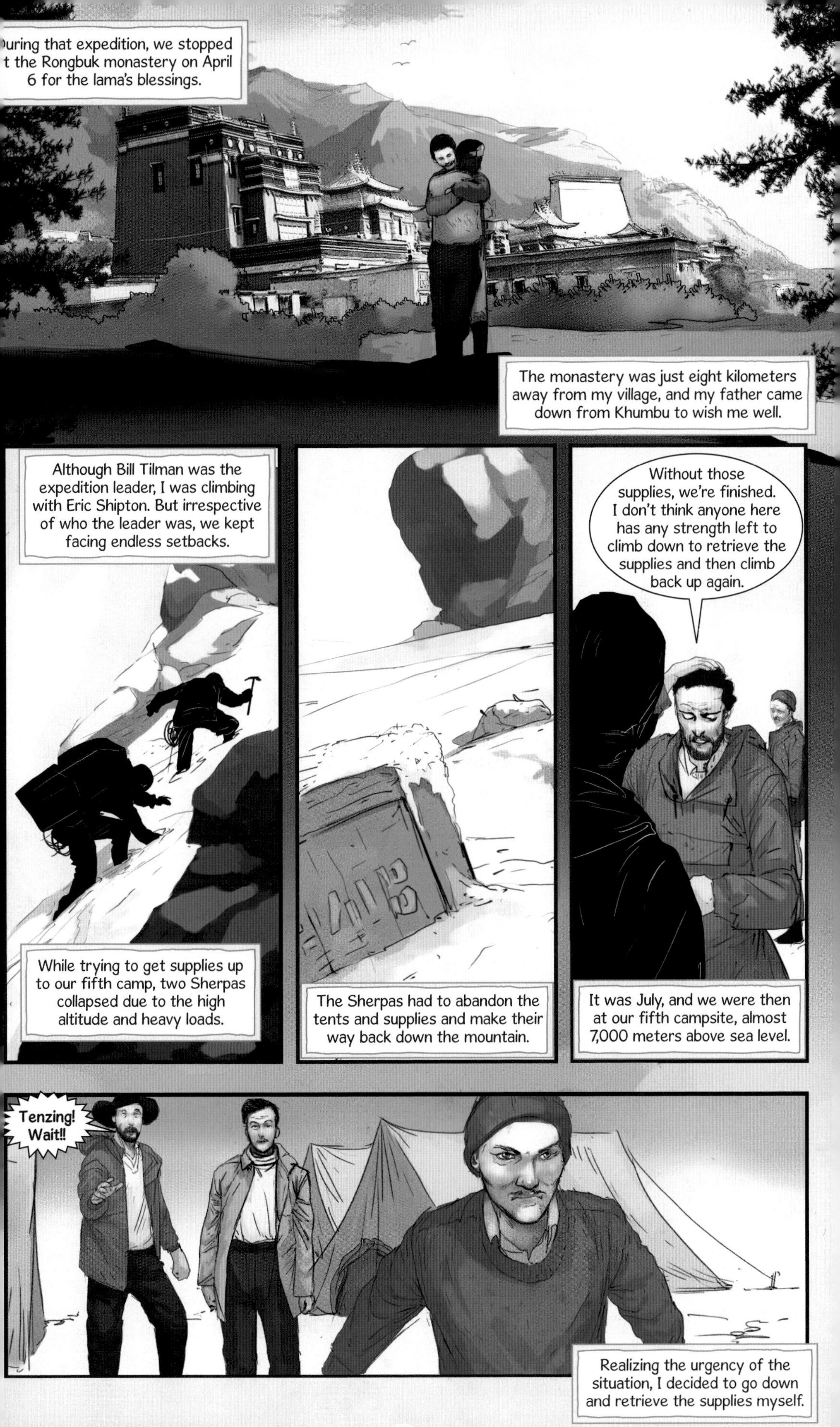
uring that expedition, we stopped t the Rongbuk monastery on April 6 for the lama's blessings.
The monastery was just eight kilometers away from my village, and my father came down from Khumbu to wish me well.
Although Bill Tilman was the expedition leader, I was climbing with Eric Shipton. But irrespective of who the leader was, we kept facing endless setbacks.
While trying to get supplies up to our fifth camp, two Sherpas collapsed due to the high altitude and heavy loads.
The Sherpas had to abandon the tents and supplies and make their way back down the mountain.
Without those supplies, we're finished. I don't think anyone here has any strength left to climb down to retrieve the supplies and then climb back up again.
It was July, and we were then at our fifth campsite, almost 7,000 meters above sea level.
Tenzing! Wait!!
Realizing the urgency of the situation, I decided to go down and retrieve the supplies myself.

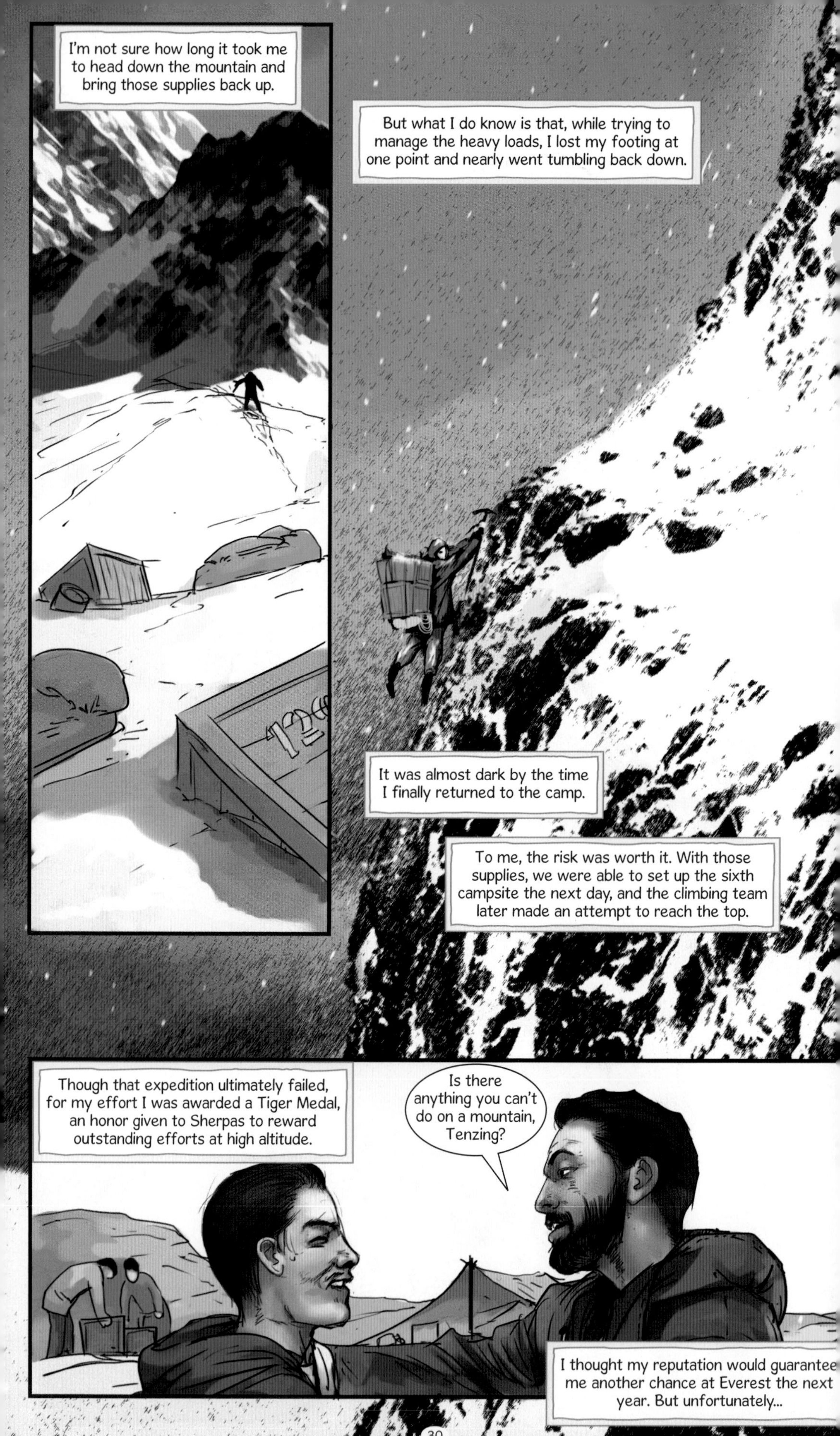

I'm not sure how long it took me to head down the mountain and bring those supplies back up.
But what I do know is that, while trying to manage the heavy loads, I lost my footing at one point and nearly went tumbling back down.
It was almost dark by the time I finally returned to the camp.
To me, the risk was worth it. With those supplies, we were able to set up the sixth campsite the next day, and the climbing team later made an attempt to reach the top.
Though that expedition ultimately failed, for my effort I was awarded a Tiger Medal, an honor given to Sherpas to reward outstanding efforts at high altitude.
Is there anything you can't do on a mountain, Tenzing?
I thought my reputation would guarantee me another chance at Everest the next year. But unfortunately...

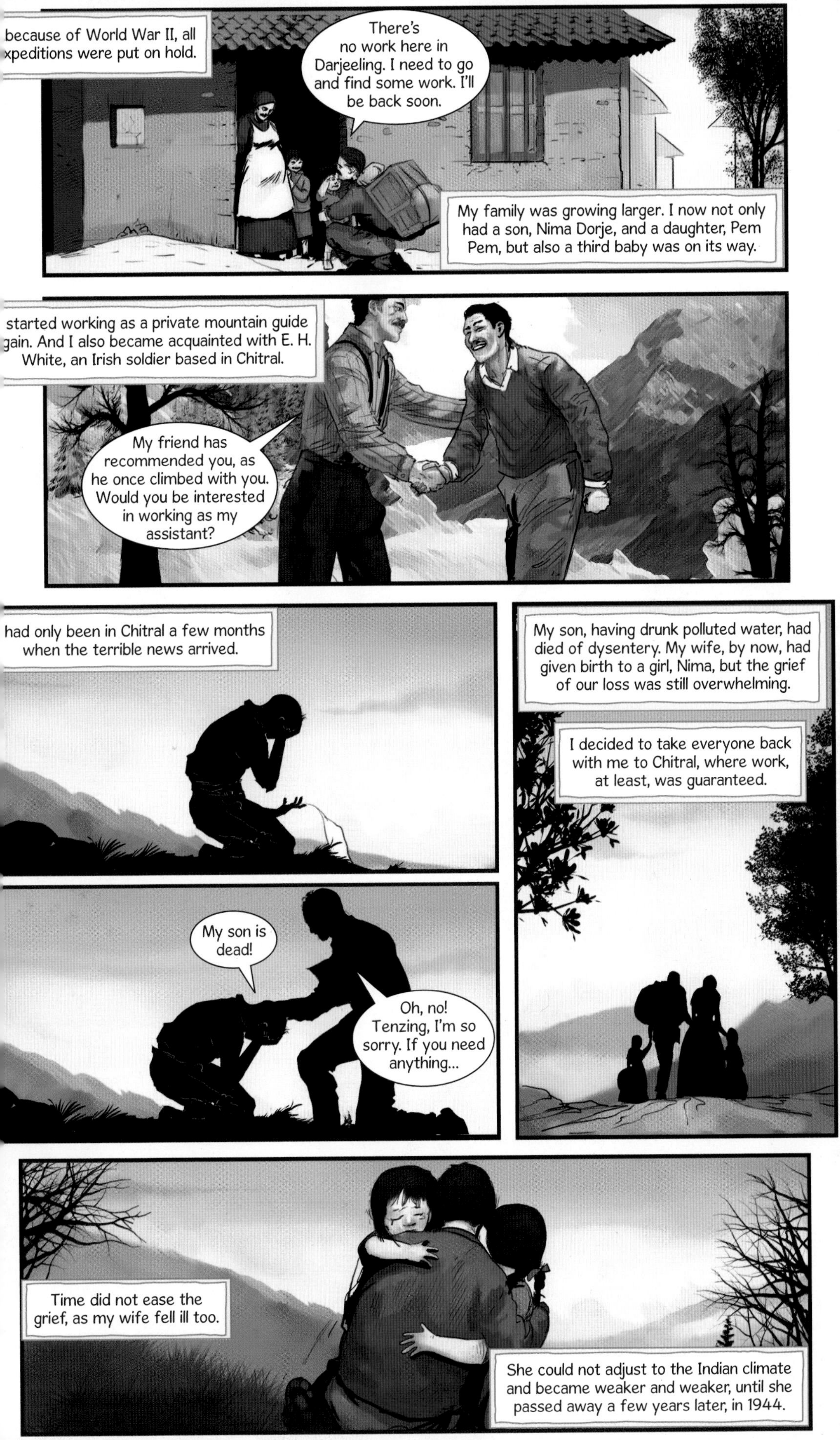
because of World War II, all
xpeditions were put on hold.
There's no work here in Darjeeling. I need to go and find some work. I'll be back soon.
My family was growing larger. I now not only had a son, Nima Dorje, and a daughter, Pem Pem, but also a third baby was on its way.
started working as a private mountain guide
gain. And I also became acquainted with E. H. White, an Irish soldier based in Chitral.
My friend has recommended you, as he once climbed with you. Would you be interested in working as my assistant?
had only been in Chitral a few months when the terrible news arrived.
My son is dead!
Oh, no! Tenzing, I'm so sorry. If you need anything...
My son, having drunk polluted water, had died of dysentery. My wife, by now, had given birth to a girl, Nima, but the grief of our loss was still overwhelming.
I decided to take everyone back with me to Chitral, where work, at least, was guaranteed.
Time did not ease the grief, as my wife fell ill too.
She could not adjust to the Indian climate and became weaker and weaker, until she passed away a few years later, in 1944.

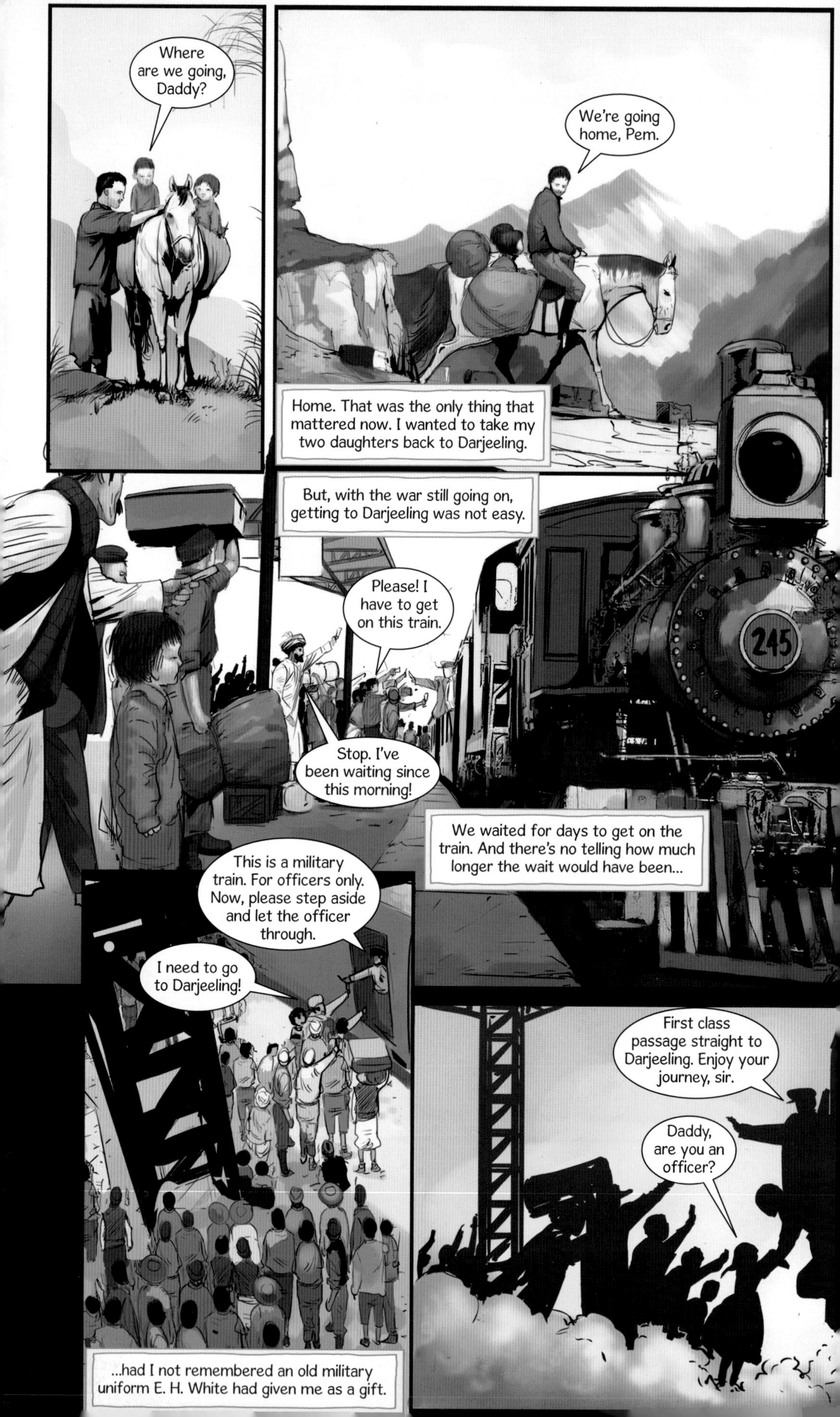
Where are we going, Daddy?
We're going home, Pem.
Home. That was the only thing that mattered now. I wanted to take my two daughters back to Darjeeling.
But, with the war still going on, getting to Darjeeling was not easy.
Please! I have to get on this train.
Stop. I've been waiting since this morning!
245
We waited for days to get on the train. And there's no telling how much longer the wait would have been...
This is a military train. For officers only. Now, please step aside and let the officer through.
I need to go to Darjeeling!
...had I not remembered an old military uniform E. H. White had given me as a gift.
First class passage straight to Darjeeling. Enjoy your journey, sir.
Daddy, are you an officer?

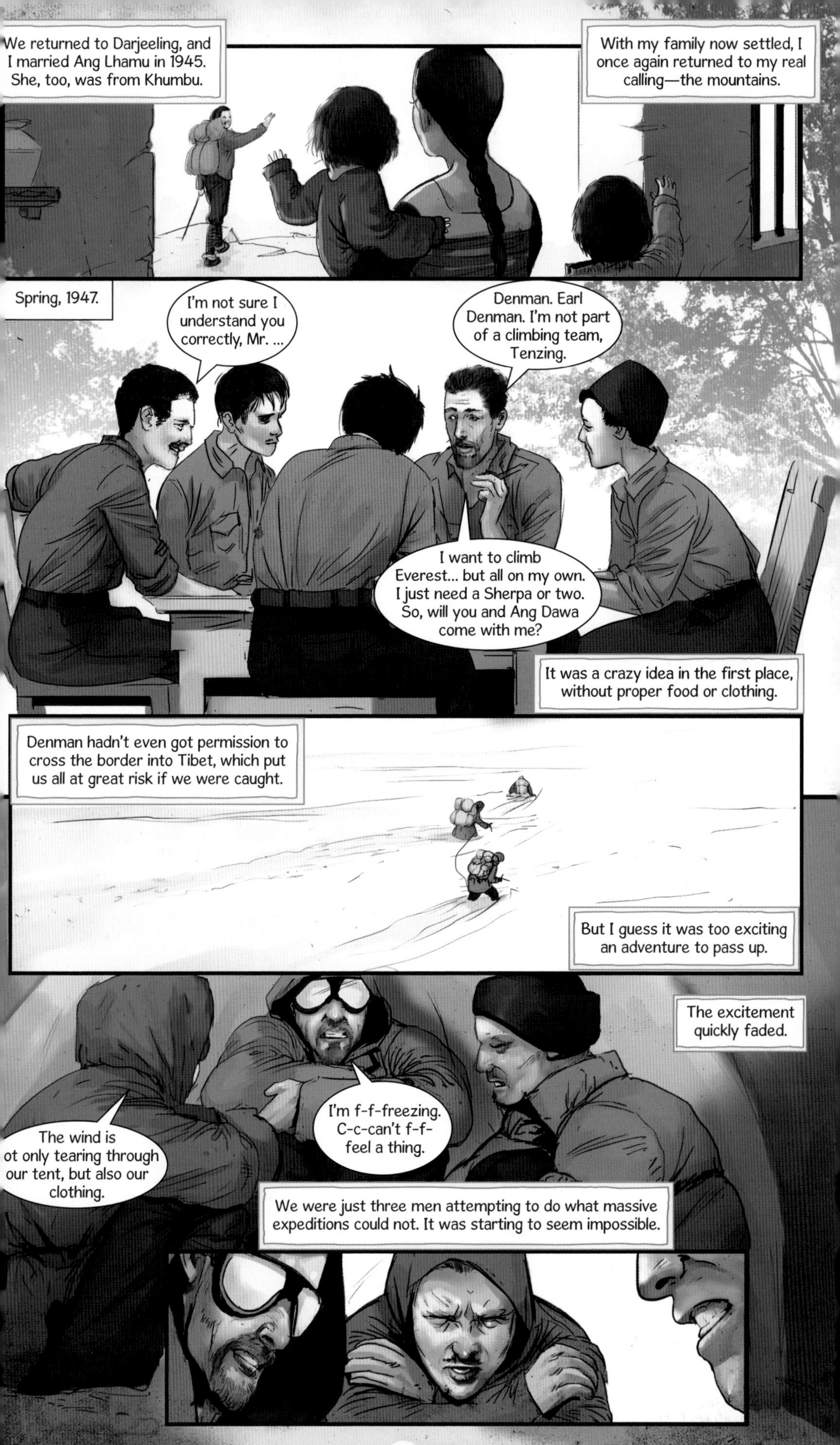
We returned to Darjeeling, and I married Ang Lhamu in 1945. She, too, was from Khumbu.
With my family now settled, I once again returned to my real calling—the mountains.
Spring, 1947.
I'm not sure I understand you correctly, Mr. ...
Denman. Earl Denman. I'm not part of a climbing team, Tenzing.
I want to climb Everest... but all on my own. I just need a Sherpa or two. So, will you and Ang Dawa come with me?
It was a crazy idea in the first place, without proper food or clothing.
Denman hadn't even got permission to cross the border into Tibet, which put us all at great risk if we were caught.
But I guess it was too exciting an adventure to pass up.
The excitement quickly faded.
The wind is ot only tearing through our tent, but also our clothing.
I'm f-f-freezing. C-c-can't f-f-feel a thing.
We were just three men attempting to do what massive expeditions could not. It was starting to seem impossible.

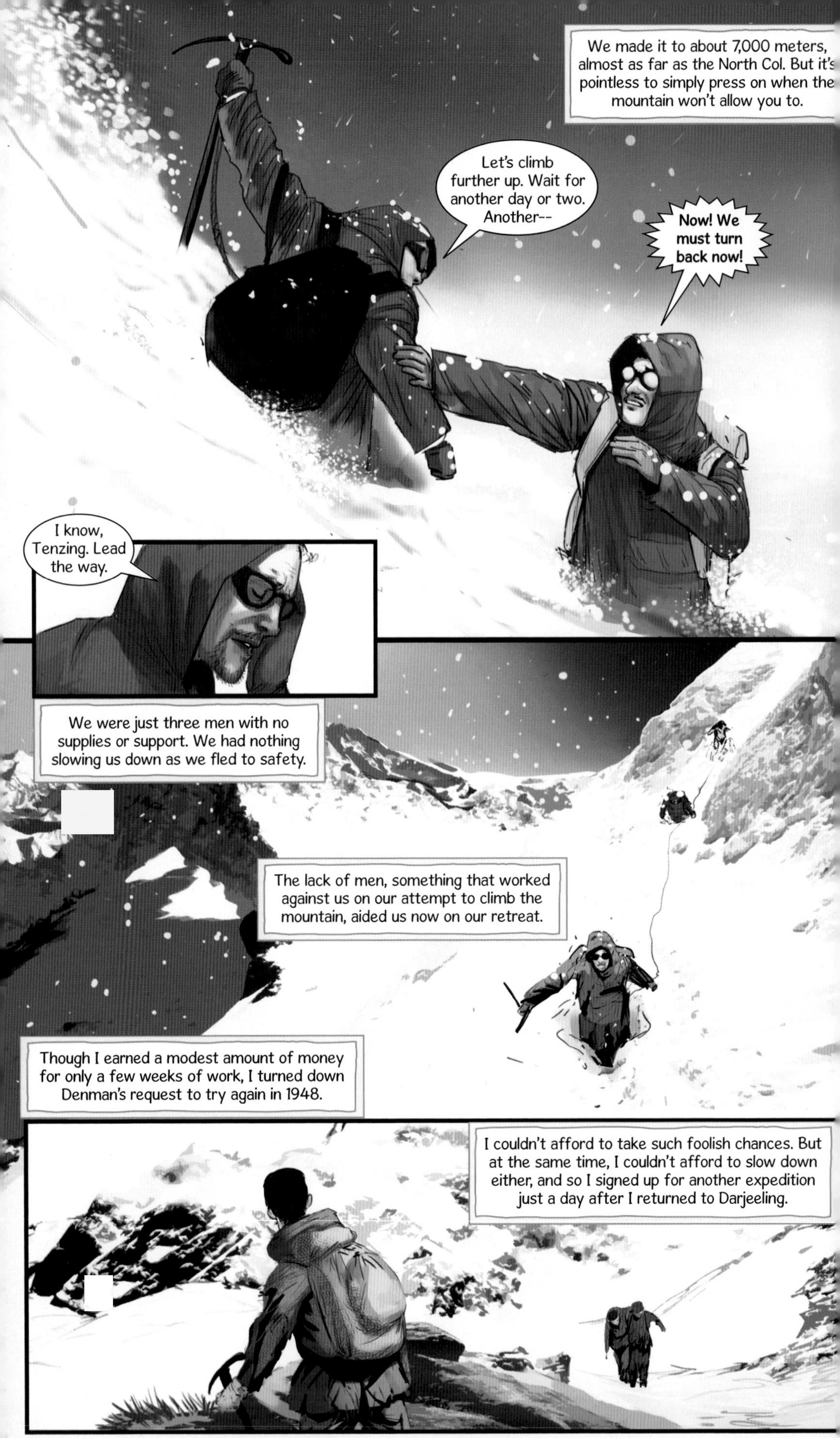

We made it to about 7,000 meters, almost as far as the North Col. But it's pointless to simply press on when the mountain won't allow you to.
Let's climb further up. Wait for another day or two. Another--
Now! We must turn back now!
I know, Tenzing. Lead the way.
We were just three men with no supplies or support. We had nothing slowing us down as we fled to safety.
The lack of men, something that worked against us on our attempt to climb the mountain, aided us now on our retreat.
Though I earned a modest amount of money for only a few weeks of work, I turned down Denman's request to try again in 1948.
I couldn't afford to take such foolish chances. But at the same time, I couldn't afford to slow down either, and so I signed up for another expedition just a day after I returned to Darjeeling.

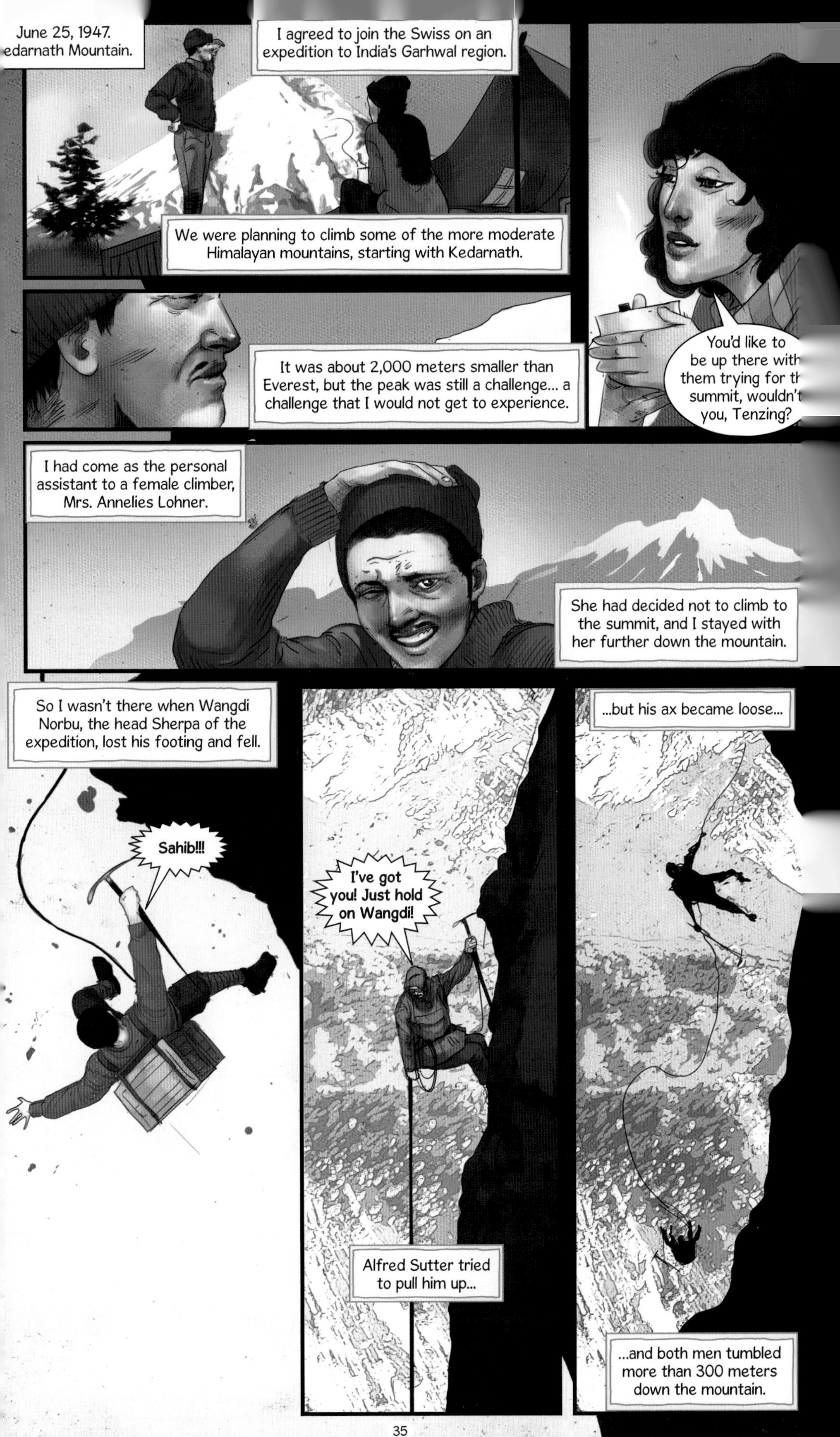
June 25, 1947.
edarnath Mountain.
I agreed to join the Swiss on an expedition to India's Garhwal region.
We were planning to climb some of the more moderate Himalayan mountains, starting with Kedarnath.
You'd like to be up there with them trying for th summit, wouldn't you, Tenzing?
It was about 2,000 meters smaller than Everest, but the peak was still a challenge... a challenge that I would not get to experience.
I had come as the personal assistant to a female climber, Mrs. Annelies Lohner.
She had decided not to climb to the summit, and I stayed with her further down the mountain.
So I wasn't there when Wangdi Norbu, the head Sherpa of the expedition, lost his footing and fell.
Sahib!!!
I've got you! Just hold on Wangdi!
Alfred Sutter tried to pull him up...
...but his ax became loose...
...and both men tumbled more than 300 meters down the mountain.

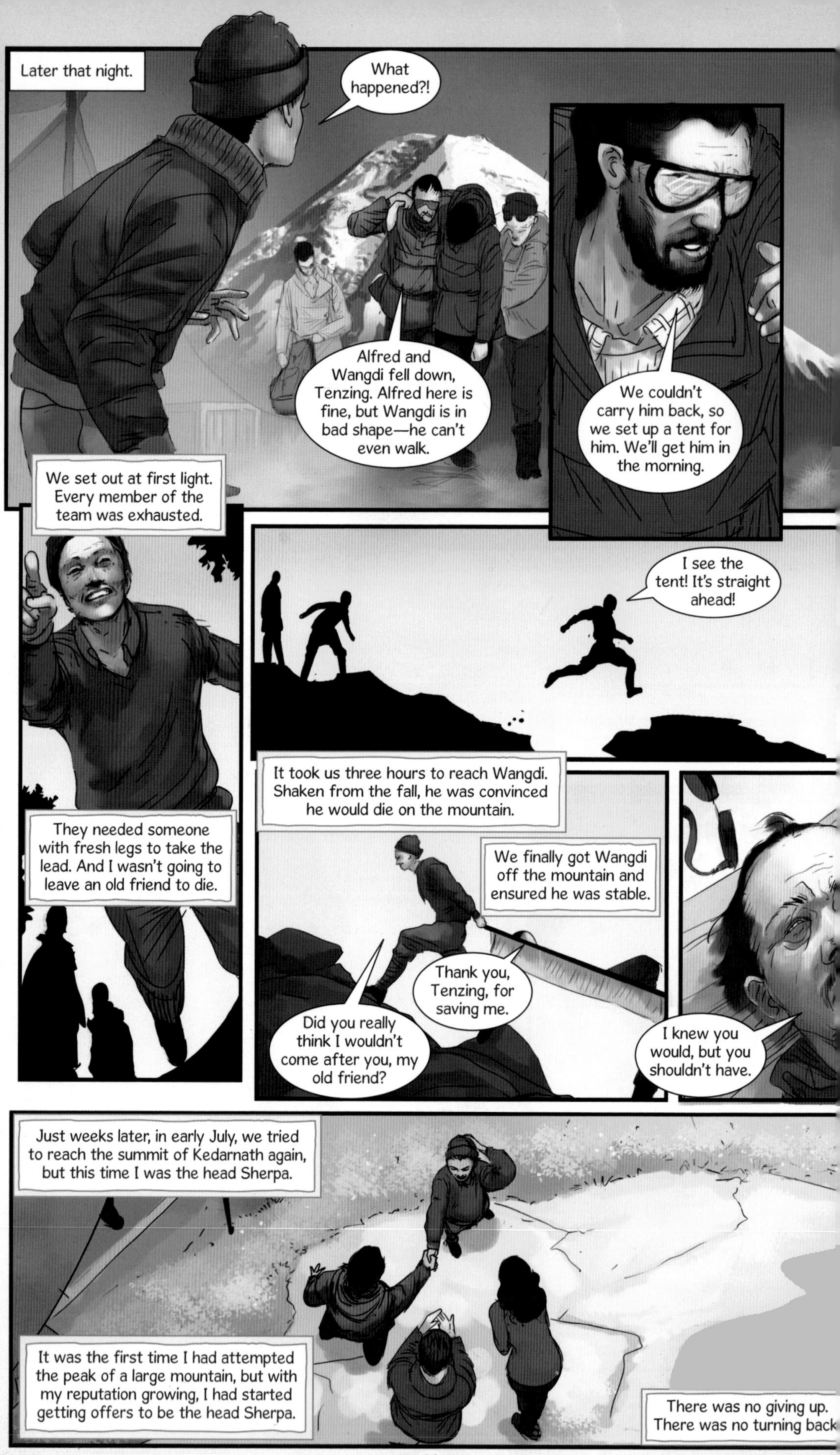

Later that night.
What happened?!
Alfred and Wangdi fell down, Tenzing. Alfred here is fine, but Wangdi is in bad shape—he can't even walk.
We couldn't carry him back, so we set up a tent for him. We'll get him in the morning.
We set out at first light. Every member of the team was exhausted.
They needed someone with fresh legs to take the lead. And I wasn't going to leave an old friend to die.
I see the tent! It's straight ahead!
It took us three hours to reach Wangdi. Shaken from the fall, he was convinced he would die on the mountain.
We finally got Wangdi off the mountain and ensured he was stable.
Thank you, Tenzing, for saving me.
Did you really think I wouldn't come after you, my old friend?
I knew you would, but you shouldn't have.
Just weeks later, in early July, we tried to reach the summit of Kedarnath again, but this time I was the head Sherpa.
It was the first time I had attempted the peak of a large mountain, but with my reputation growing, I had started getting offers to be the head Sherpa.
There was no giving up. There was no turning back

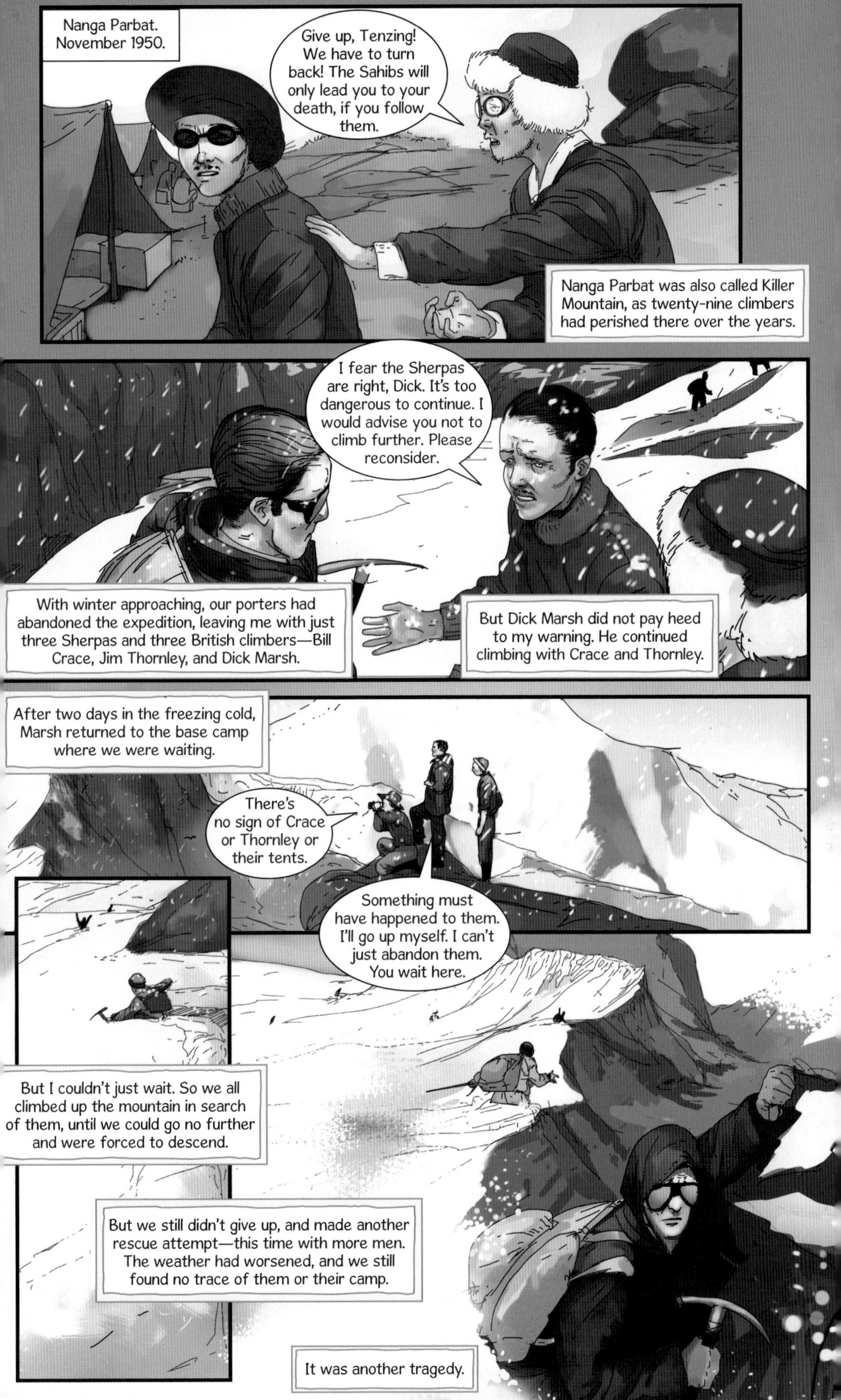

Nanga Parbat. November 1950.
Give up, Tenzing! We have to turn back! The Sahibs will only lead you to your death, if you follow them.
Nanga Parbat was also called Killer Mountain, as twenty-nine climbers had perished there over the years.
I fear the Sherpas are right, Dick. It's too dangerous to continue. I would advise you not to climb further. Please reconsider.
With winter approaching, our porters had abandoned the expedition, leaving me with just three Sherpas and three British climbers—Bill Crace, Jim Thornley, and Dick Marsh.
But Dick Marsh did not pay heed to my warning. He continued climbing with Crace and Thornley.
After two days in the freezing cold, Marsh returned to the base camp where we were waiting.
There's no sign of Crace or Thornley or their tents.
Something must have happened to them. I'll go up myself. I can't just abandon them. You wait here.
But I couldn't just wait. So we all climbed up the mountain in search of them, until we could go no further and were forced to descend.
But we still didn't give up, and made another rescue attempt—this time with more men. The weather had worsened, and we still found no trace of them or their camp.
It was another tragedy.

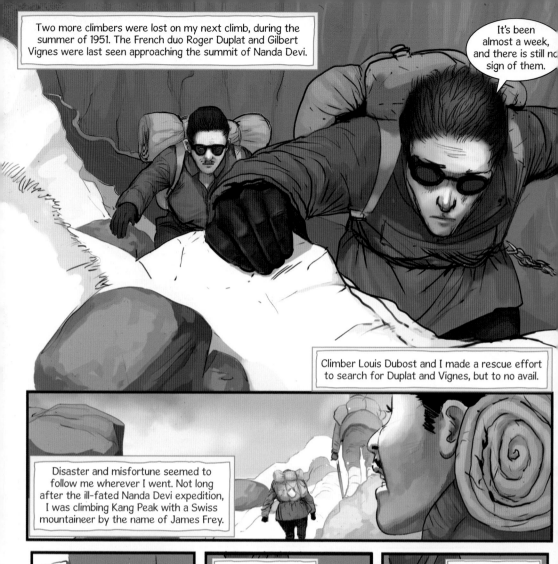

Two more climbers were lost on my next climb, during the summer of 1951. The French duo Roger Duplat and Gilbert Vignes were last seen approaching the summit of Nanda Devi.

It's been almost a week, and there is still no sign of them.

Climber Louis Dubost and I made a rescue effort to search for Duplat and Vignes, but to no avail.

Disaster and misfortune seemed to follow me wherever I went. Not long after the ill-fated Nanda Devi expedition, I was climbing Kang Peak with a Swiss mountaineer by the name of James Frey.

He suddenly slipped.

I broke my finger trying to save him...

...but it was in vain.

Tragedy and death showed their faces on every expedition.

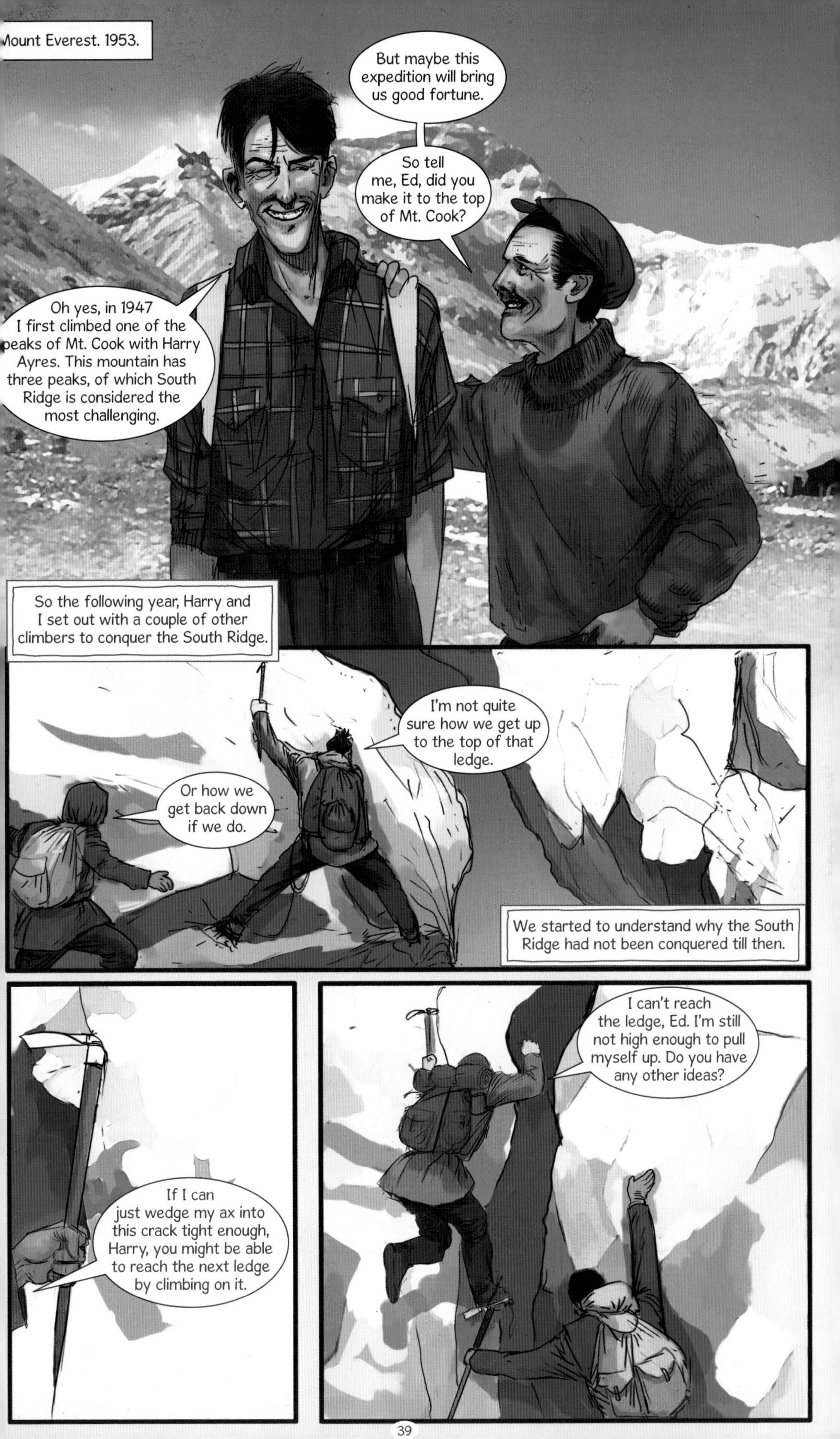
Mount Everest. 1953.
But maybe this expedition will bring us good fortune.
So tell me, Ed, did you make it to the top of Mt. Cook?
Oh yes, in 1947 I first climbed one of the peaks of Mt. Cook with Harry Ayres. This mountain has three peaks, of which South Ridge is considered the most challenging.
So the following year, Harry and I set out with a couple of other climbers to conquer the South Ridge.
I'm not quite sure how we get up to the top of that ledge.
Or how we get back down if we do.
We started to understand why the South Ridge had not been conquered till then.
If I can just wedge my ax into this crack tight enough, Harry, you might be able to reach the next ledge by climbing on it.
I can't reach the ledge, Ed. I'm still not high enough to pull myself up. Do you have any other ideas?

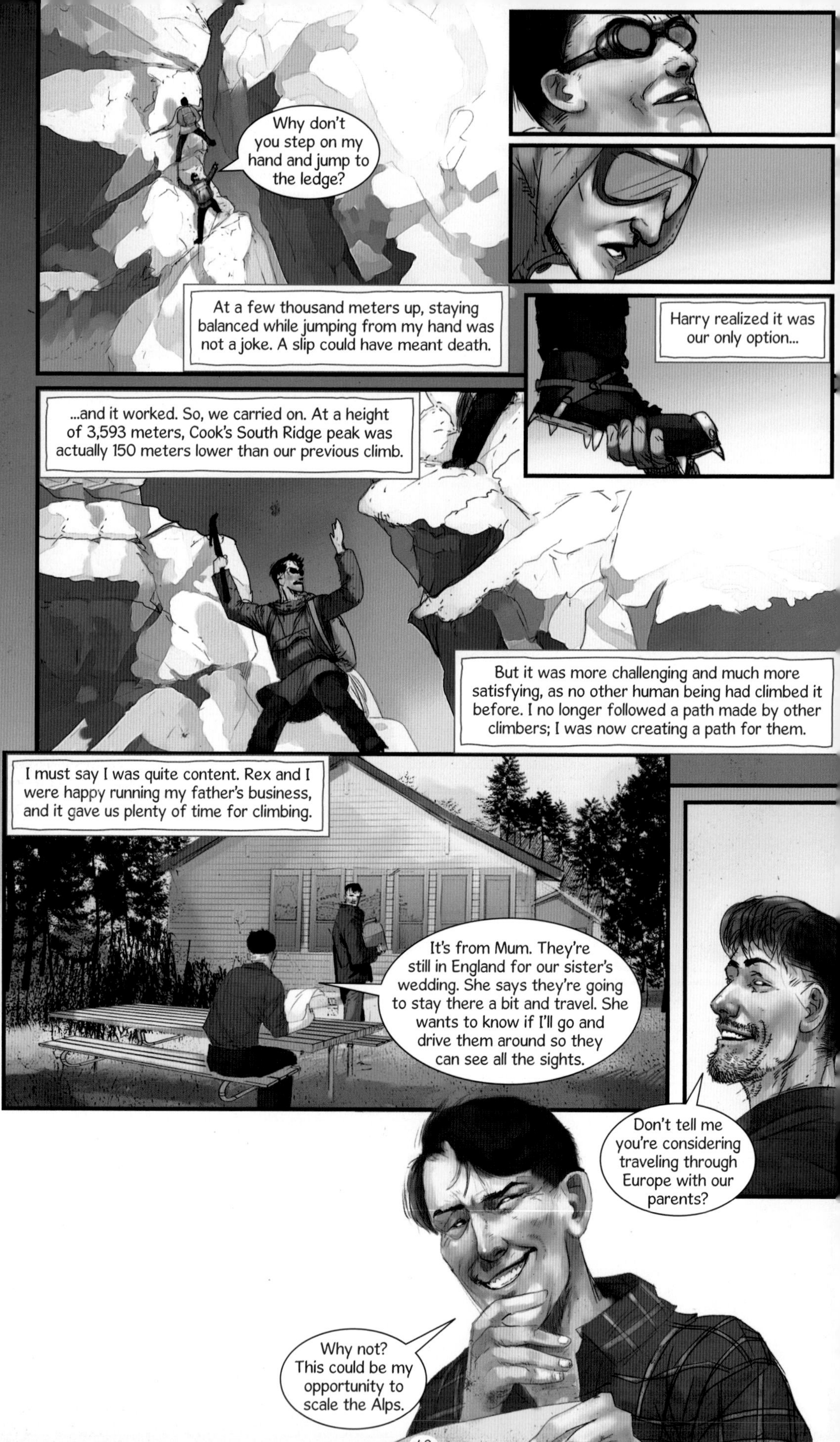
Why don't you step on my hand and jump to the ledge?
At a few thousand meters up, staying balanced while jumping from my hand was not a joke. A slip could have meant death.
Harry realized it was our only option...
...and it worked. So, we carried on. At a height of 3,593 meters, Cook's South Ridge peak was actually 150 meters lower than our previous climb.
But it was more challenging and much more satisfying, as no other human being had climbed it before. I no longer followed a path made by other climbers; I was now creating a path for them.
I must say I was quite content. Rex and I were happy running my father's business, and it gave us plenty of time for climbing.
It's from Mum. They're still in England for our sister's wedding. She says they're going to stay there a bit and travel. She wants to know if I'll go and drive them around so they can see all the sights.
Don't tell me you're considering traveling through Europe with our parents?
Why not? This could be my opportunity to scale the Alps.

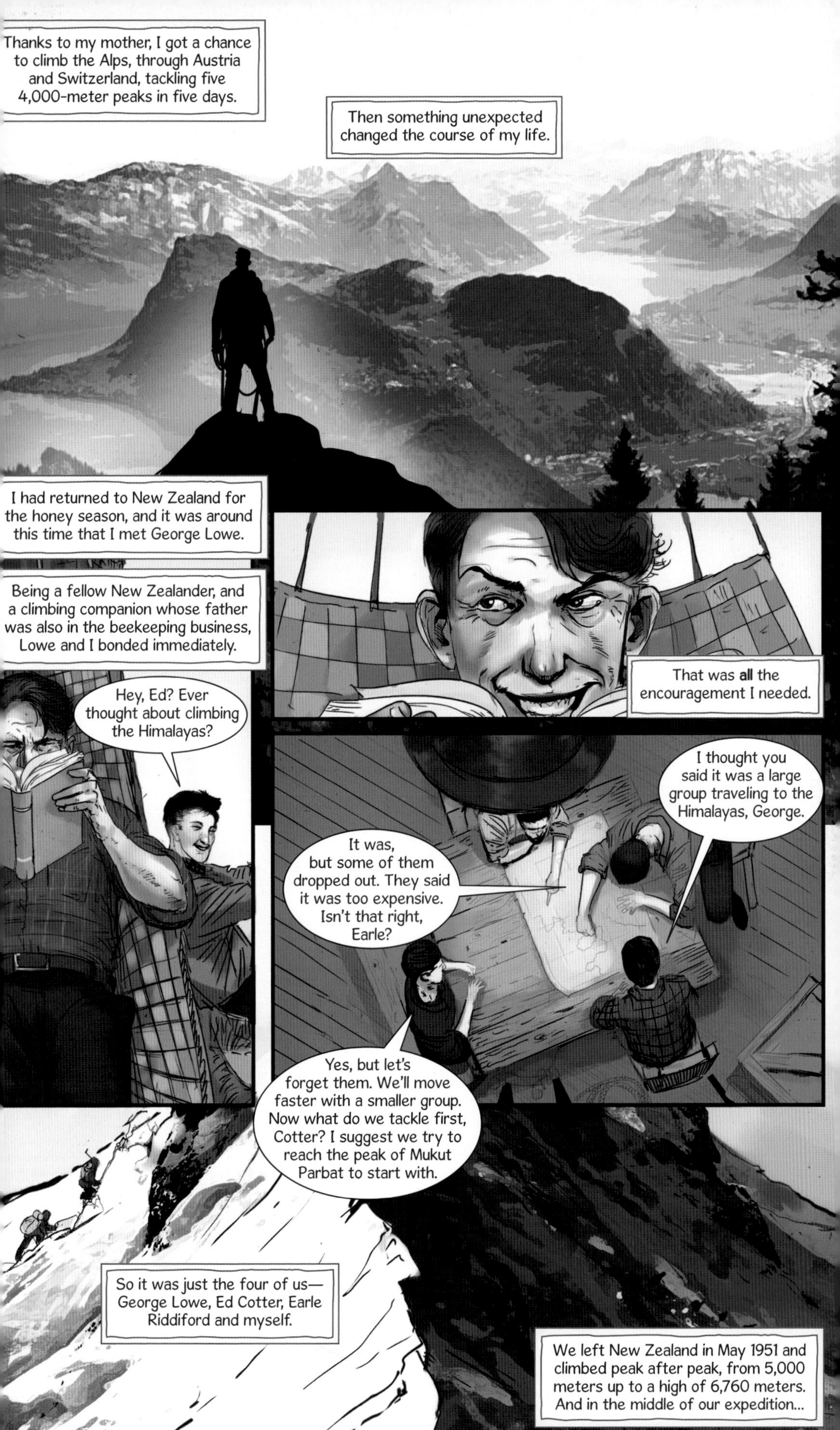

Thanks to my mother, I got a chance to climb the Alps, through Austria and Switzerland, tackling five 4,000-meter peaks in five days.
Then something unexpected changed the course of my life.
I had returned to New Zealand for the honey season, and it was around this time that I met George Lowe.
Being a fellow New Zealander, and a climbing companion whose father was also in the beekeeping business, Lowe and I bonded immediately.
Hey, Ed? Ever thought about climbing the Himalayas?
That was **all** the encouragement I needed.
I thought you said it was a large group traveling to the Himalayas, George.
It was, but some of them dropped out. They said it was too expensive. Isn't that right, Earle?
Yes, but let's forget them. We'll move faster with a smaller group. Now what do we tackle first, Cotter? I suggest we try to reach the peak of Mukut Parbat to start with.
So it was just the four of us—George Lowe, Ed Cotter, Earle Riddiford and myself.
We left New Zealand in May 1951 and climbed peak after peak, from 5,000 meters up to a high of 6,760 meters. And in the middle of our expedition...

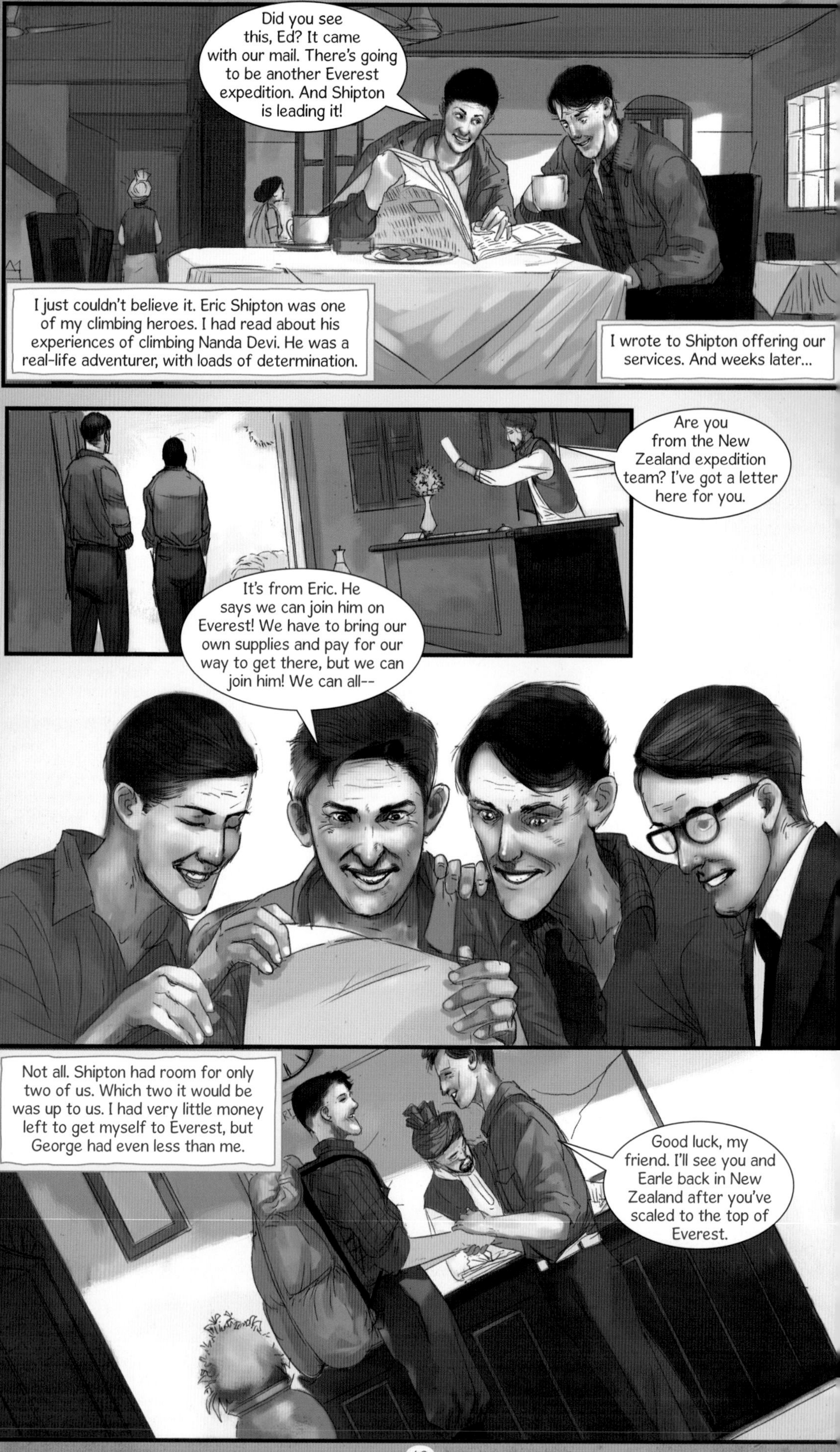

Did you see this, Ed? It came with our mail. There's going to be another Everest expedition. And Shipton is leading it!
I just couldn't believe it. Eric Shipton was one of my climbing heroes. I had read about his experiences of climbing Nanda Devi. He was a real-life adventurer, with loads of determination.
I wrote to Shipton offering our services. And weeks later...
Are you from the New Zealand expedition team? I've got a letter here for you.
It's from Eric. He says we can join him on Everest! We have to bring our own supplies and pay for our way to get there, but we can join him! We can all--
Not all. Shipton had room for only two of us. Which two it would be was up to us. I had very little money left to get myself to Everest, but George had even less than me.
Good luck, my friend. I'll see you and Earle back in New Zealand after you've scaled to the top of Everest.

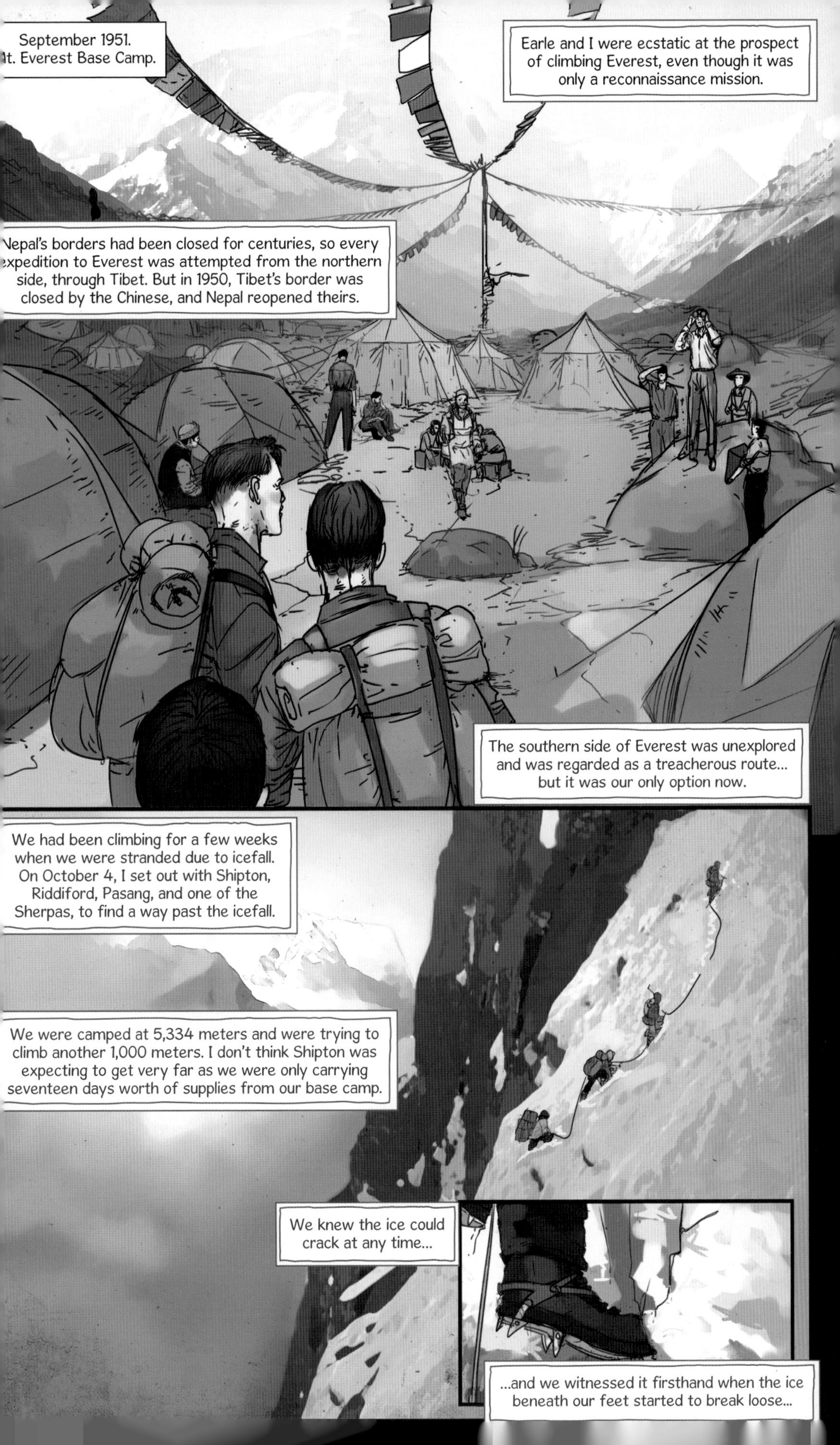
September 1951.
Mt. Everest Base Camp.
Earle and I were ecstatic at the prospect of climbing Everest, even though it was only a reconnaissance mission.
Nepal's borders had been closed for centuries, so every expedition to Everest was attempted from the northern side, through Tibet. But in 1950, Tibet's border was closed by the Chinese, and Nepal reopened theirs.
The southern side of Everest was unexplored and was regarded as a treacherous route... but it was our only option now.
We had been climbing for a few weeks when we were stranded due to icefall. On October 4, I set out with Shipton, Riddiford, Pasang, and one of the Sherpas, to find a way past the icefall.
We were camped at 5,334 meters and were trying to climb another 1,000 meters. I don't think Shipton was expecting to get very far as we were only carrying seventeen days worth of supplies from our base camp.
We knew the ice could crack at any time...
...and we witnessed it firsthand when the ice beneath our feet started to break loose...

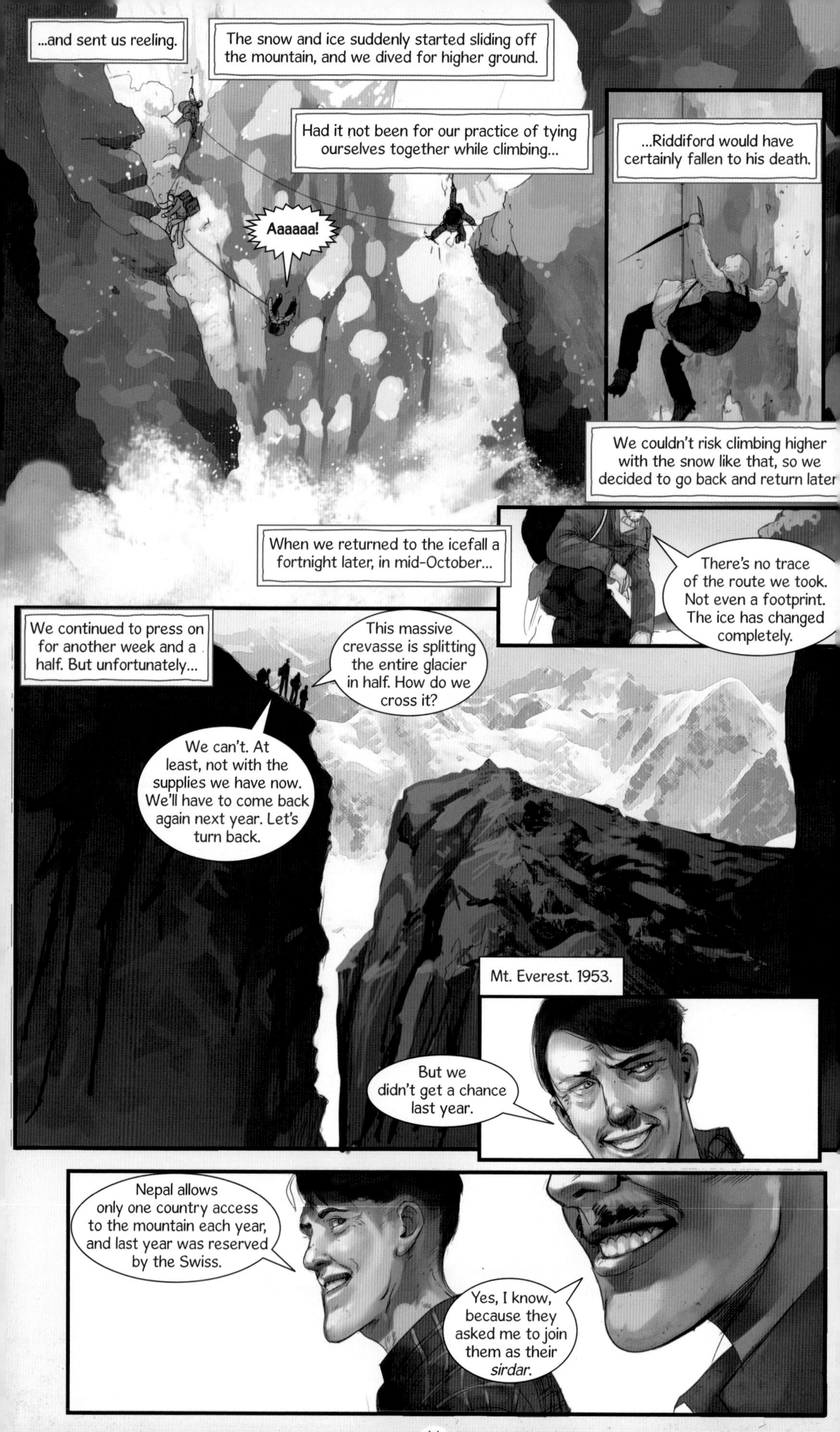

...and sent us reeling.
The snow and ice suddenly started sliding off the mountain, and we dived for higher ground.
Had it not been for our practice of tying ourselves together while climbing...
Aaaaaa!
...Riddiford would have certainly fallen to his death.
We couldn't risk climbing higher with the snow like that, so we decided to go back and return later
When we returned to the icefall a fortnight later, in mid-October...
There's no trace of the route we took. Not even a footprint. The ice has changed completely.
We continued to press on for another week and a half. But unfortunately...
This massive crevasse is splitting the entire glacier in half. How do we cross it?
We can't. At least, not with the supplies we have now. We'll have to come back again next year. Let's turn back.
Mt. Everest. 1953.
But we didn't get a chance last year.
Nepal allows only one country access to the mountain each year, and last year was reserved by the Swiss.
Yes, I know, because they asked me to join them as their *sirdar*.

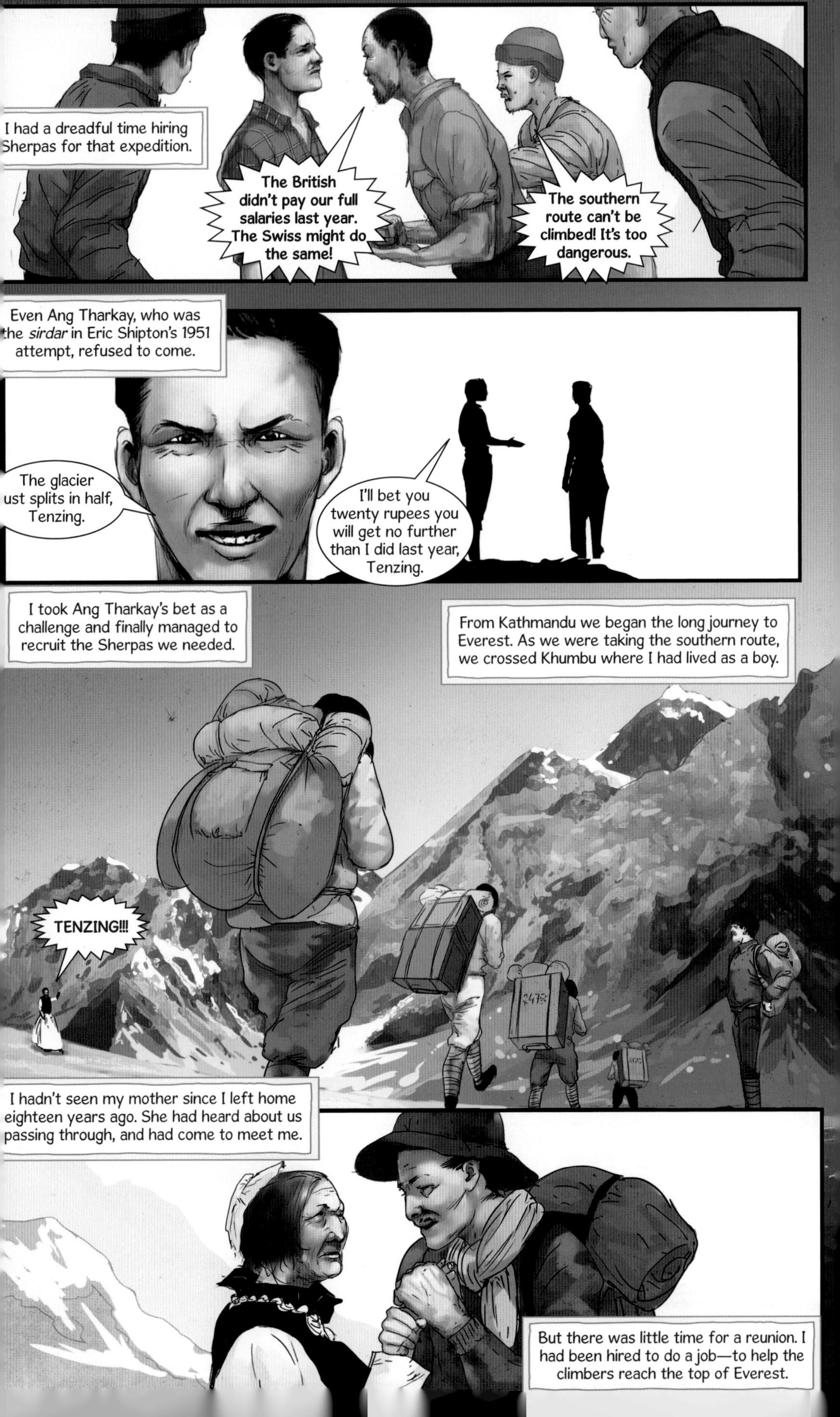

I had a dreadful time hiring Sherpas for that expedition.
The British didn't pay our full salaries last year. The Swiss might do the same!
The southern route can't be climbed! It's too dangerous.
Even Ang Tharkay, who was the *sirdar* in Eric Shipton's 1951 attempt, refused to come.
The glacier ust splits in half, Tenzing.
I'll bet you twenty rupees you will get no further than I did last year, Tenzing.
I took Ang Tharkay's bet as a challenge and finally managed to recruit the Sherpas we needed.
From Kathmandu we began the long journey to Everest. As we were taking the southern route, we crossed Khumbu where I had lived as a boy.
TENZING!!!
I hadn't seen my mother since I left home eighteen years ago. She had heard about us passing through, and had come to meet me.
But there was little time for a reunion. I had been hired to do a job—to help the climbers reach the top of Everest.

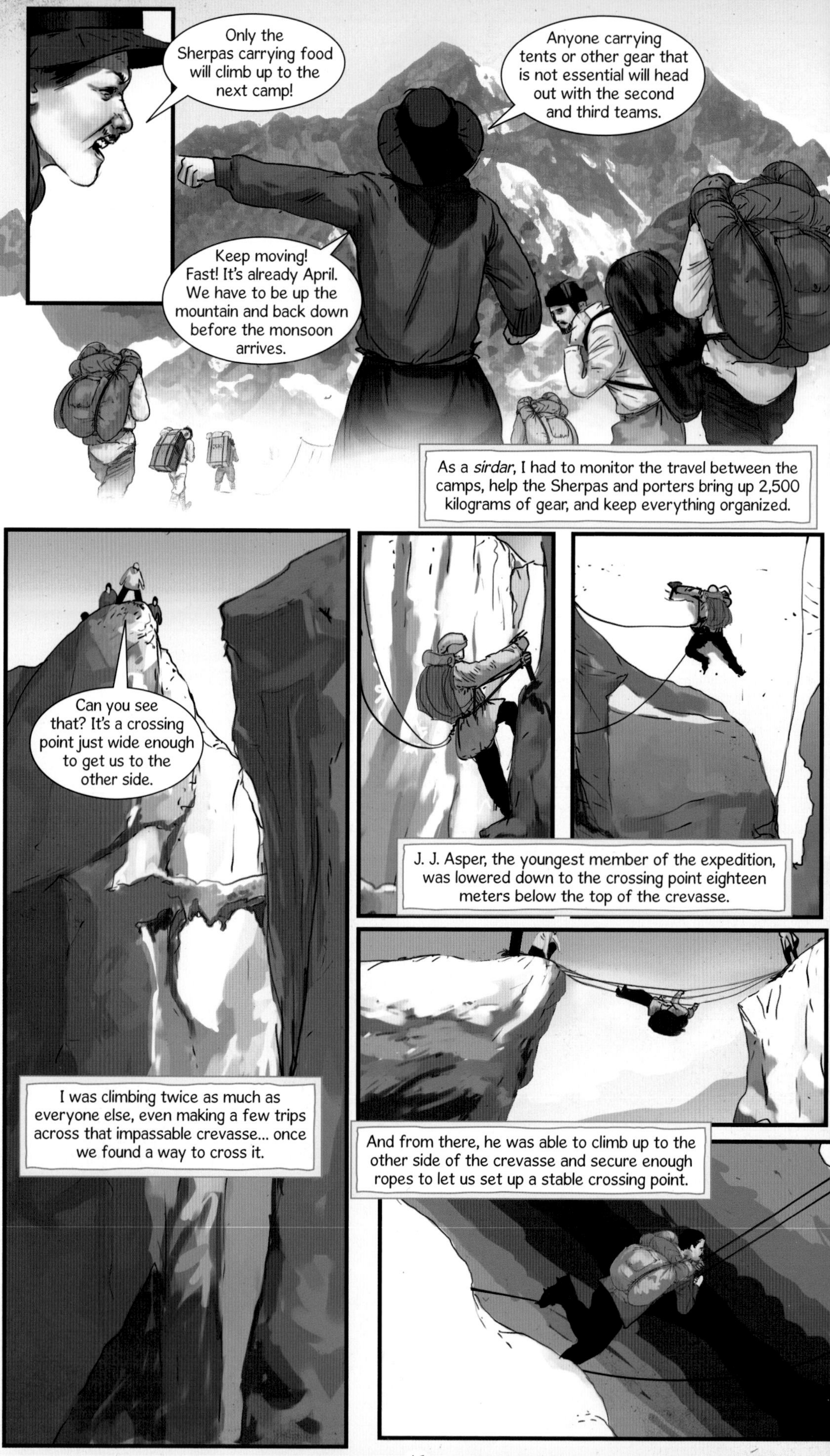

Only the Sherpas carrying food will climb up to the next camp!
Anyone carrying tents or other gear that is not essential will head out with the second and third teams.
Keep moving! Fast! It's already April. We have to be up the mountain and back down before the monsoon arrives.
As a *sirdar*, I had to monitor the travel between the camps, help the Sherpas and porters bring up 2,500 kilograms of gear, and keep everything organized.
Can you see that? It's a crossing point just wide enough to get us to the other side.
I was climbing twice as much as everyone else, even making a few trips across that impassable crevasse... once we found a way to cross it.
J. J. Asper, the youngest member of the expedition, was lowered down to the crossing point eighteen meters below the top of the crevasse.
And from there, he was able to climb up to the other side of the crevasse and secure enough ropes to let us set up a stable crossing point.

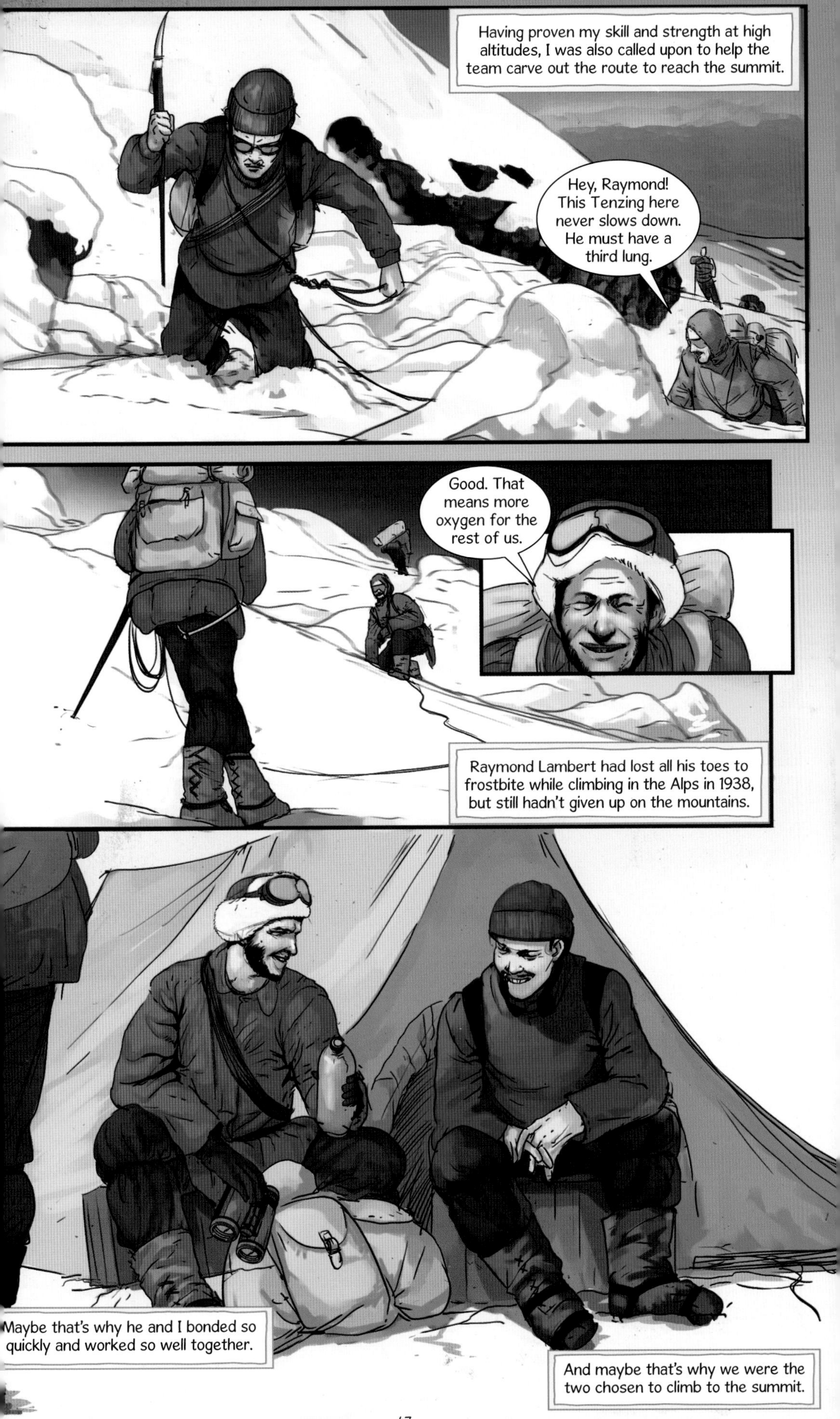
Having proven my skill and strength at high altitudes, I was also called upon to help the team carve out the route to reach the summit.
Hey, Raymond! This Tenzing here never slows down. He must have a third lung.
Good. That means more oxygen for the rest of us.
Raymond Lambert had lost all his toes to frostbite while climbing in the Alps in 1938, but still hadn't given up on the mountains.
Maybe that's why he and I bonded so quickly and worked so well together.
And maybe that's why we were the two chosen to climb to the summit.

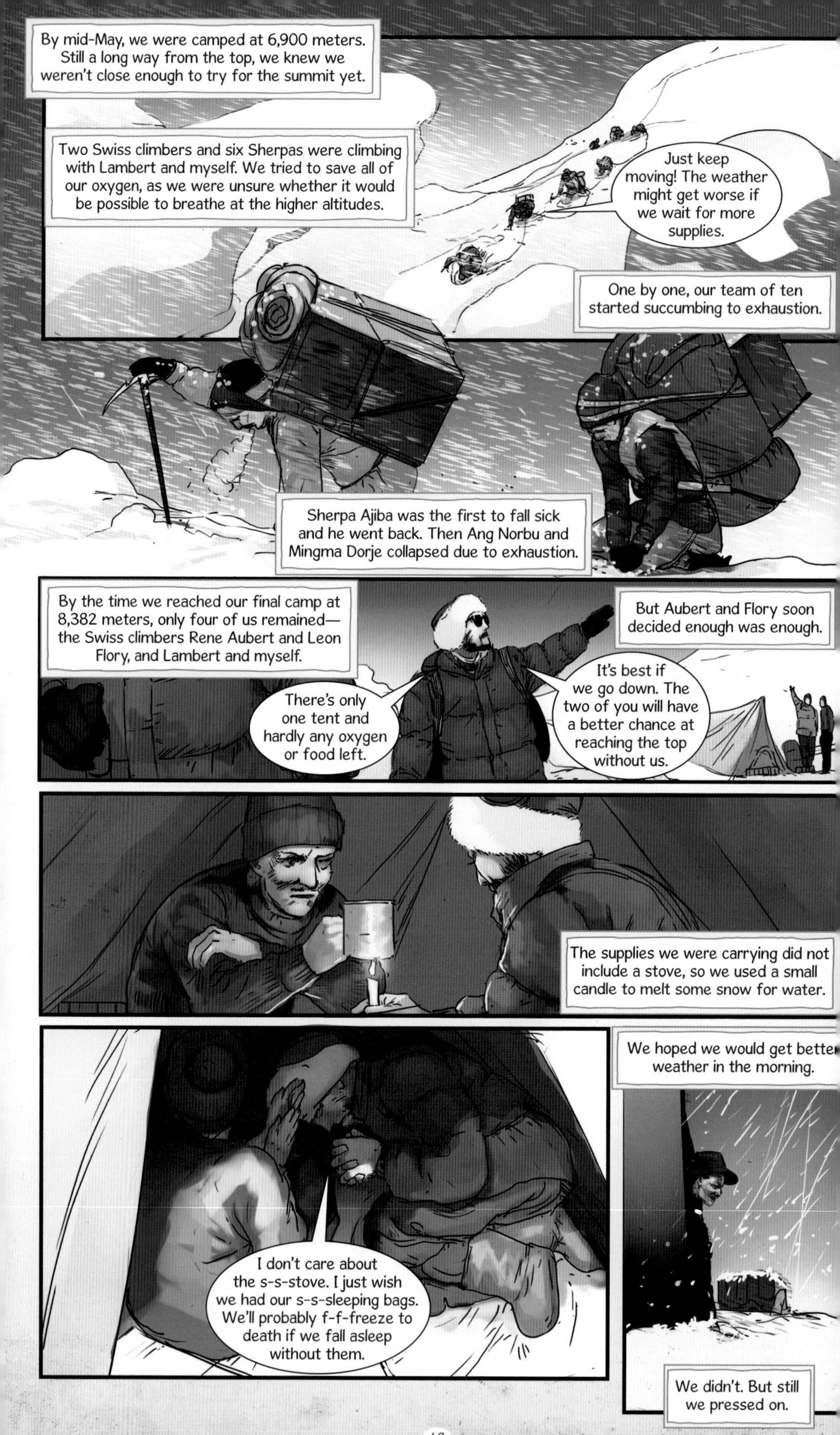

By mid-May, we were camped at 6,900 meters. Still a long way from the top, we knew we weren't close enough to try for the summit yet.
Two Swiss climbers and six Sherpas were climbing with Lambert and myself. We tried to save all of our oxygen, as we were unsure whether it would be possible to breathe at the higher altitudes.
Just keep moving! The weather might get worse if we wait for more supplies.
One by one, our team of ten started succumbing to exhaustion.
Sherpa Ajiba was the first to fall sick and he went back. Then Ang Norbu and Mingma Dorje collapsed due to exhaustion.
By the time we reached our final camp at 8,382 meters, only four of us remained—the Swiss climbers Rene Aubert and Leon Flory, and Lambert and myself.
But Aubert and Flory soon decided enough was enough.
There's only one tent and hardly any oxygen or food left.
It's best if we go down. The two of you will have a better chance at reaching the top without us.
The supplies we were carrying did not include a stove, so we used a small candle to melt some snow for water.
I don't care about the s-s-stove. I just wish we had our s-s-sleeping bags. We'll probably f-f-freeze to death if we fall asleep without them.
We hoped we would get better weather in the morning.
We didn't. But still we pressed on.

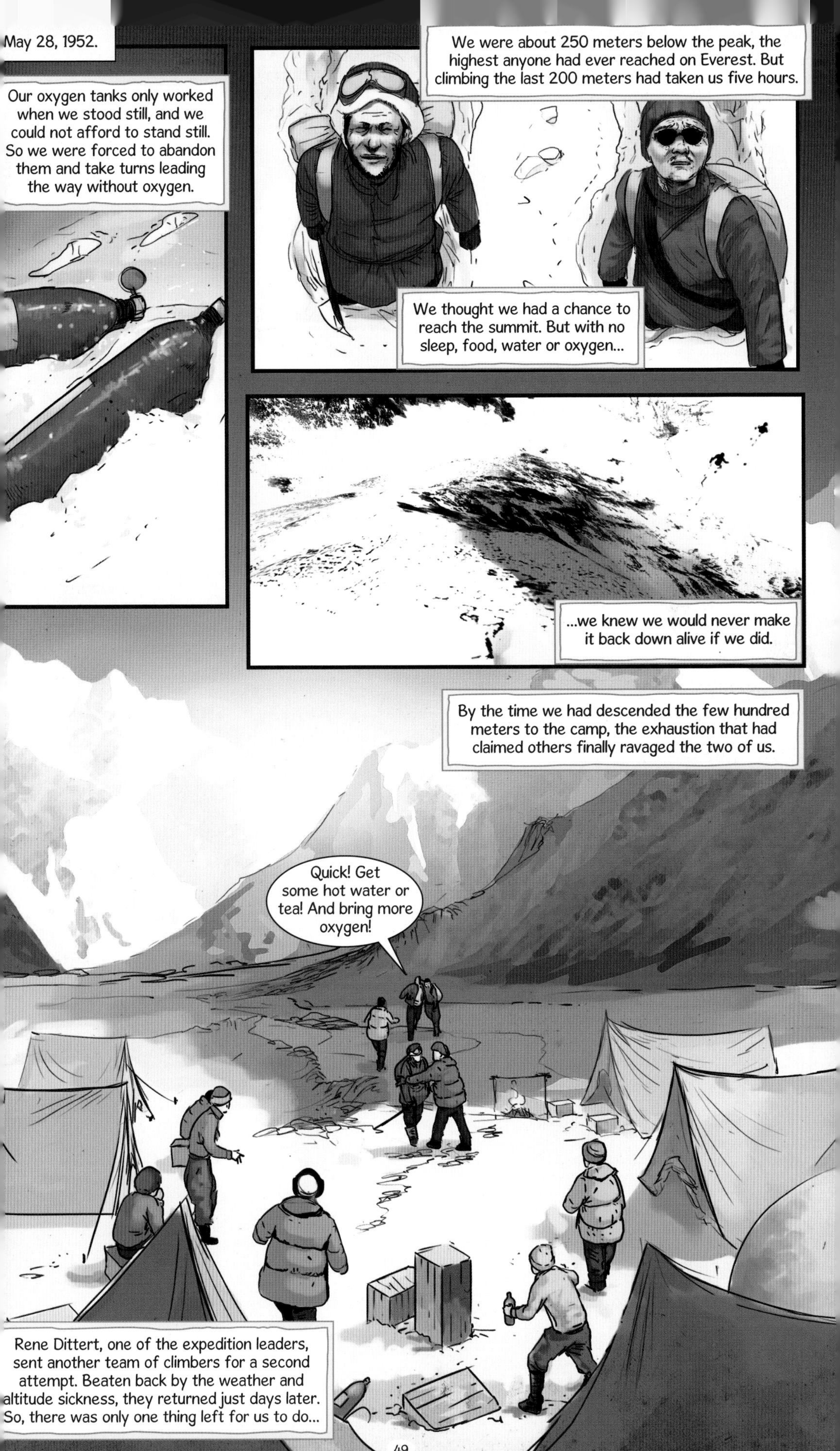
May 28, 1952.
Our oxygen tanks only worked when we stood still, and we could not afford to stand still. So we were forced to abandon them and take turns leading the way without oxygen.
We were about 250 meters below the peak, the highest anyone had ever reached on Everest. But climbing the last 200 meters had taken us five hours.
We thought we had a chance to reach the summit. But with no sleep, food, water or oxygen...
...we knew we would never make it back down alive if we did.
By the time we had descended the few hundred meters to the camp, the exhaustion that had claimed others finally ravaged the two of us.
Quick! Get some hot water or tea! And bring more oxygen!
Rene Dittert, one of the expedition leaders, sent another team of climbers for a second attempt. Beaten back by the weather and altitude sickness, they returned just days later. So, there was only one thing left for us to do...

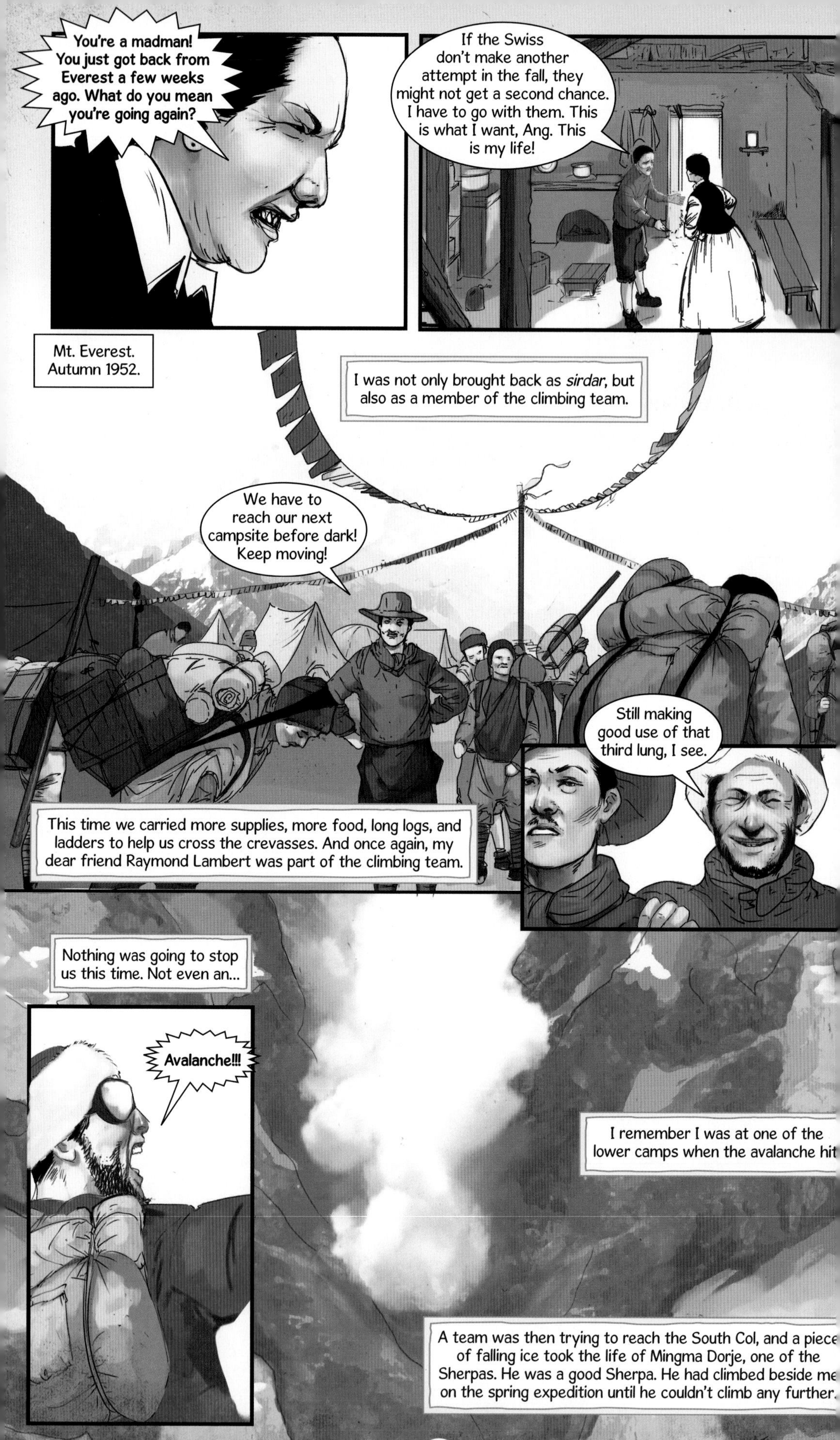

You're a madman! You just got back from Everest a few weeks ago. What do you mean you're going again?
If the Swiss don't make another attempt in the fall, they might not get a second chance. I have to go with them. This is what I want, Ang. This is my life!
Mt. Everest. Autumn 1952.
I was not only brought back as *sirdar*, but also as a member of the climbing team.
We have to reach our next campsite before dark! Keep moving!
This time we carried more supplies, more food, long logs, and ladders to help us cross the crevasses. And once again, my dear friend Raymond Lambert was part of the climbing team.
Still making good use of that third lung, I see.
Nothing was going to stop us this time. Not even an...
Avalanche!!!
I remember I was at one of the lower camps when the avalanche hit
A team was then trying to reach the South Col, and a piece of falling ice took the life of Mingma Dorje, one of the Sherpas. He was a good Sherpa. He had climbed beside me on the spring expedition until he couldn't climb any further.

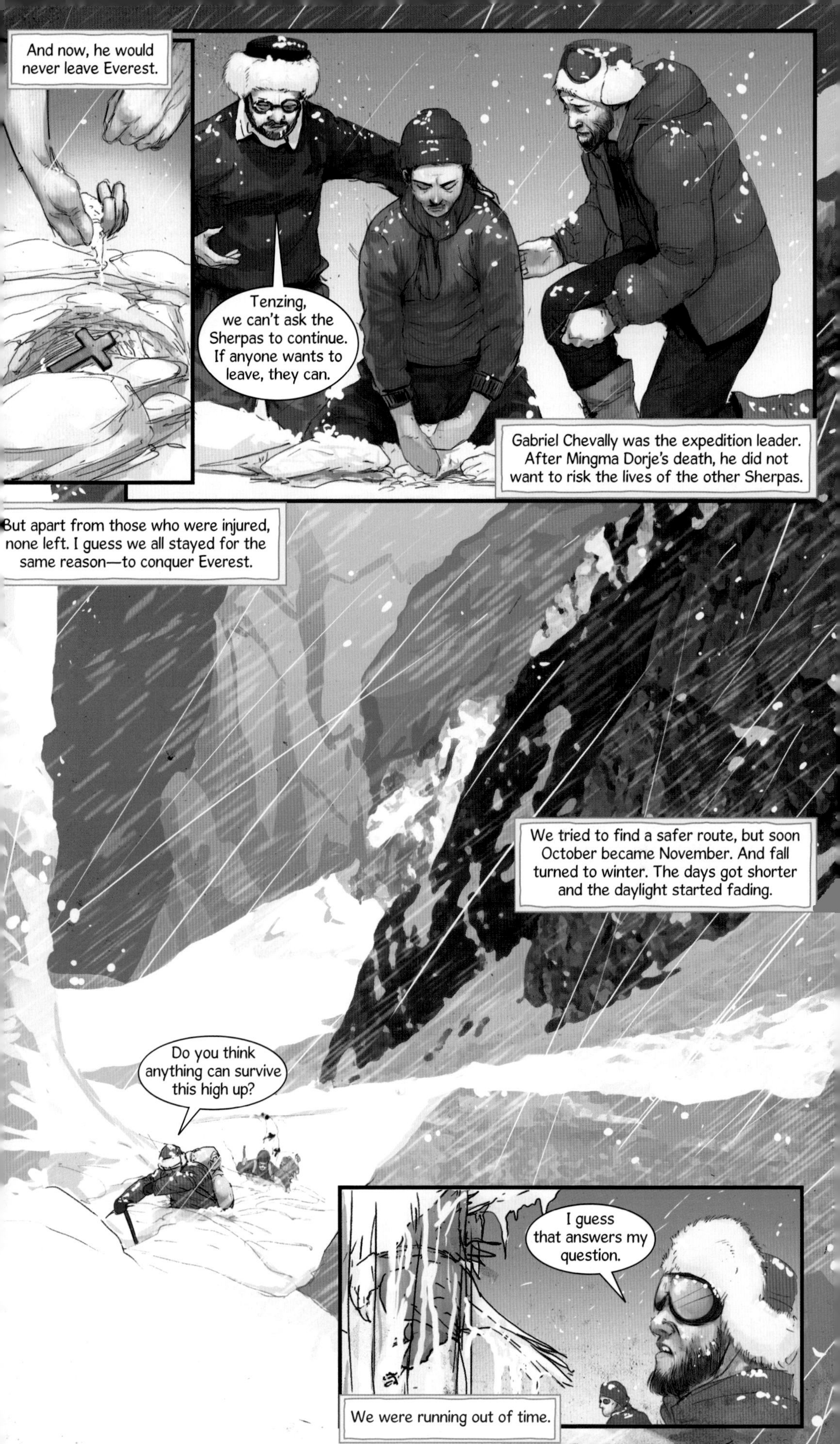
And now, he would never leave Everest.
Tenzing, we can't ask the Sherpas to continue. If anyone wants to leave, they can.
Gabriel Chevally was the expedition leader. After Mingma Dorje's death, he did not want to risk the lives of the other Sherpas.
But apart from those who were injured, none left. I guess we all stayed for the same reason—to conquer Everest.
We tried to find a safer route, but soon October became November. And fall turned to winter. The days got shorter and the daylight started fading.
Do you think anything can survive this high up?
I guess that answers my question.
We were running out of time.

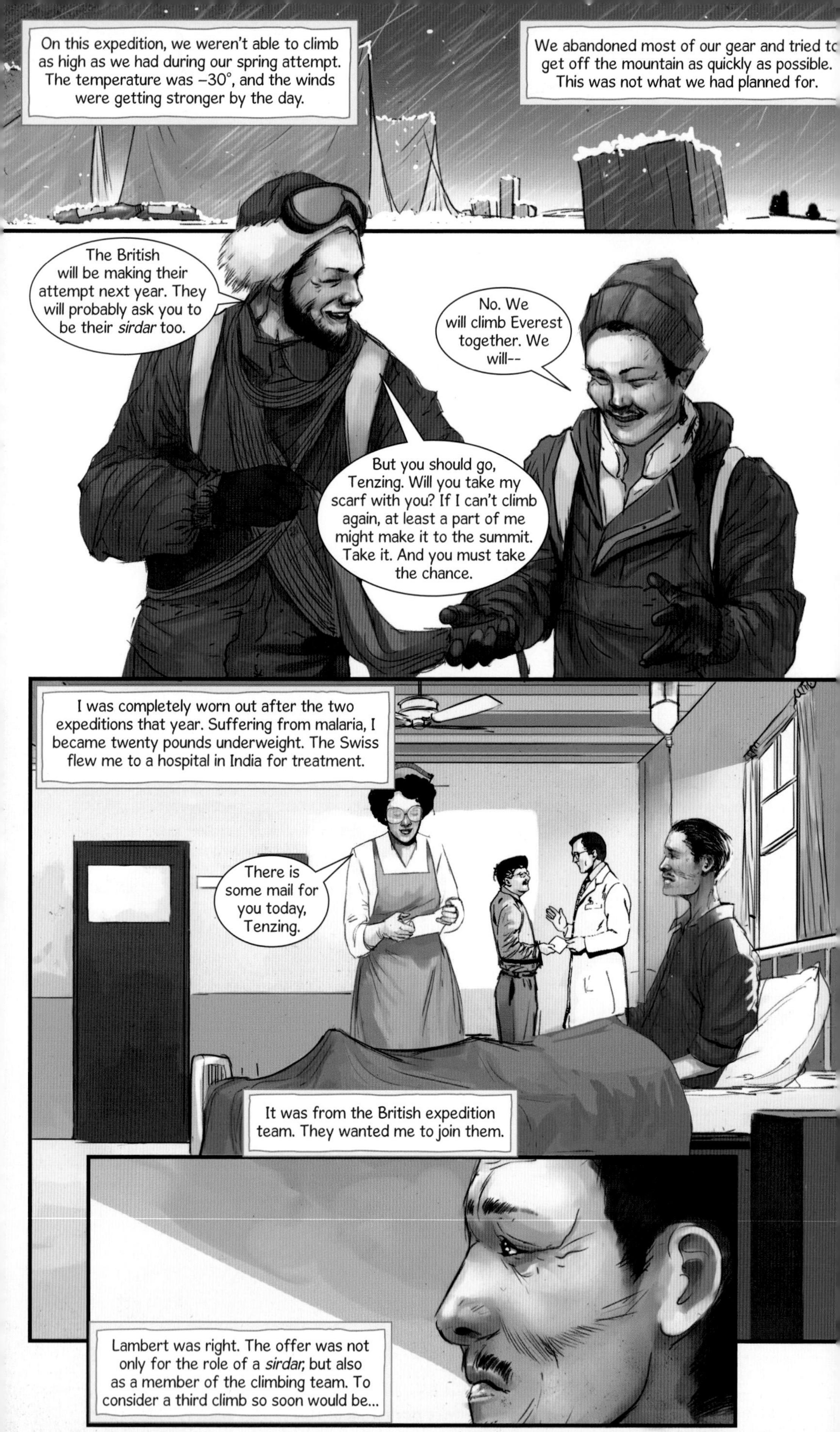

On this expedition, we weren't able to climb as high as we had during our spring attempt. The temperature was –30°, and the winds were getting stronger by the day.
We abandoned most of our gear and tried to get off the mountain as quickly as possible. This was not what we had planned for.
The British will be making their attempt next year. They will probably ask you to be their *sirdar* too.
No. We will climb Everest together. We will--
But you should go, Tenzing. Will you take my scarf with you? If I can't climb again, at least a part of me might make it to the summit. Take it. And you must take the chance.
I was completely worn out after the two expeditions that year. Suffering from malaria, I became twenty pounds underweight. The Swiss flew me to a hospital in India for treatment.
There is some mail for you today, Tenzing.
It was from the British expedition team. They wanted me to join them.
Lambert was right. The offer was not only for the role of a *sirdar,* but also as a member of the climbing team. To consider a third climb so soon would be...

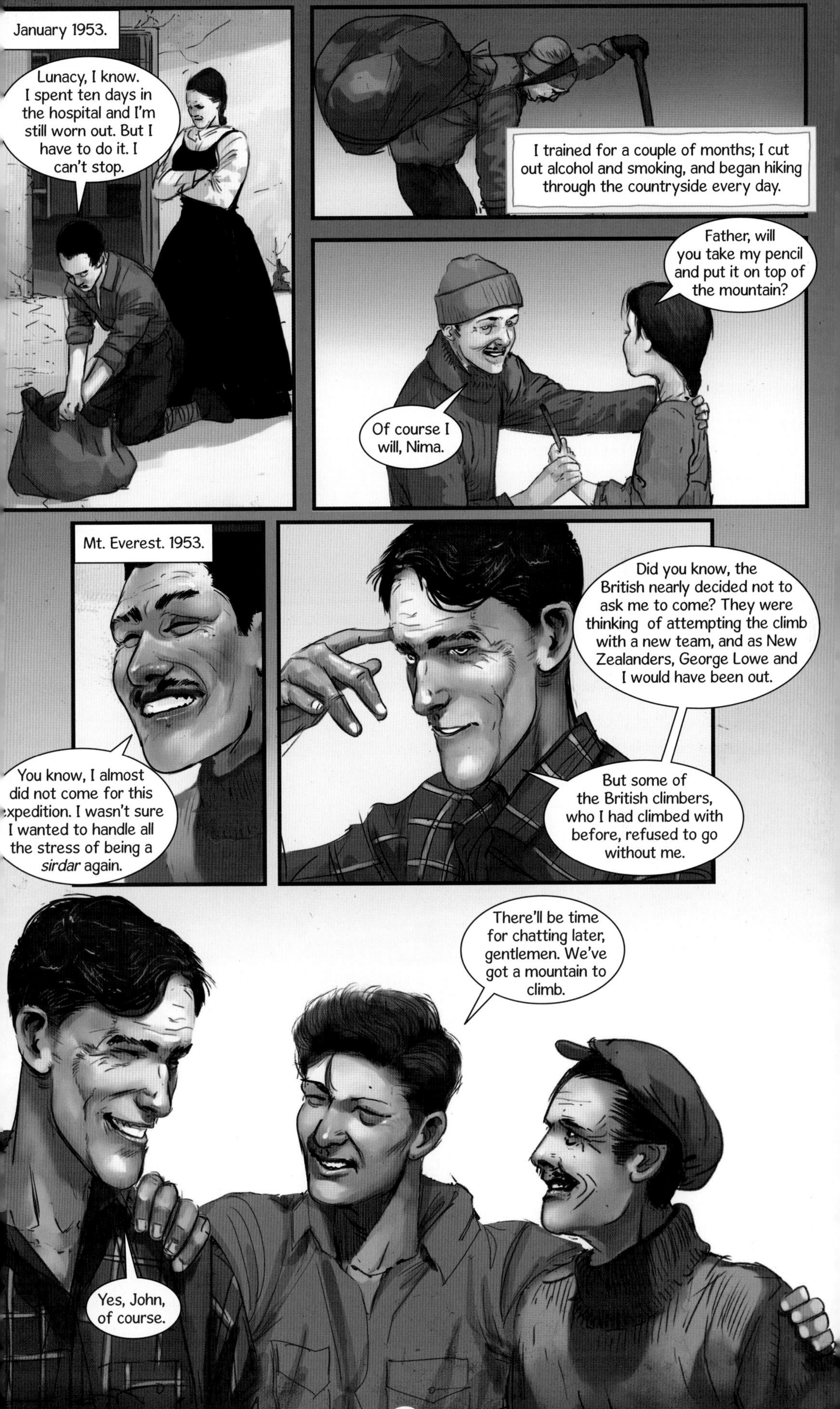

January 1953.
Lunacy, I know. I spent ten days in the hospital and I'm still worn out. But I have to do it. I can't stop.
I trained for a couple of months; I cut out alcohol and smoking, and began hiking through the countryside every day.
Father, will you take my pencil and put it on top of the mountain?
Of course I will, Nima.
Mt. Everest. 1953.
You know, I almost did not come for this expedition. I wasn't sure I wanted to handle all the stress of being a *sirdar* again.
Did you know, the British nearly decided not to ask me to come? They were thinking of attempting the climb with a new team, and as New Zealanders, George Lowe and I would have been out.
But some of the British climbers, who I had climbed with before, refused to go without me.
There'll be time for chatting later, gentlemen. We've got a mountain to climb.
Yes, John, of course.

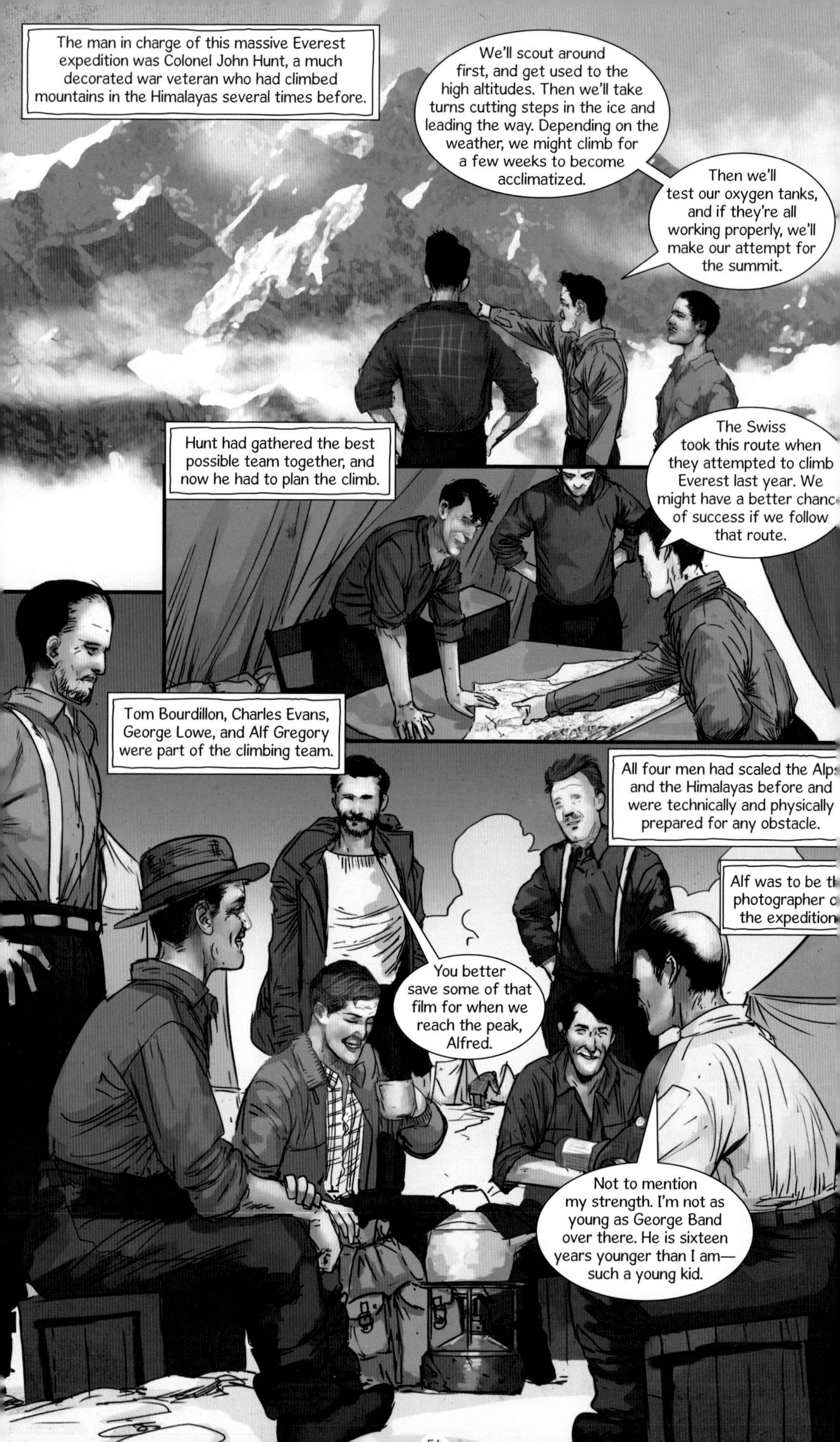
The man in charge of this massive Everest expedition was Colonel John Hunt, a much decorated war veteran who had climbed mountains in the Himalayas several times before.
We'll scout around first, and get used to the high altitudes. Then we'll take turns cutting steps in the ice and leading the way. Depending on the weather, we might climb for a few weeks to become acclimatized.
Then we'll test our oxygen tanks, and if they're all working properly, we'll make our attempt for the summit.
Hunt had gathered the best possible team together, and now he had to plan the climb.
The Swiss took this route when they attempted to climb Everest last year. We might have a better chanc of success if we follow that route.
Tom Bourdillon, Charles Evans, George Lowe, and Alf Gregory were part of the climbing team.
All four men had scaled the Alp and the Himalayas before and were technically and physically prepared for any obstacle.
Alf was to be t photographer o the expedition
You better save some of that film for when we reach the peak, Alfred.
Not to mention my strength. I'm not as young as George Band over there. He is sixteen years younger than I am— such a young kid.

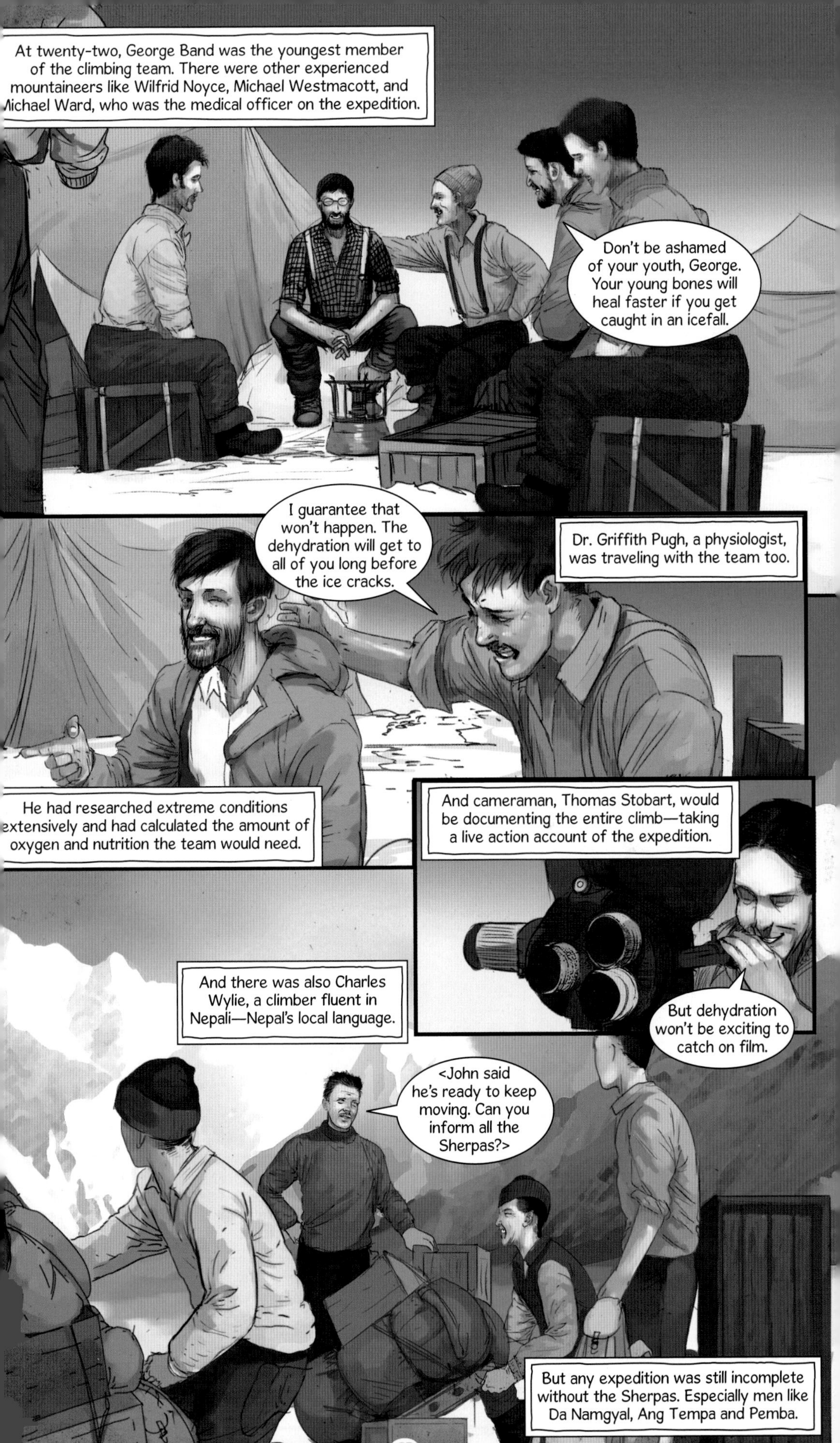
At twenty-two, George Band was the youngest member of the climbing team. There were other experienced mountaineers like Wilfrid Noyce, Michael Westmacott, and Michael Ward, who was the medical officer on the expedition.
Don't be ashamed of your youth, George. Your young bones will heal faster if you get caught in an icefall.
I guarantee that won't happen. The dehydration will get to all of you long before the ice cracks.
Dr. Griffith Pugh, a physiologist, was traveling with the team too.
He had researched extreme conditions extensively and had calculated the amount of oxygen and nutrition the team would need.
And cameraman, Thomas Stobart, would be documenting the entire climb—taking a live action account of the expedition.
But dehydration won't be exciting to catch on film.
And there was also Charles Wylie, a climber fluent in Nepali—Nepal's local language.
<John said he's ready to keep moving. Can you inform all the Sherpas?>
But any expedition was still incomplete without the Sherpas. Especially men like Da Namgyal, Ang Tempa and Pemba.

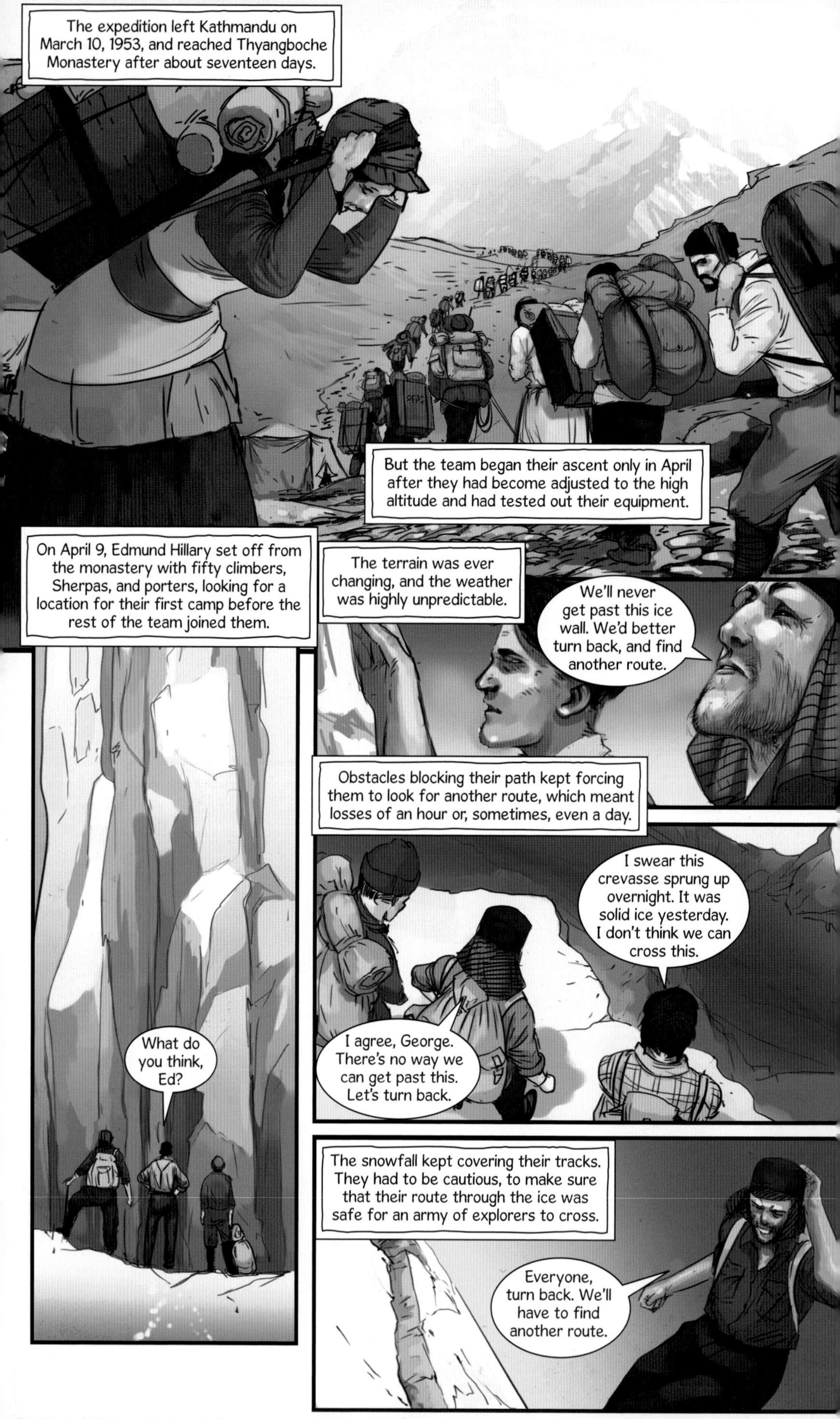
The expedition left Kathmandu on March 10, 1953, and reached Thyangboche Monastery after about seventeen days.
But the team began their ascent only in April after they had become adjusted to the high altitude and had tested out their equipment.
On April 9, Edmund Hillary set off from the monastery with fifty climbers, Sherpas, and porters, looking for a location for their first camp before the rest of the team joined them.
What do you think, Ed?
The terrain was ever changing, and the weather was highly unpredictable.
We'll never get past this ice wall. We'd better turn back, and find another route.
Obstacles blocking their path kept forcing them to look for another route, which meant losses of an hour or, sometimes, even a day.
I swear this crevasse sprung up overnight. It was solid ice yesterday. I don't think we can cross this.
I agree, George. There's no way we can get past this. Let's turn back.
The snowfall kept covering their tracks. They had to be cautious, to make sure that their route through the ice was safe for an army of explorers to cross.
Everyone, turn back. We'll have to find another route.

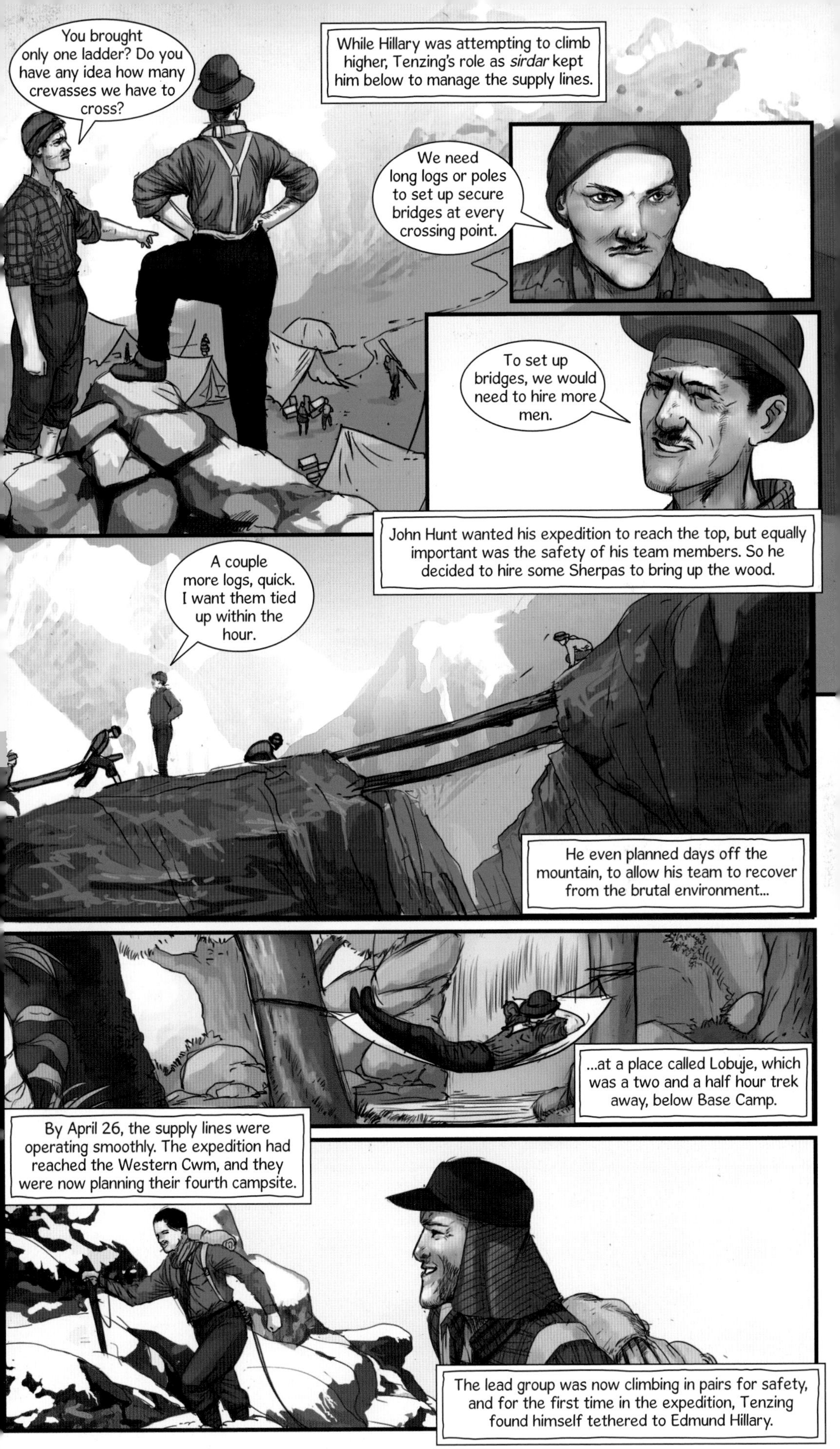
You brought only one ladder? Do you have any idea how many crevasses we have to cross?
While Hillary was attempting to climb higher, Tenzing's role as *sirdar* kept him below to manage the supply lines.
We need long logs or poles to set up secure bridges at every crossing point.
To set up bridges, we would need to hire more men.
John Hunt wanted his expedition to reach the top, but equally important was the safety of his team members. So he decided to hire some Sherpas to bring up the wood.
A couple more logs, quick. I want them tied up within the hour.
He even planned days off the mountain, to allow his team to recover from the brutal environment...
...at a place called Lobuje, which was a two and a half hour trek away, below Base Camp.
By April 26, the supply lines were operating smoothly. The expedition had reached the Western Cwm, and they were now planning their fourth campsite.
The lead group was now climbing in pairs for safety, and for the first time in the expedition, Tenzing found himself tethered to Edmund Hillary.

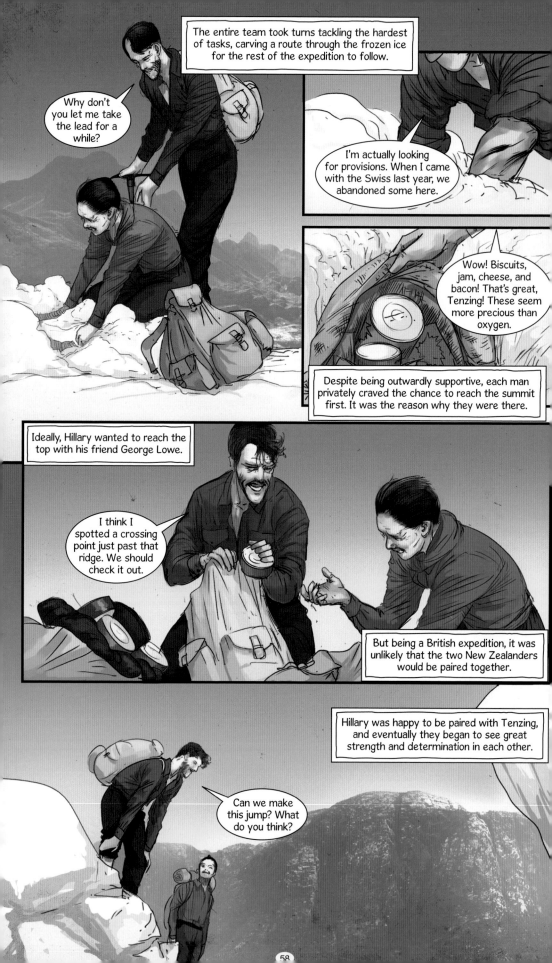

The entire team took turns tackling the hardest of tasks, carving a route through the frozen ice for the rest of the expedition to follow.

Why don't you let me take the lead for a while?

I'm actually looking for provisions. When I came with the Swiss last year, we abandoned some here.

Wow! Biscuits, jam, cheese, and bacon! That's great, Tenzing! These seem more precious than oxygen.

Despite being outwardly supportive, each man privately craved the chance to reach the summit first. It was the reason why they were there.

Ideally, Hillary wanted to reach the top with his friend George Lowe.

I think I spotted a crossing point just past that ridge. We should check it out.

But being a British expedition, it was unlikely that the two New Zealanders would be paired together.

Hillary was happy to be paired with Tenzing, and eventually they began to see great strength and determination in each other.

Can we make this jump? What do you think?

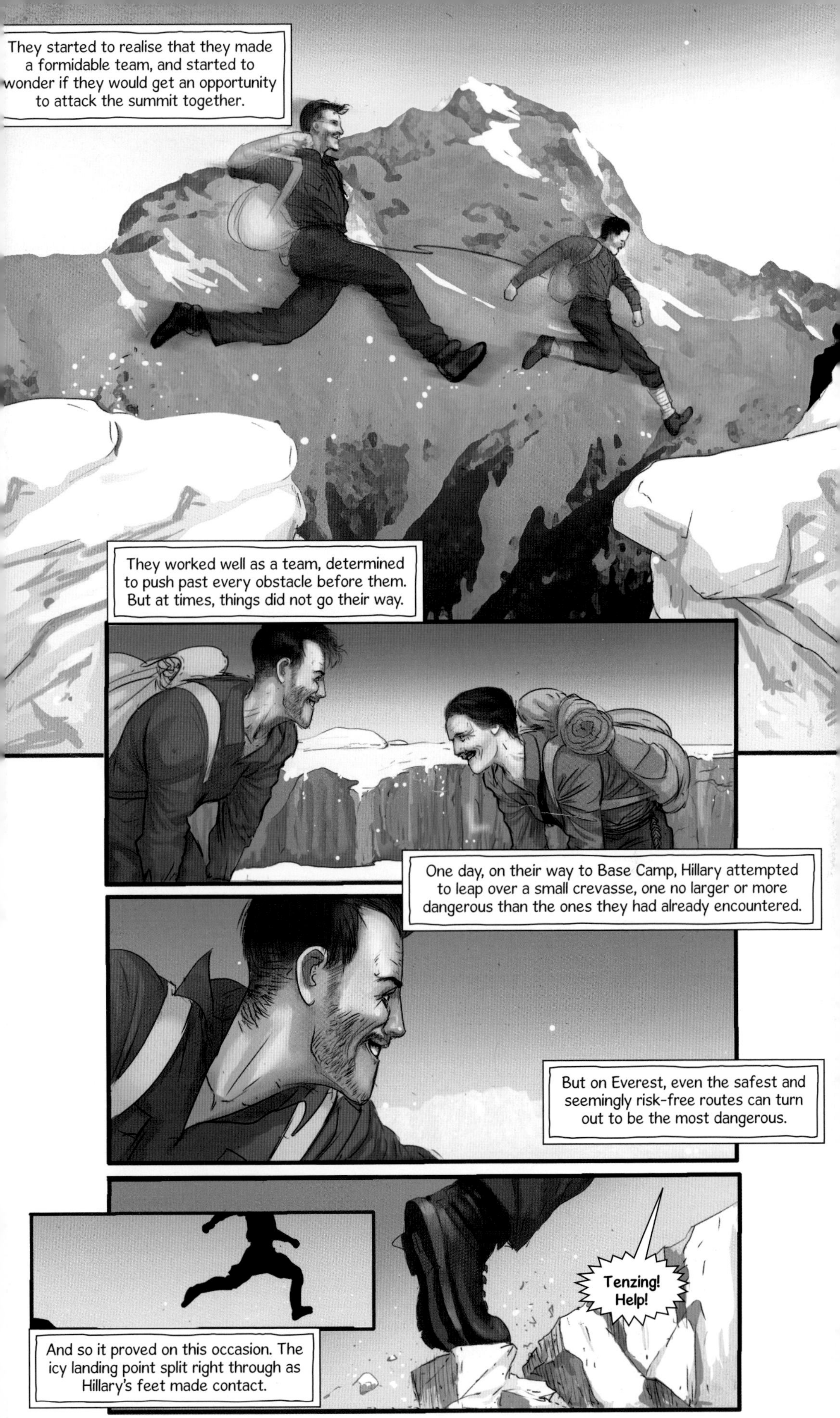
They started to realise that they made a formidable team, and started to wonder if they would get an opportunity to attack the summit together.
They worked well as a team, determined to push past every obstacle before them. But at times, things did not go their way.
One day, on their way to Base Camp, Hillary attempted to leap over a small crevasse, one no larger or more dangerous than the ones they had already encountered.
But on Everest, even the safest and seemingly risk-free routes can turn out to be the most dangerous.
And so it proved on this occasion. The icy landing point split right through as Hillary's feet made contact.
Tenzing! Help!

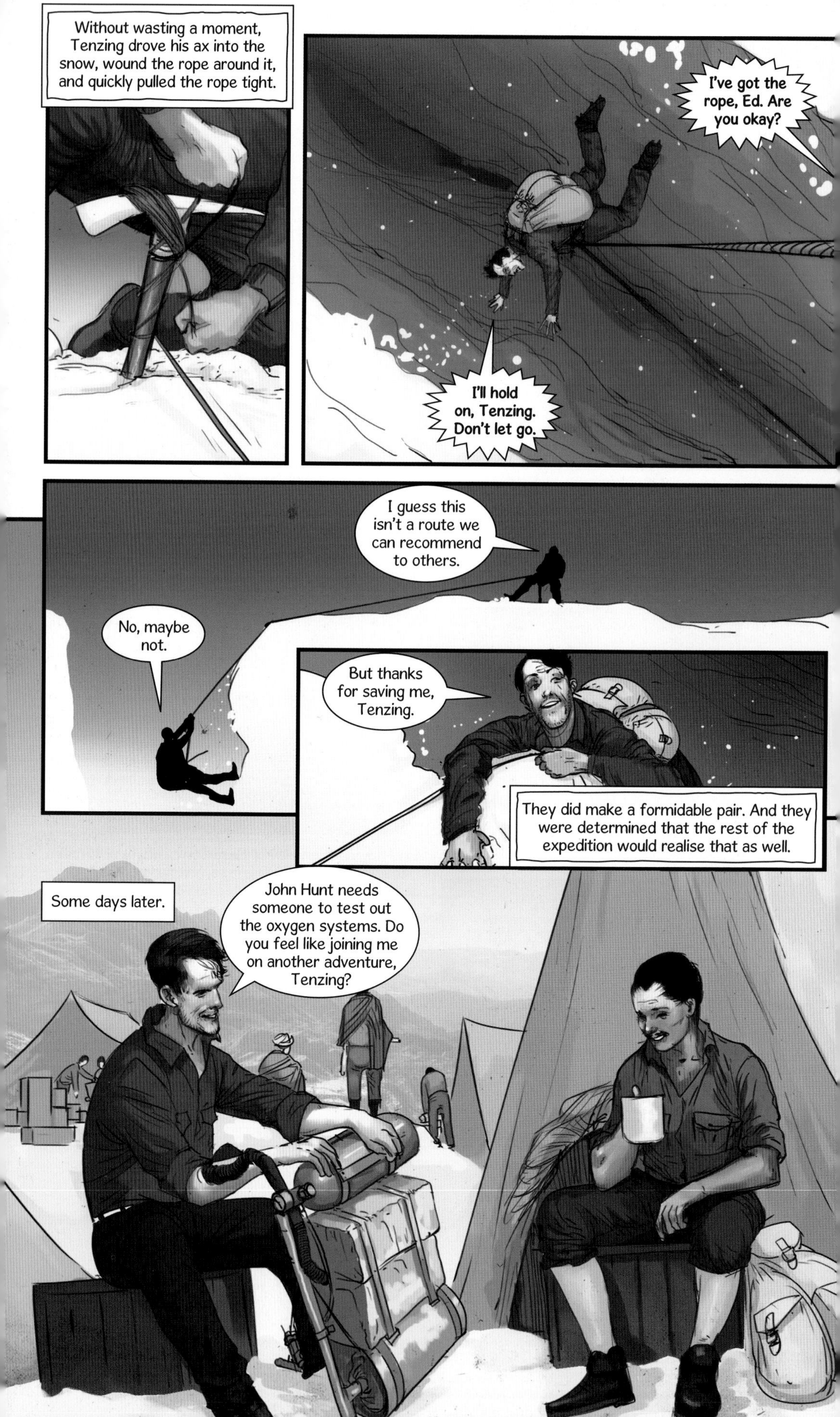
Without wasting a moment, Tenzing drove his ax into the snow, wound the rope around it, and quickly pulled the rope tight.
I've got the rope, Ed. Are you okay?
I'll hold on, Tenzing. Don't let go.
I guess this isn't a route we can recommend to others.
No, maybe not.
But thanks for saving me, Tenzing.
They did make a formidable pair. And they were determined that the rest of the expedition would realise that as well.
Some days later.
John Hunt needs someone to test out the oxygen systems. Do you feel like joining me on another adventure, Tenzing?

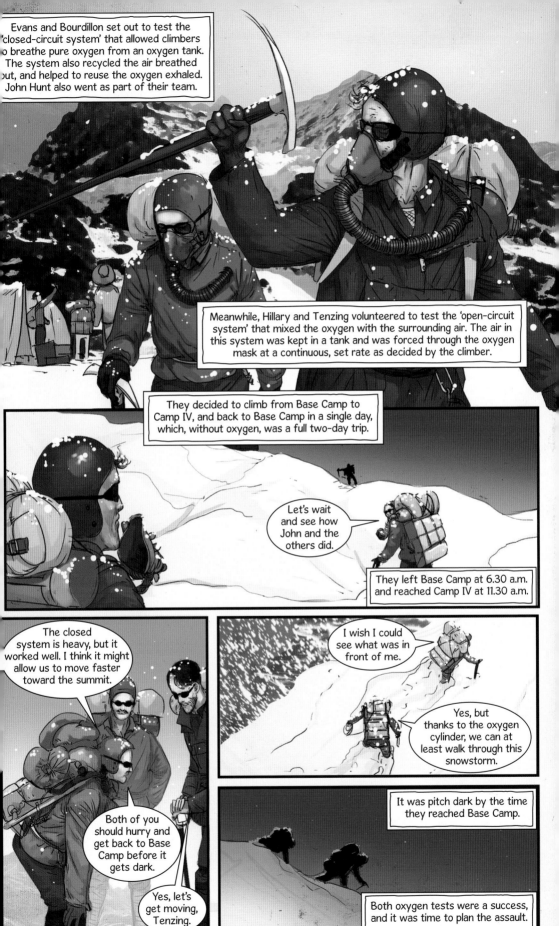

Evans and Bourdillon set out to test the 'closed-circuit system' that allowed climbers to breathe pure oxygen from an oxygen tank. The system also recycled the air breathed out, and helped to reuse the oxygen exhaled. John Hunt also went as part of their team.

Meanwhile, Hillary and Tenzing volunteered to test the 'open-circuit system' that mixed the oxygen with the surrounding air. The air in this system was kept in a tank and was forced through the oxygen mask at a continuous, set rate as decided by the climber.

They decided to climb from Base Camp to Camp IV, and back to Base Camp in a single day, which, without oxygen, was a full two-day trip.

Let's wait and see how John and the others did.

They left Base Camp at 6.30 a.m. and reached Camp IV at 11.30 a.m.

The closed system is heavy, but it worked well. I think it might allow us to move faster toward the summit.

I wish I could see what was in front of me.

Yes, but thanks to the oxygen cylinder, we can at least walk through this snowstorm.

Both of you should hurry and get back to Base Camp before it gets dark.

Yes, let's get moving, Tenzing.

It was pitch dark by the time they reached Base Camp.

Both oxygen tests were a success, and it was time to plan the assault.

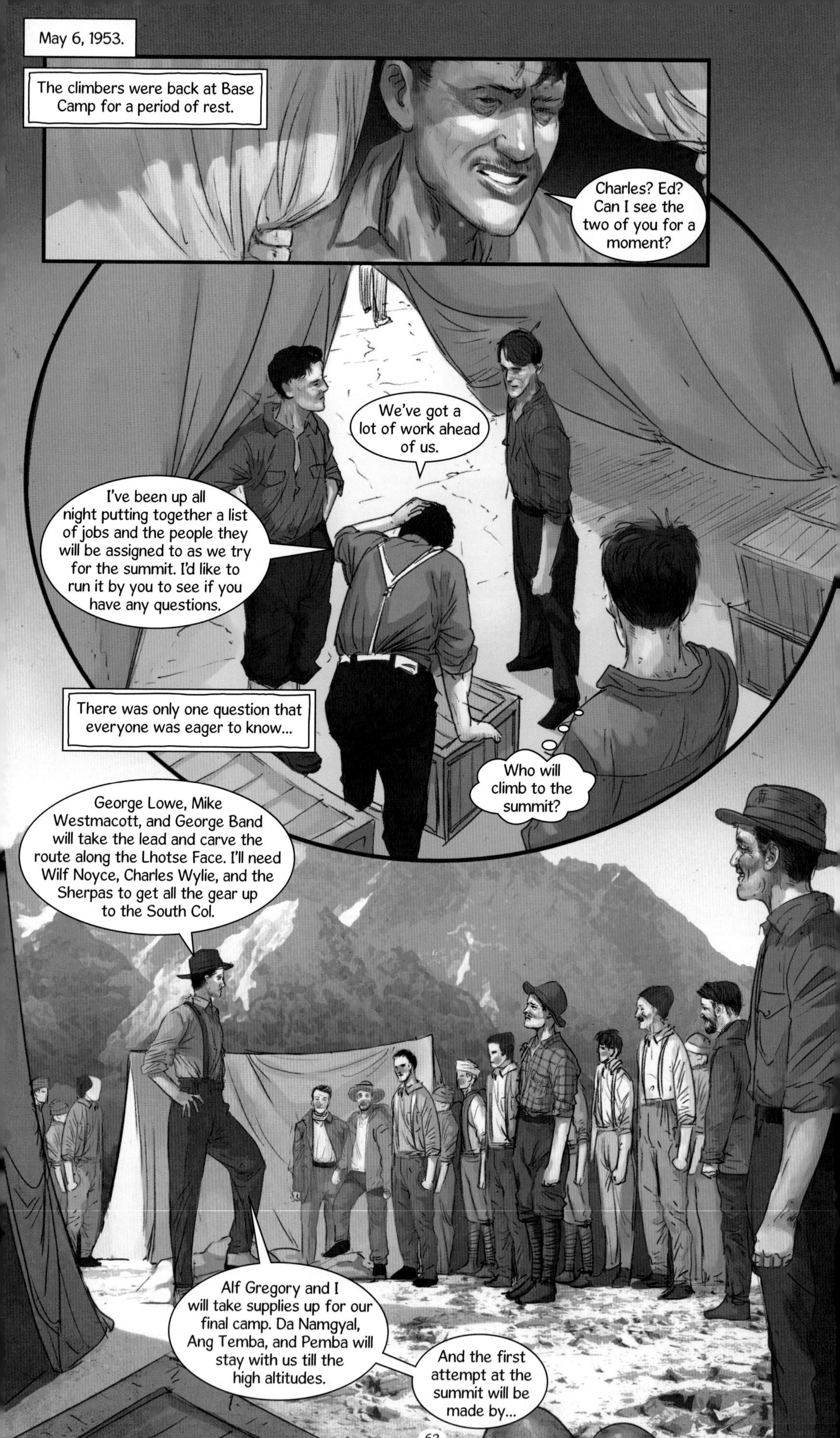
May 6, 1953.
The climbers were back at Base Camp for a period of rest.
Charles? Ed? Can I see the two of you for a moment?
We've got a lot of work ahead of us.
I've been up all night putting together a list of jobs and the people they will be assigned to as we try for the summit. I'd like to run it by you to see if you have any questions.
There was only one question that everyone was eager to know...
Who will climb to the summit?
George Lowe, Mike Westmacott, and George Band will take the lead and carve the route along the Lhotse Face. I'll need Wilf Noyce, Charles Wylie, and the Sherpas to get all the gear up to the South Col.
Alf Gregory and I will take supplies up for our final camp. Da Namgyal, Ang Temba, and Pemba will stay with us till the high altitudes.
And the first attempt at the summit will be made by...

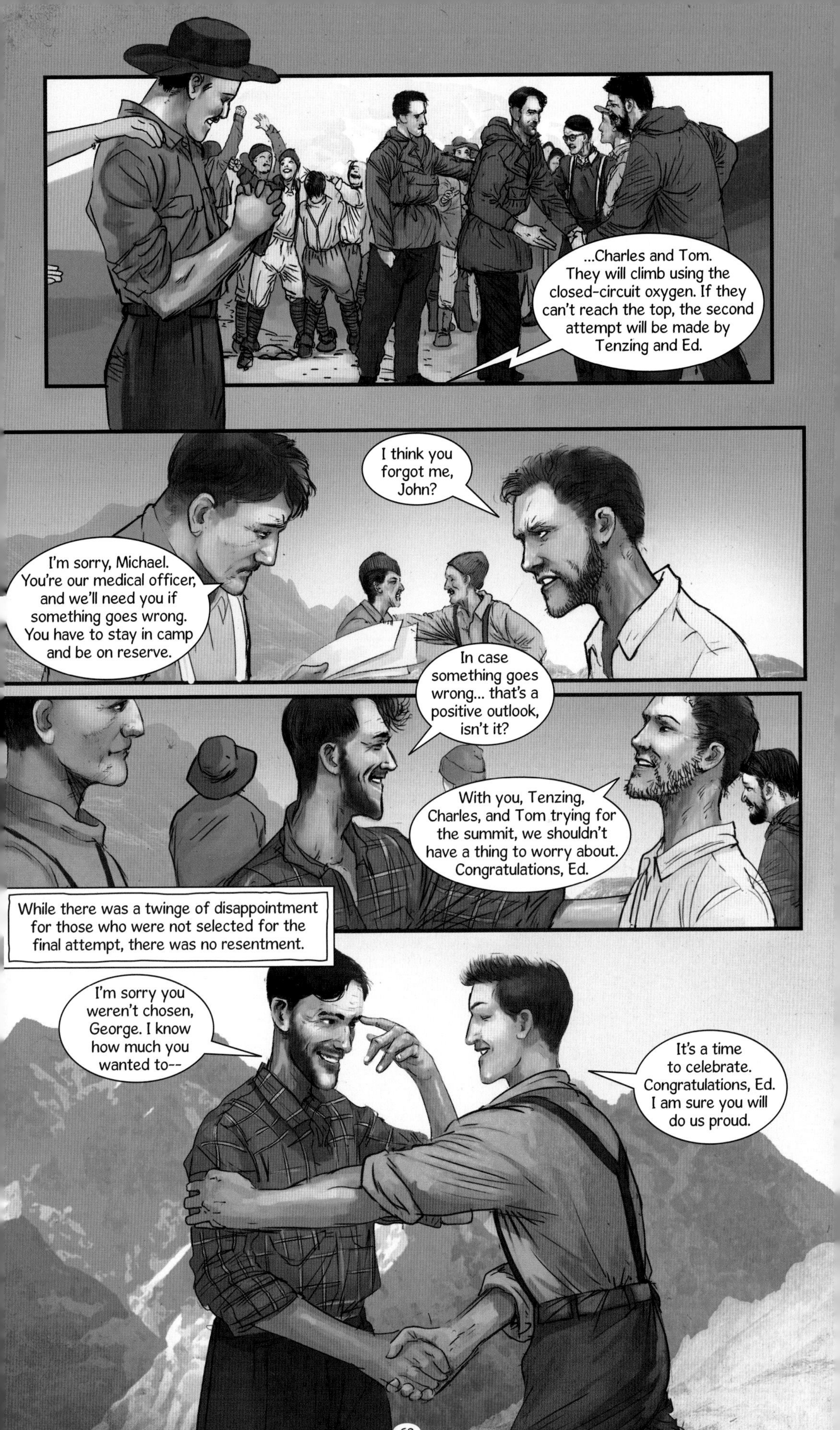
...Charles and Tom. They will climb using the closed-circuit oxygen. If they can't reach the top, the second attempt will be made by Tenzing and Ed.
I think you forgot me, John?
I'm sorry, Michael. You're our medical officer, and we'll need you if something goes wrong. You have to stay in camp and be on reserve.
In case something goes wrong... that's a positive outlook, isn't it?
With you, Tenzing, Charles, and Tom trying for the summit, we shouldn't have a thing to worry about. Congratulations, Ed.
While there was a twinge of disappointment for those who were not selected for the final attempt, there was no resentment.
I'm sorry you weren't chosen, George. I know how much you wanted to--
It's a time to celebrate. Congratulations, Ed. I am sure you will do us proud.

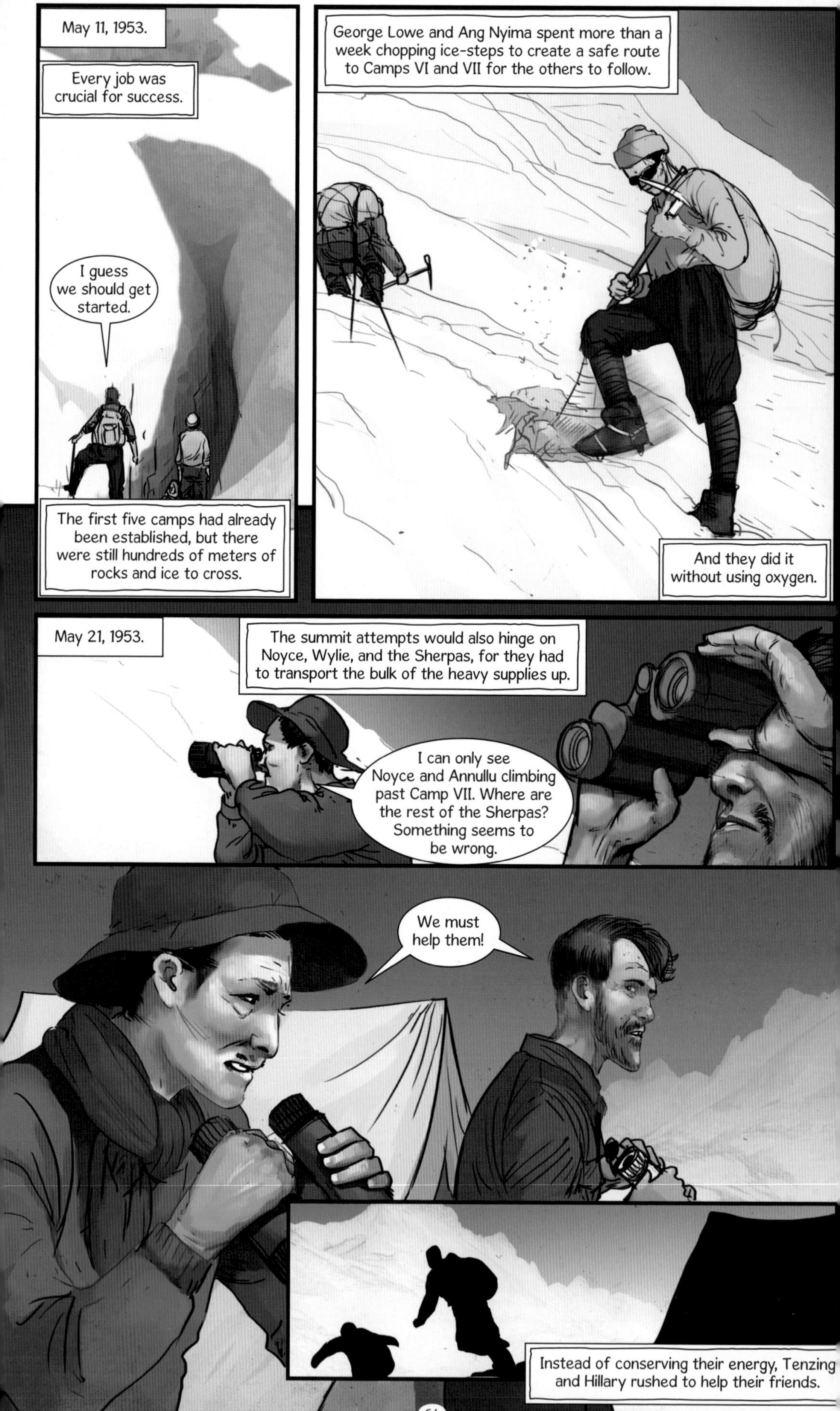
May 11, 1953.
Every job was crucial for success.
I guess we should get started.
The first five camps had already been established, but there were still hundreds of meters of rocks and ice to cross.
George Lowe and Ang Nyima spent more than a week chopping ice-steps to create a safe route to Camps VI and VII for the others to follow.
And they did it without using oxygen.
May 21, 1953.
The summit attempts would also hinge on Noyce, Wylie, and the Sherpas, for they had to transport the bulk of the heavy supplies up.
I can only see Noyce and Annullu climbing past Camp VII. Where are the rest of the Sherpas? Something seems to be wrong.
We must help them!
Instead of conserving their energy, Tenzing and Hillary rushed to help their friends.

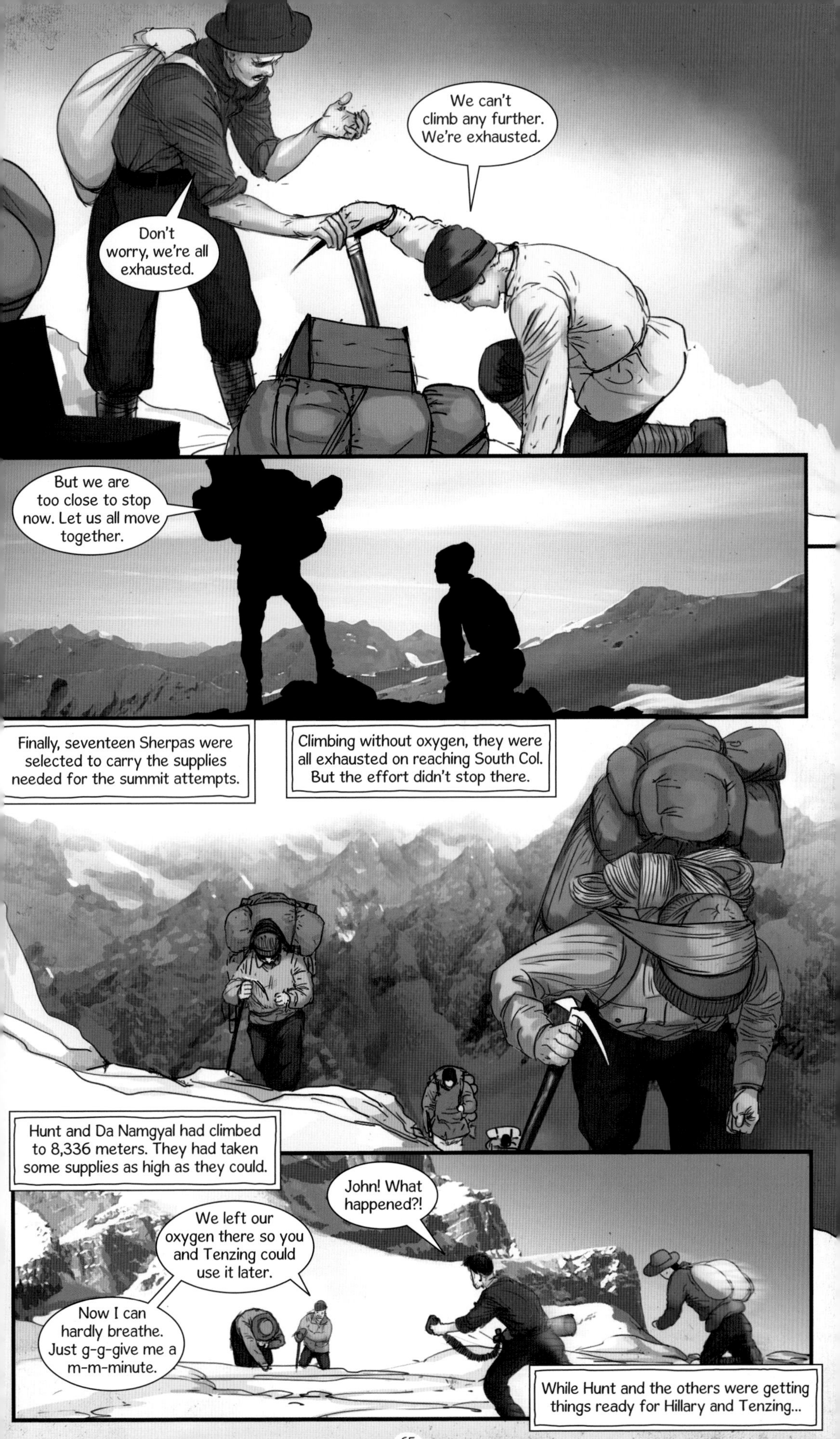

We can't climb any further. We're exhausted.
Don't worry, we're all exhausted.
But we are too close to stop now. Let us all move together.
Finally, seventeen Sherpas were selected to carry the supplies needed for the summit attempts.
Climbing without oxygen, they were all exhausted on reaching South Col. But the effort didn't stop there.
Hunt and Da Namgyal had climbed to 8,336 meters. They had taken some supplies as high as they could.
John! What happened?!
We left our oxygen there so you and Tenzing could use it later.
Now I can hardly breathe. Just g-g-give me a m-m-minute.
While Hunt and the others were getting things ready for Hillary and Tenzing...

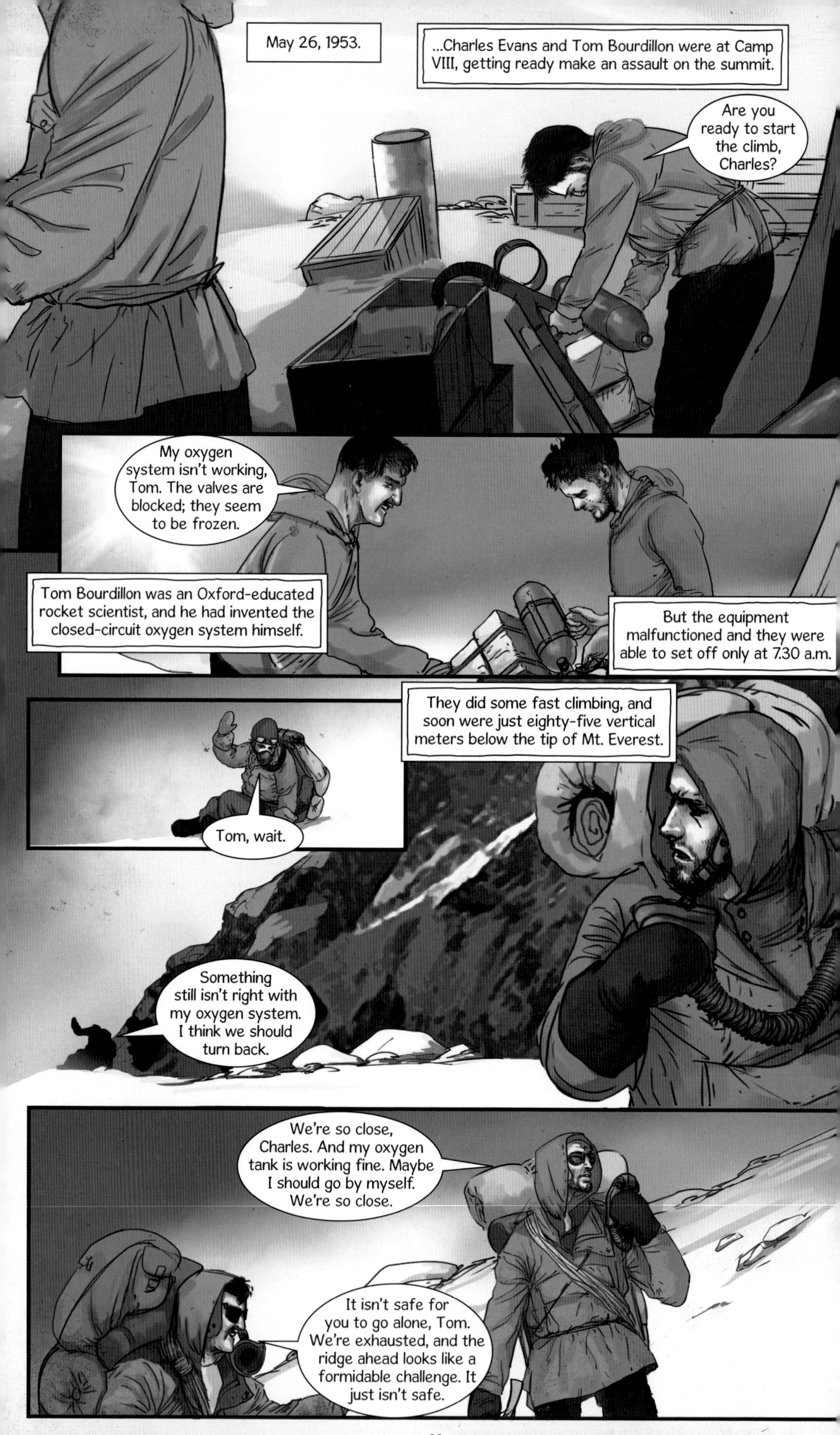
May 26, 1953.
...Charles Evans and Tom Bourdillon were at Camp VIII, getting ready make an assault on the summit.
Are you ready to start the climb, Charles?
My oxygen system isn't working, Tom. The valves are blocked; they seem to be frozen.
Tom Bourdillon was an Oxford-educated rocket scientist, and he had invented the closed-circuit oxygen system himself.
But the equipment malfunctioned and they were able to set off only at 7.30 a.m.
Tom, wait.
They did some fast climbing, and soon were just eighty-five vertical meters below the tip of Mt. Everest.
Something still isn't right with my oxygen system. I think we should turn back.
We're so close, Charles. And my oxygen tank is working fine. Maybe I should go by myself. We're so close.
It isn't safe for you to go alone, Tom. We're exhausted, and the ridge ahead looks like a formidable challenge. It just isn't safe.

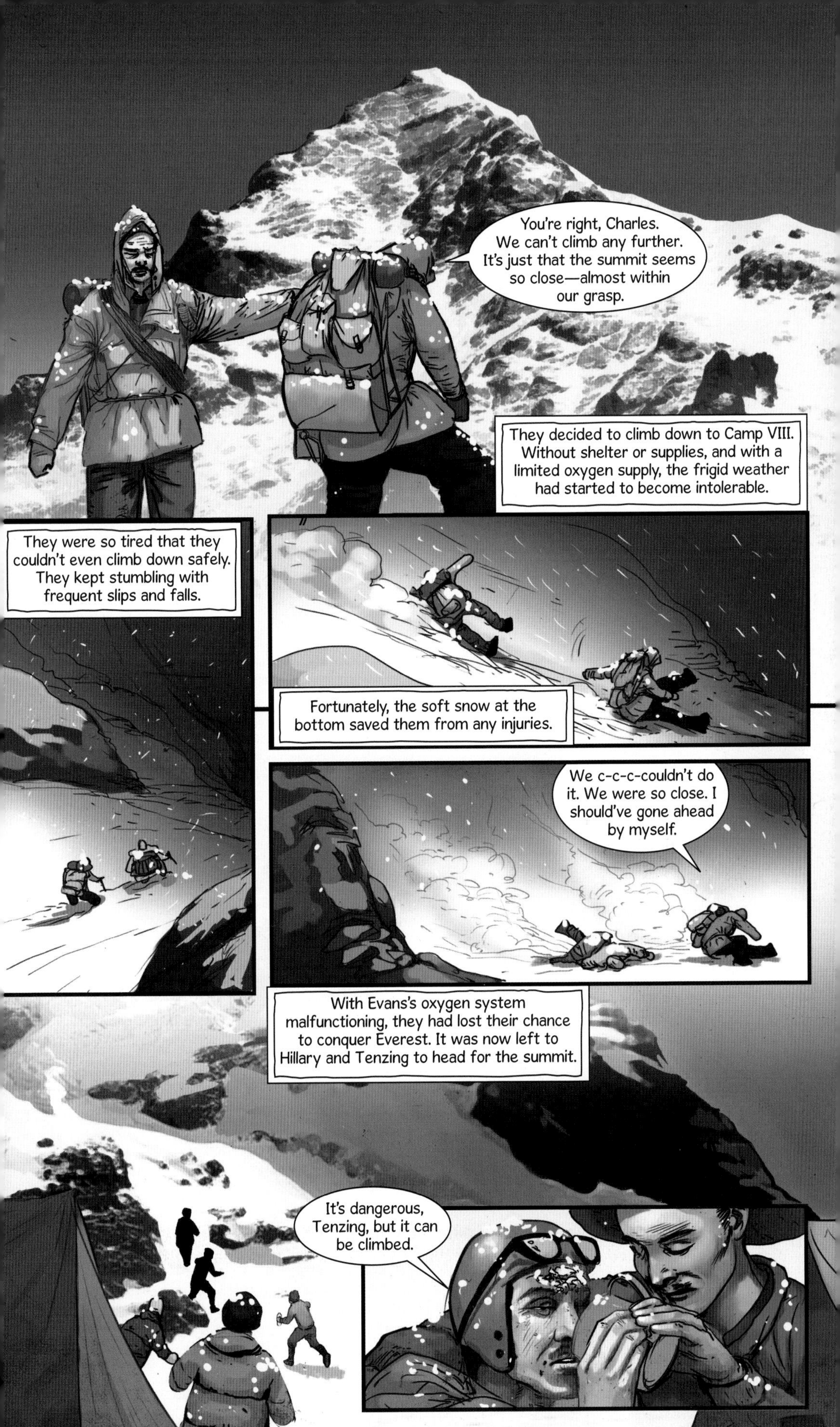
You're right, Charles. We can't climb any further. It's just that the summit seems so close—almost within our grasp.
They decided to climb down to Camp VIII. Without shelter or supplies, and with a limited oxygen supply, the frigid weather had started to become intolerable.
They were so tired that they couldn't even climb down safely. They kept stumbling with frequent slips and falls.
Fortunately, the soft snow at the bottom saved them from any injuries.
We c-c-c-couldn't do it. We were so close. I should've gone ahead by myself.
With Evans's oxygen system malfunctioning, they had lost their chance to conquer Everest. It was now left to Hillary and Tenzing to head for the summit.
It's dangerous, Tenzing, but it can be climbed.

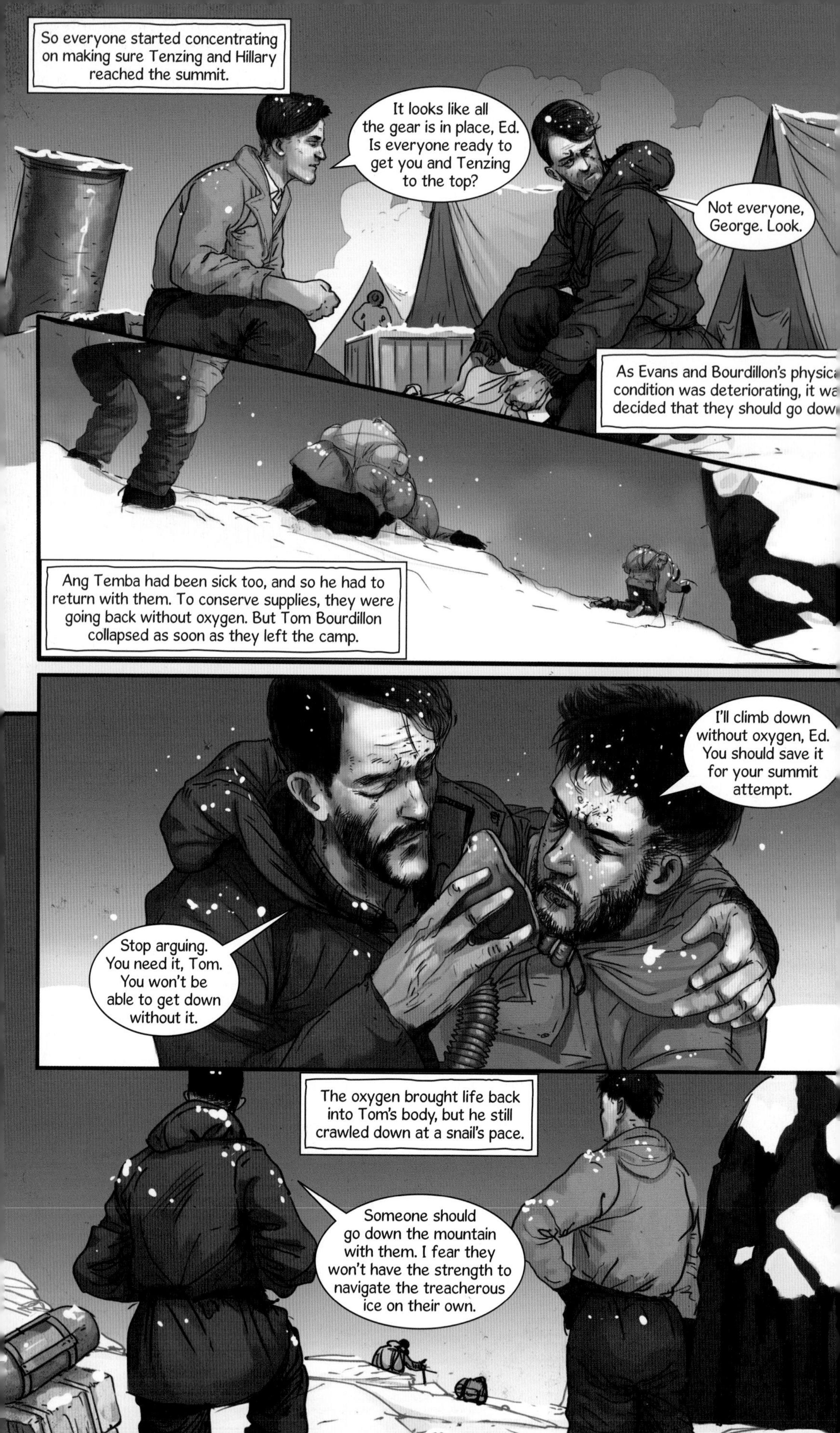

So everyone started concentrating on making sure Tenzing and Hillary reached the summit.
It looks like all the gear is in place, Ed. Is everyone ready to get you and Tenzing to the top?
Not everyone, George. Look.
As Evans and Bourdillon's physica condition was deteriorating, it wa decided that they should go dow
Ang Temba had been sick too, and so he had to return with them. To conserve supplies, they were going back without oxygen. But Tom Bourdillon collapsed as soon as they left the camp.
I'll climb down without oxygen, Ed. You should save it for your summit attempt.
Stop arguing. You need it, Tom. You won't be able to get down without it.
The oxygen brought life back into Tom's body, but he still crawled down at a snail's pace.
Someone should go down the mountain with them. I fear they won't have the strength to navigate the treacherous ice on their own.

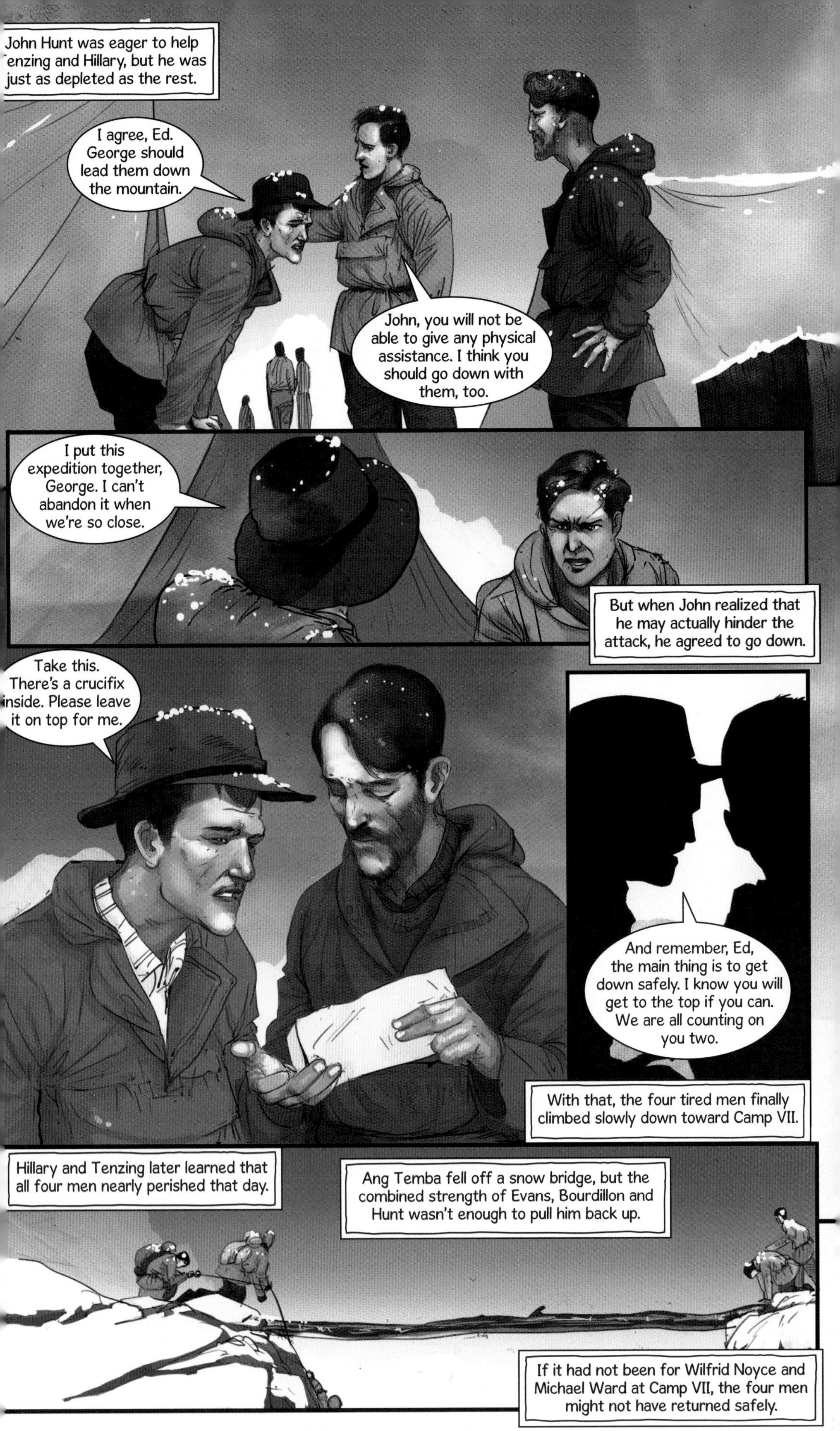
John Hunt was eager to help Tenzing and Hillary, but he was just as depleted as the rest.
I agree, Ed. George should lead them down the mountain.
John, you will not be able to give any physical assistance. I think you should go down with them, too.
I put this expedition together, George. I can't abandon it when we're so close.
But when John realized that he may actually hinder the attack, he agreed to go down.
Take this. There's a crucifix inside. Please leave it on top for me.
And remember, Ed, the main thing is to get down safely. I know you will get to the top if you can. We are all counting on you two.
With that, the four tired men finally climbed slowly down toward Camp VII.
Hillary and Tenzing later learned that all four men nearly perished that day.
Ang Temba fell off a snow bridge, but the combined strength of Evans, Bourdillon and Hunt wasn't enough to pull him back up.
If it had not been for Wilfrid Noyce and Michael Ward at Camp VII, the four men might not have returned safely.

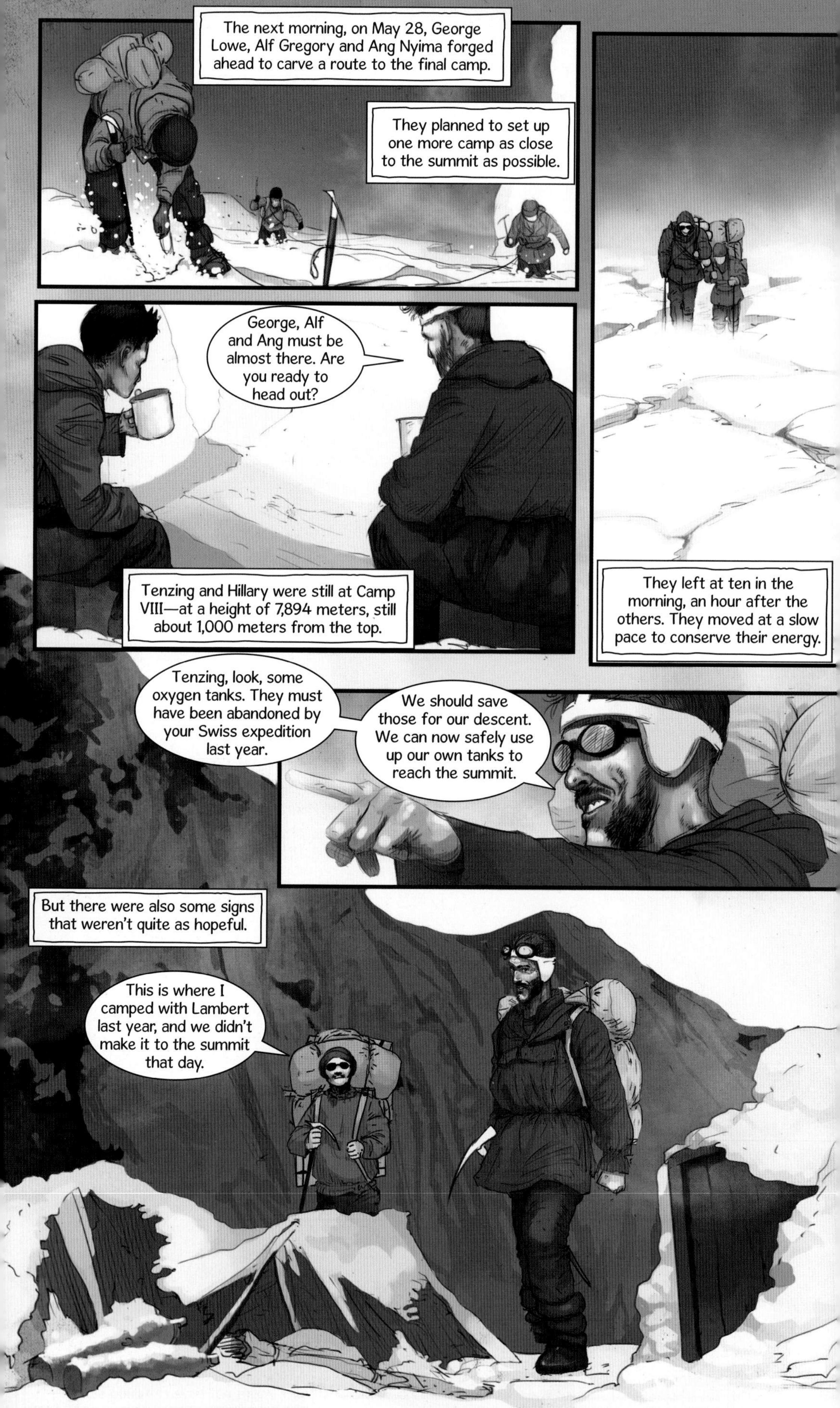

The next morning, on May 28, George Lowe, Alf Gregory and Ang Nyima forged ahead to carve a route to the final camp.
They planned to set up one more camp as close to the summit as possible.
George, Alf and Ang must be almost there. Are you ready to head out?
Tenzing and Hillary were still at Camp VIII—at a height of 7,894 meters, still about 1,000 meters from the top.
They left at ten in the morning, an hour after the others. They moved at a slow pace to conserve their energy.
Tenzing, look, some oxygen tanks. They must have been abandoned by your Swiss expedition last year.
We should save those for our descent. We can now safely use up our own tanks to reach the summit.
But there were also some signs that weren't quite as hopeful.
This is where I camped with Lambert last year, and we didn't make it to the summit that day.

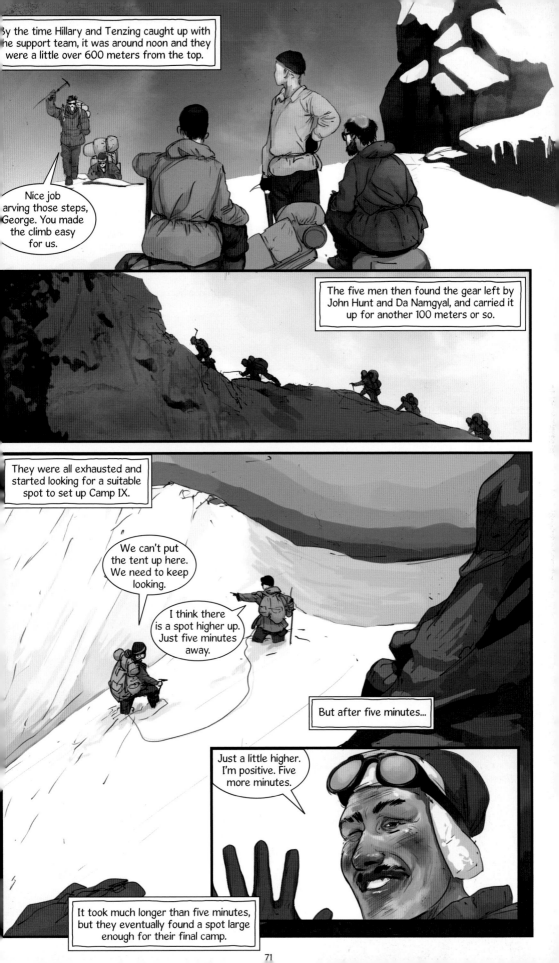

By the time Hillary and Tenzing caught up with the support team, it was around noon and they were a little over 600 meters from the top.

Nice job carving those steps, George. You made the climb easy for us.

The five men then found the gear left by John Hunt and Da Namgyal, and carried it up for another 100 meters or so.

They were all exhausted and started looking for a suitable spot to set up Camp IX.

We can't put the tent up here. We need to keep looking.

I think there is a spot higher up. Just five minutes away.

But after five minutes...

Just a little higher. I'm positive. Five more minutes.

It took much longer than five minutes, but they eventually found a spot large enough for their final camp.

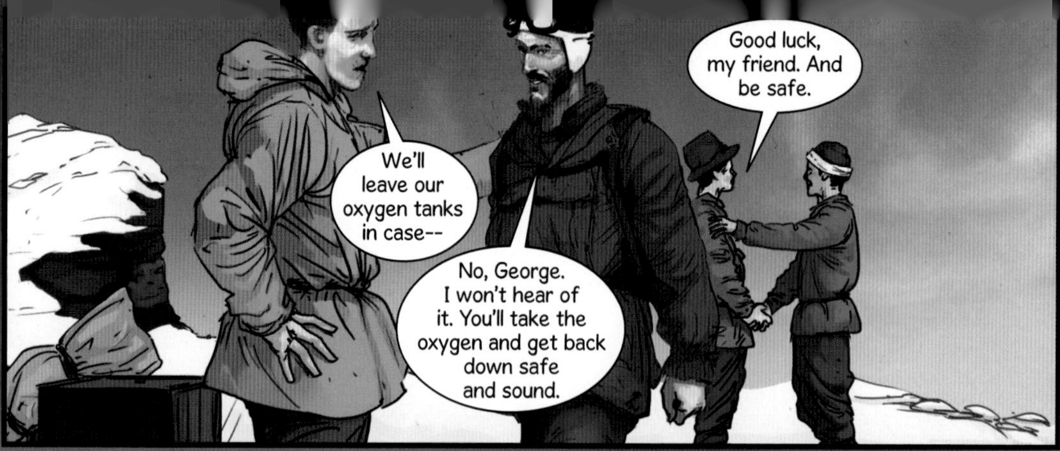
We'll leave our oxygen tanks in case--
No, George. I won't hear of it. You'll take the oxygen and get back down safe and sound.
Good luck, my friend. And be safe.

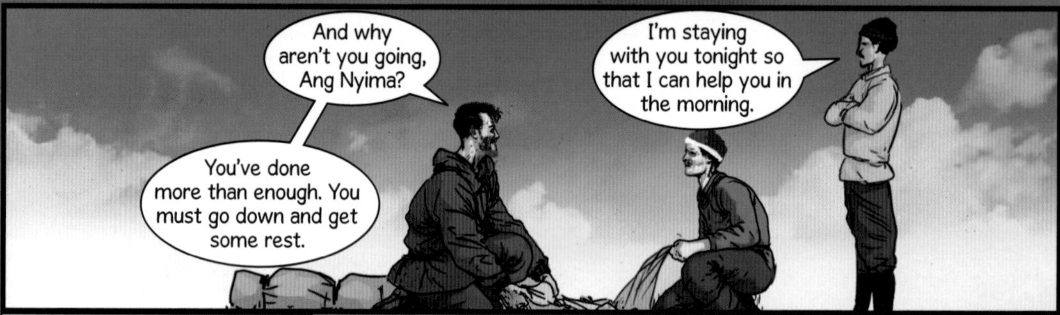
And why aren't you going, Ang Nyima?
You've done more than enough. You must go down and get some rest.
I'm staying with you tonight so that I can help you in the morning.

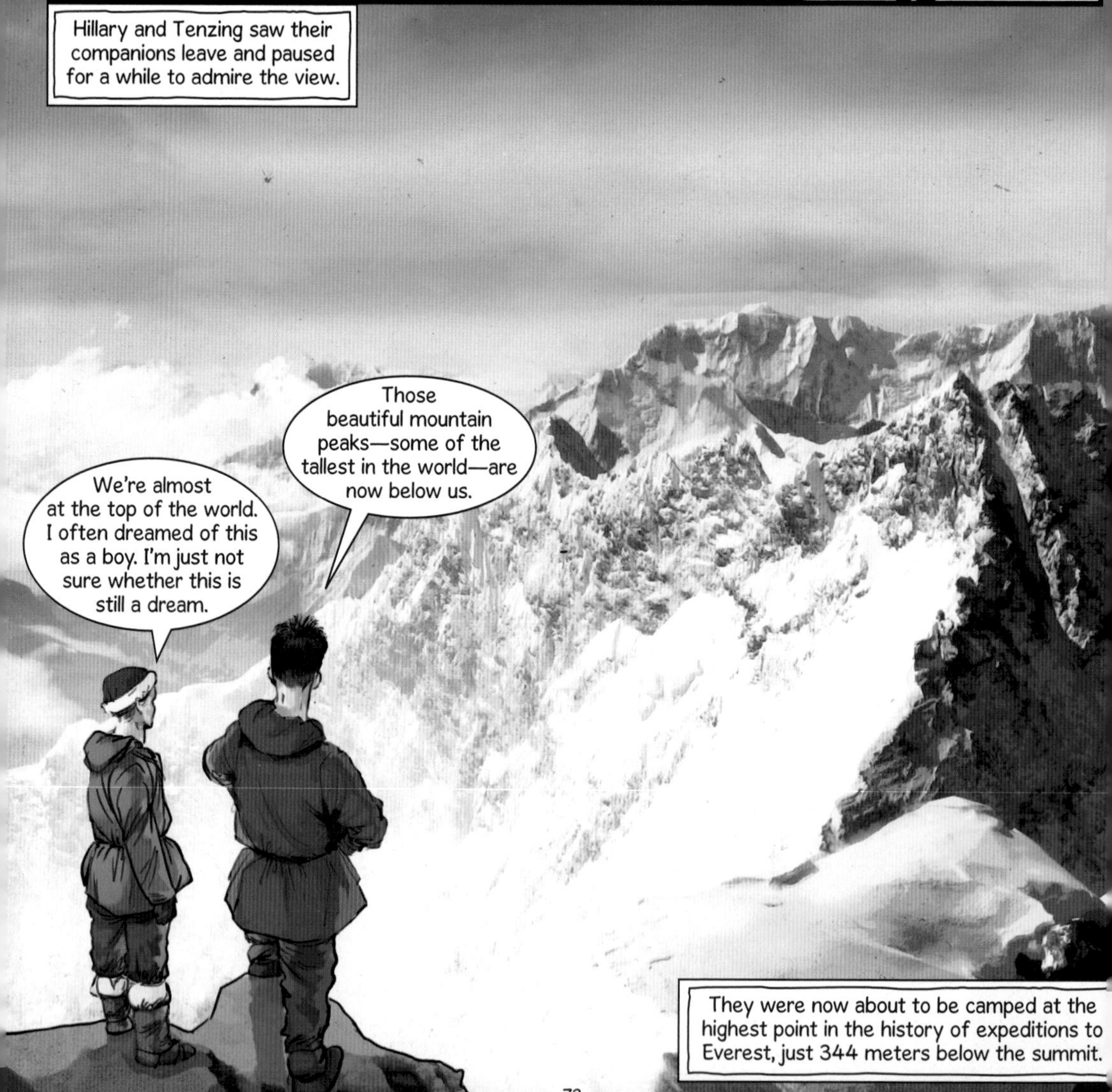
Hillary and Tenzing saw their companions leave and paused for a while to admire the view.
We're almost at the top of the world. I often dreamed of this as a boy. I'm just not sure whether this is still a dream.
Those beautiful mountain peaks—some of the tallest in the world—are now below us.
They were now about to be camped at the highest point in the history of expeditions to Everest, just 344 meters below the summit.

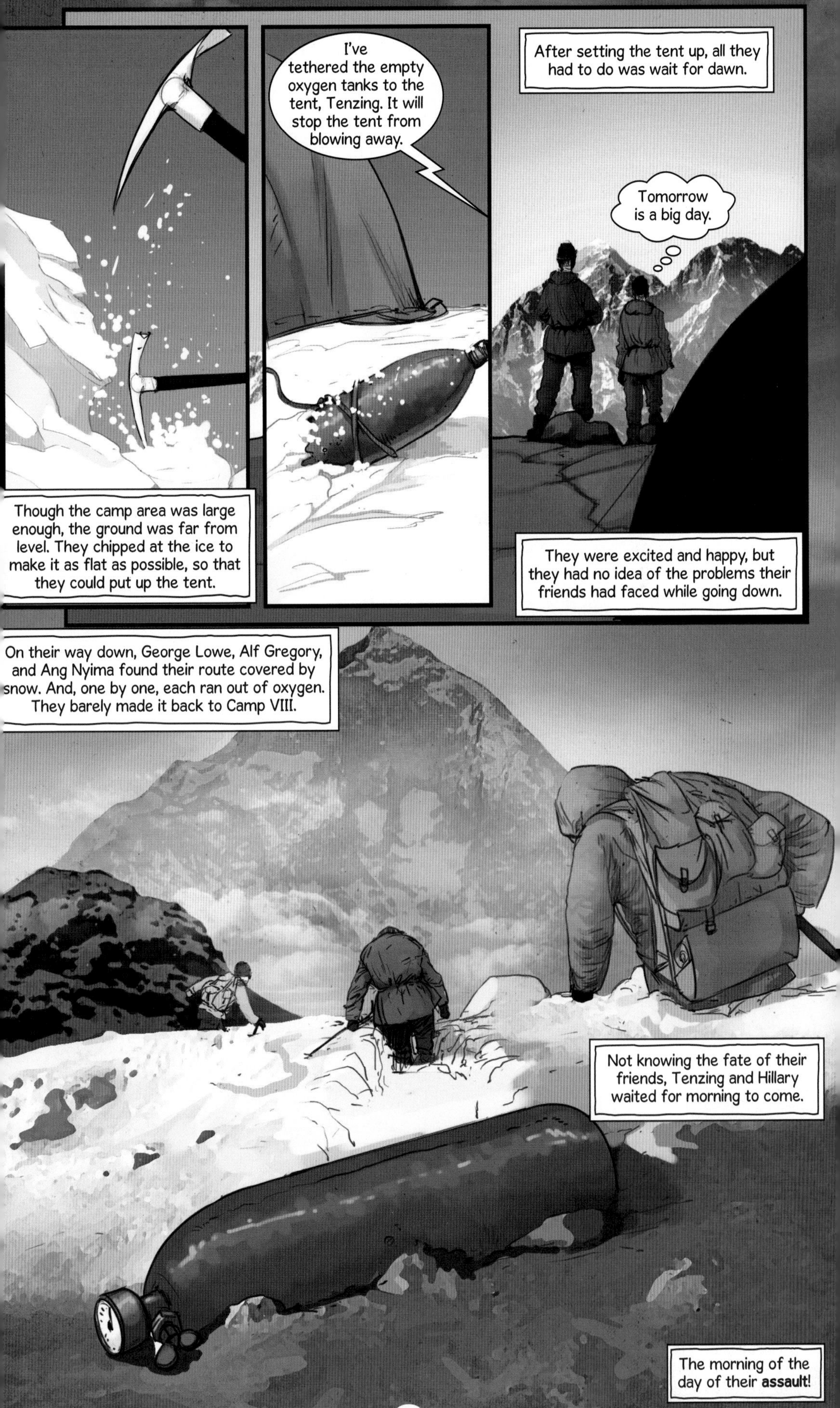
Though the camp area was large enough, the ground was far from level. They chipped at the ice to make it as flat as possible, so that they could put up the tent.
I've tethered the empty oxygen tanks to the tent, Tenzing. It will stop the tent from blowing away.
After setting the tent up, all they had to do was wait for dawn.
Tomorrow is a big day.
They were excited and happy, but they had no idea of the problems their friends had faced while going down.
On their way down, George Lowe, Alf Gregory, and Ang Nyima found their route covered by snow. And, one by one, each ran out of oxygen. They barely made it back to Camp VIII.
Not knowing the fate of their friends, Tenzing and Hillary waited for morning to come.
The morning of the day of their **assault**!

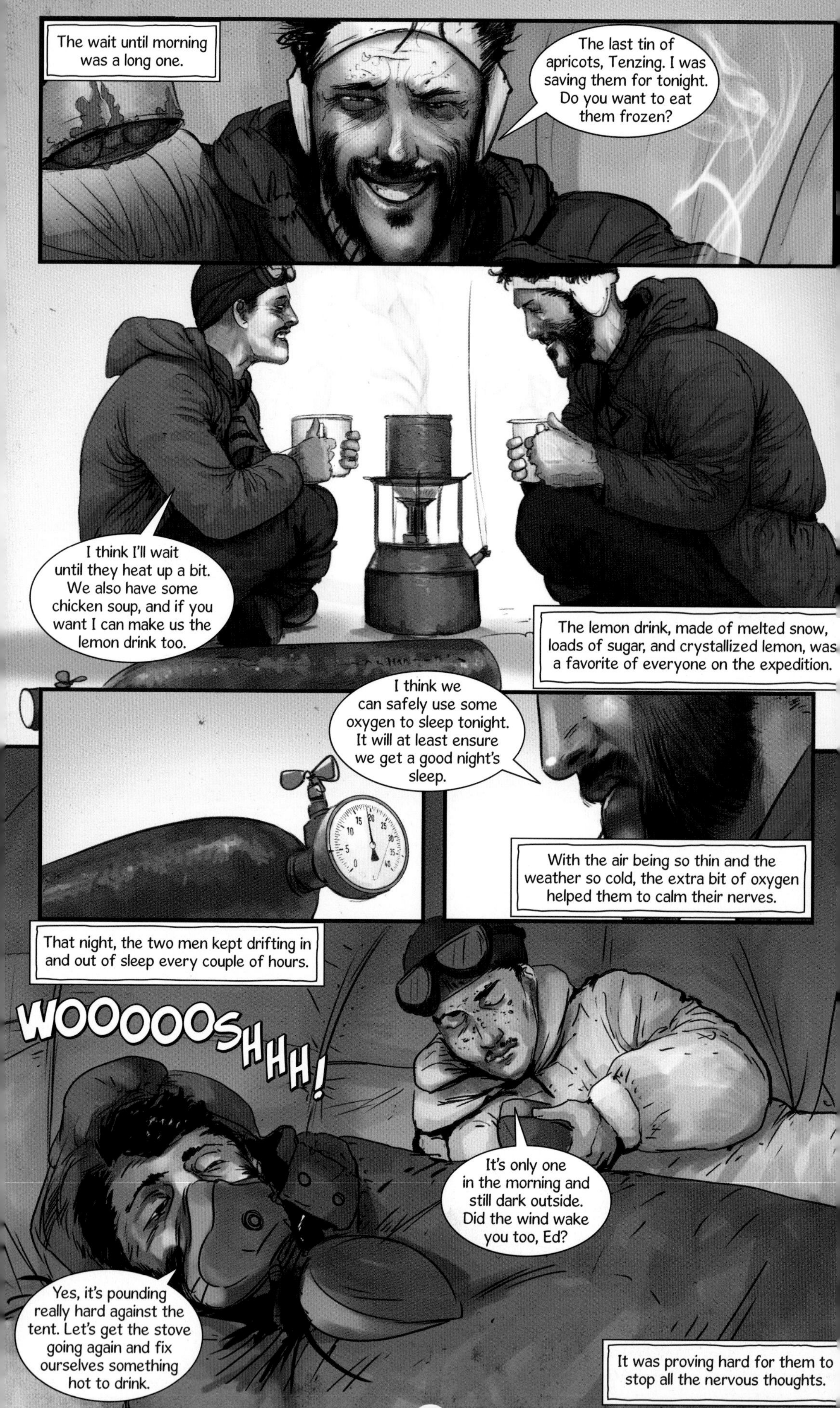

The wait until morning was a long one.
The last tin of apricots, Tenzing. I was saving them for tonight. Do you want to eat them frozen?
I think I'll wait until they heat up a bit. We also have some chicken soup, and if you want I can make us the lemon drink too.
The lemon drink, made of melted snow, loads of sugar, and crystallized lemon, was a favorite of everyone on the expedition.
I think we can safely use some oxygen to sleep tonight. It will at least ensure we get a good night's sleep.
With the air being so thin and the weather so cold, the extra bit of oxygen helped them to calm their nerves.
That night, the two men kept drifting in and out of sleep every couple of hours.
WOOOOOSHHH!
It's only one in the morning and still dark outside. Did the wind wake you too, Ed?
Yes, it's pounding really hard against the tent. Let's get the stove going again and fix ourselves something hot to drink.
It was proving hard for them to stop all the nervous thoughts.

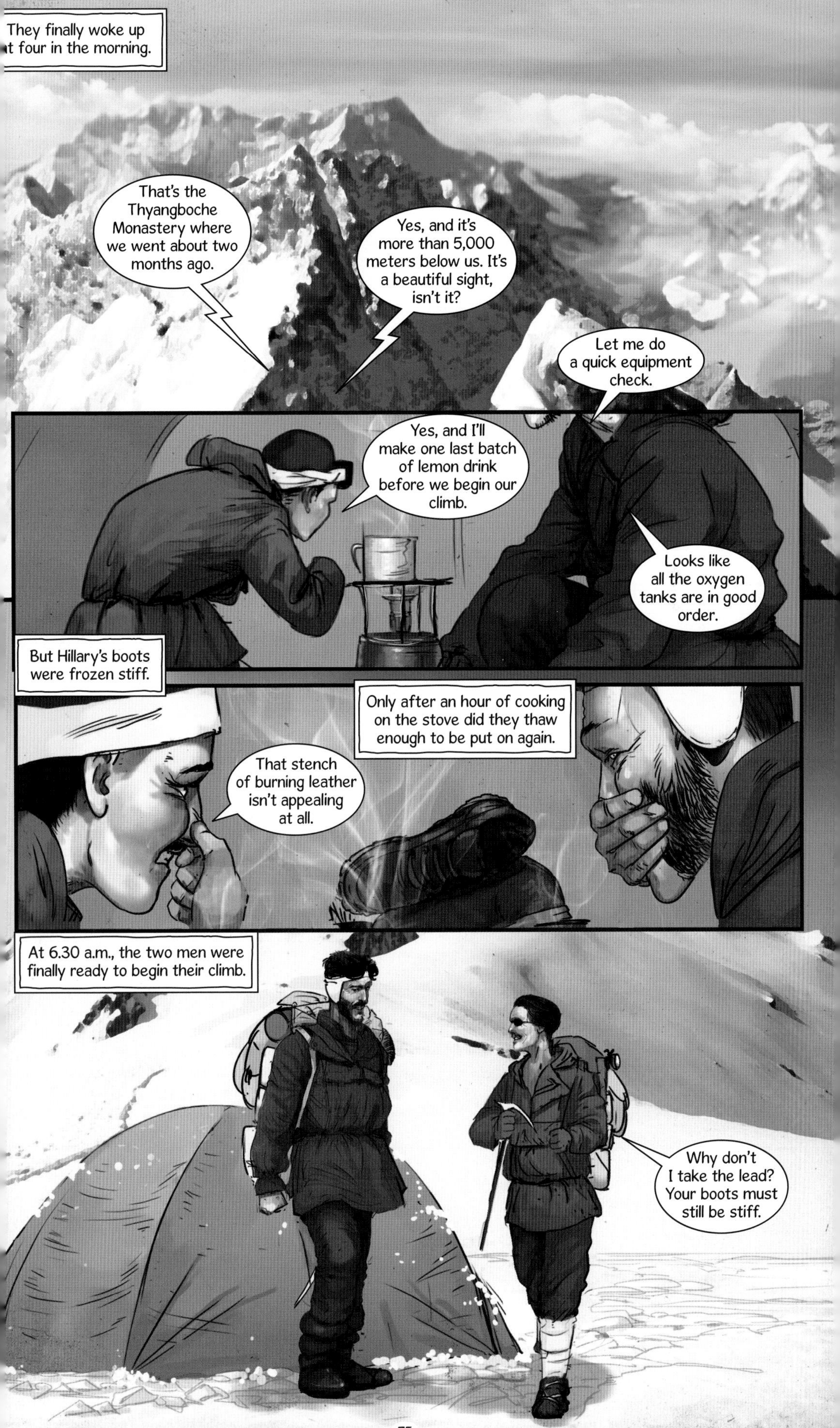

They finally woke up at four in the morning.
That's the Thyangboche Monastery where we went about two months ago.
Yes, and it's more than 5,000 meters below us. It's a beautiful sight, isn't it?
Let me do a quick equipment check.
Yes, and I'll make one last batch of lemon drink before we begin our climb.
Looks like all the oxygen tanks are in good order.
But Hillary's boots were frozen stiff.
Only after an hour of cooking on the stove did they thaw enough to be put on again.
That stench of burning leather isn't appealing at all.
At 6.30 a.m., the two men were finally ready to begin their climb.
Why don't I take the lead? Your boots must still be stiff.

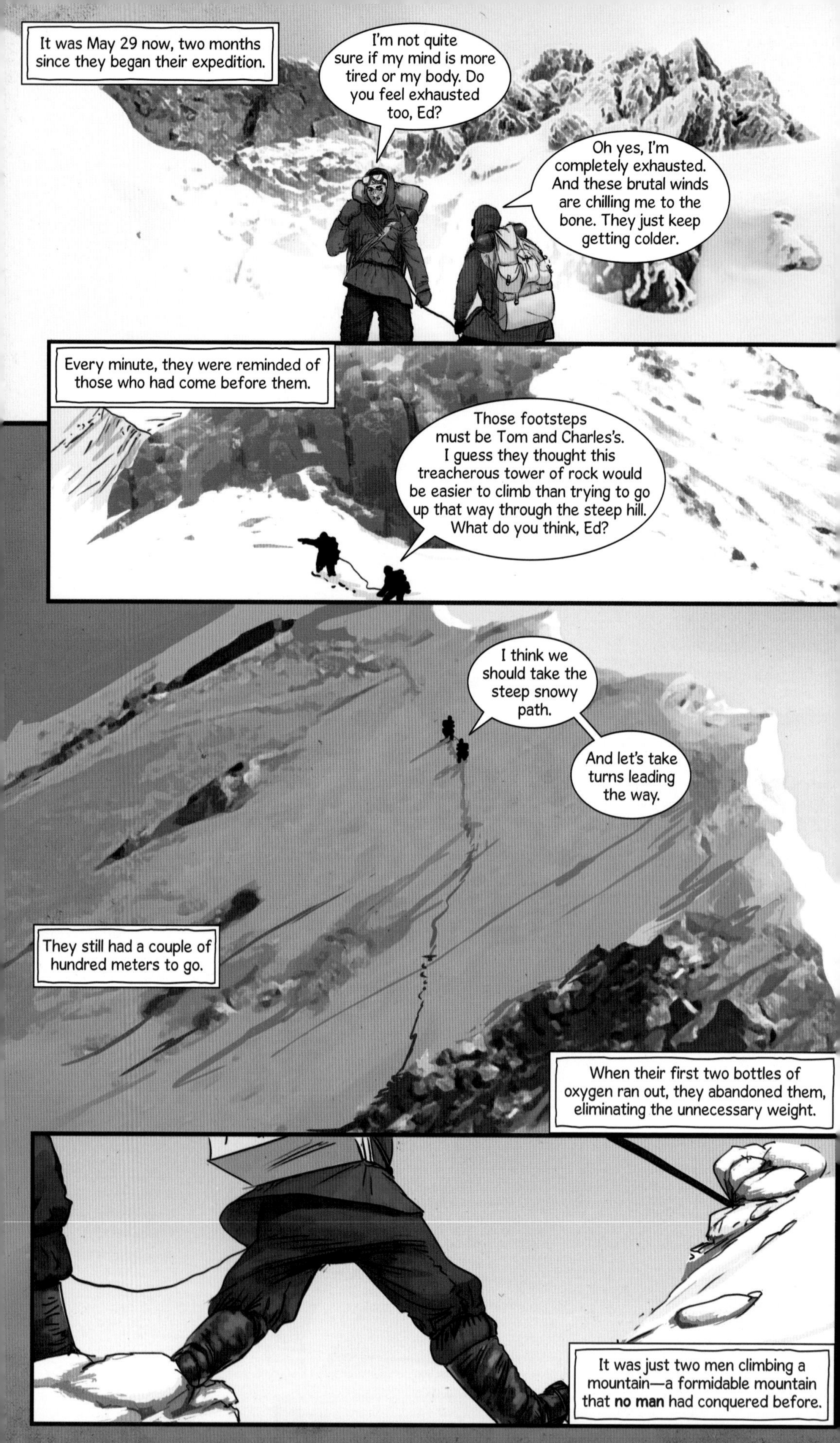

It was May 29 now, two months since they began their expedition.
I'm not quite sure if my mind is more tired or my body. Do you feel exhausted too, Ed?
Oh yes, I'm completely exhausted. And these brutal winds are chilling me to the bone. They just keep getting colder.
Every minute, they were reminded of those who had come before them.
Those footsteps must be Tom and Charles's. I guess they thought this treacherous tower of rock would be easier to climb than trying to go up that way through the steep hill. What do you think, Ed?
I think we should take the steep snowy path.
And let's take turns leading the way.
They still had a couple of hundred meters to go.
When their first two bottles of oxygen ran out, they abandoned them, eliminating the unnecessary weight.
It was just two men climbing a mountain—a formidable mountain that **no man** had conquered before.

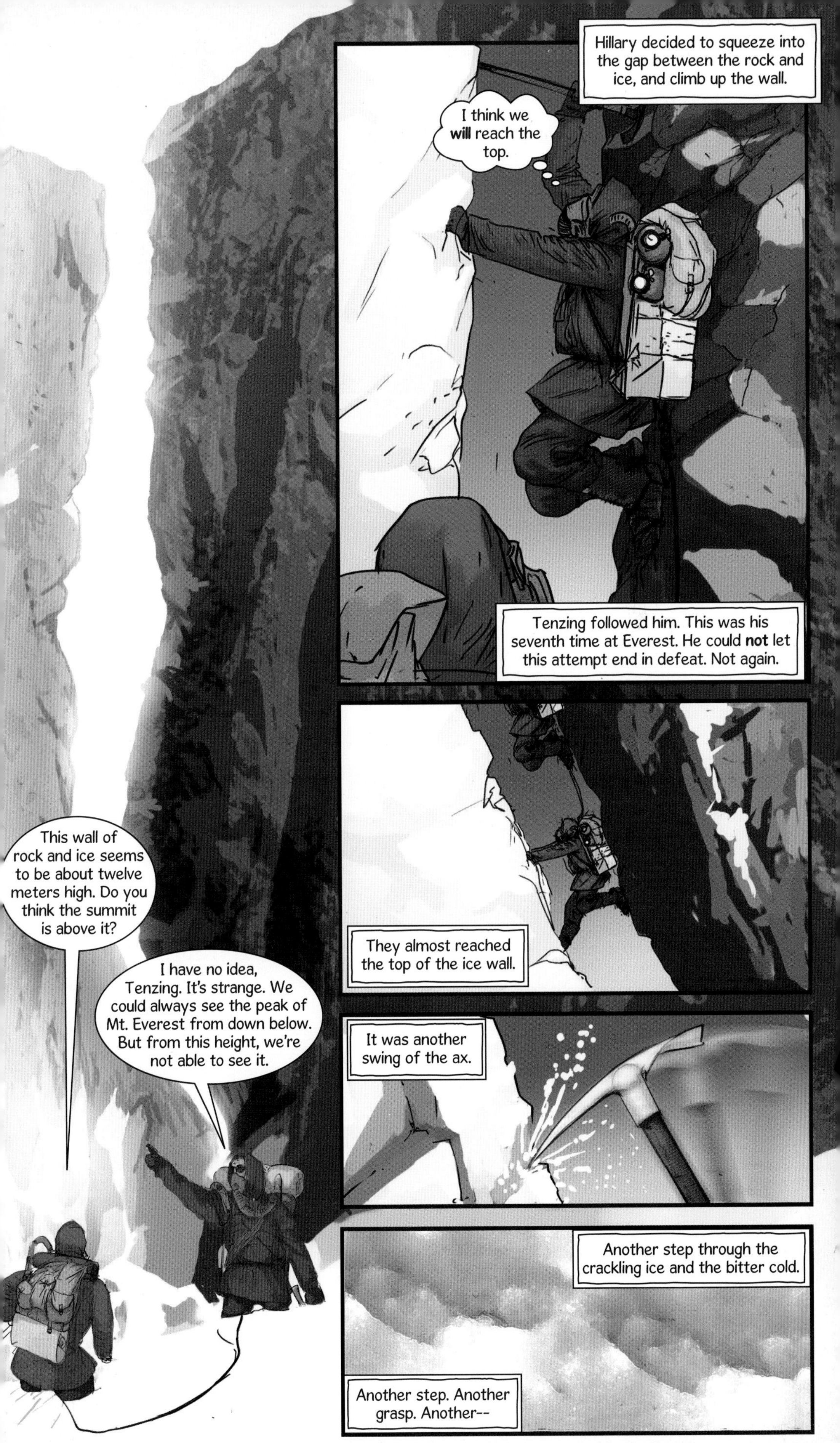

Hillary decided to squeeze into the gap between the rock and ice, and climb up the wall.
I think we **will** reach the top.
Tenzing followed him. This was his seventh time at Everest. He could **not** let this attempt end in defeat. Not again.
They almost reached the top of the ice wall.
It was another swing of the ax.
Another step through the crackling ice and the bitter cold.
Another step. Another grasp. Another--
This wall of rock and ice seems to be about twelve meters high. Do you think the summit is above it?
I have no idea, Tenzing. It's strange. We could always see the peak of Mt. Everest from down below. But from this height, we're not able to see it.

They had done it. They had reached the top. Their dream had finally come true.

At 11.30 a.m. on May 29, they were atop the highest point in the world.

Two shy young boys, from different parts of the world, had conquered Mt. Everest.

They took a moment to think of all those who had come before them. They even looked for traces of Mallory and Irvine, to see if they had reached the top in 1924 before they disappeared, but they found nothing.

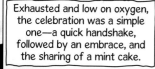

Exhausted and low on oxygen, the celebration was a simple one—a quick handshake, followed by an embrace, and the sharing of a mint cake.

They buried Tenzing's daughter's pencil, John Hunt's crucifix, and a bit of chocolate as an offering to the mountain and the gods.

Hillary took in a deep breath of the air, a pocketful of stones...

Thuji chey*, Chomolungma.

*I am grateful

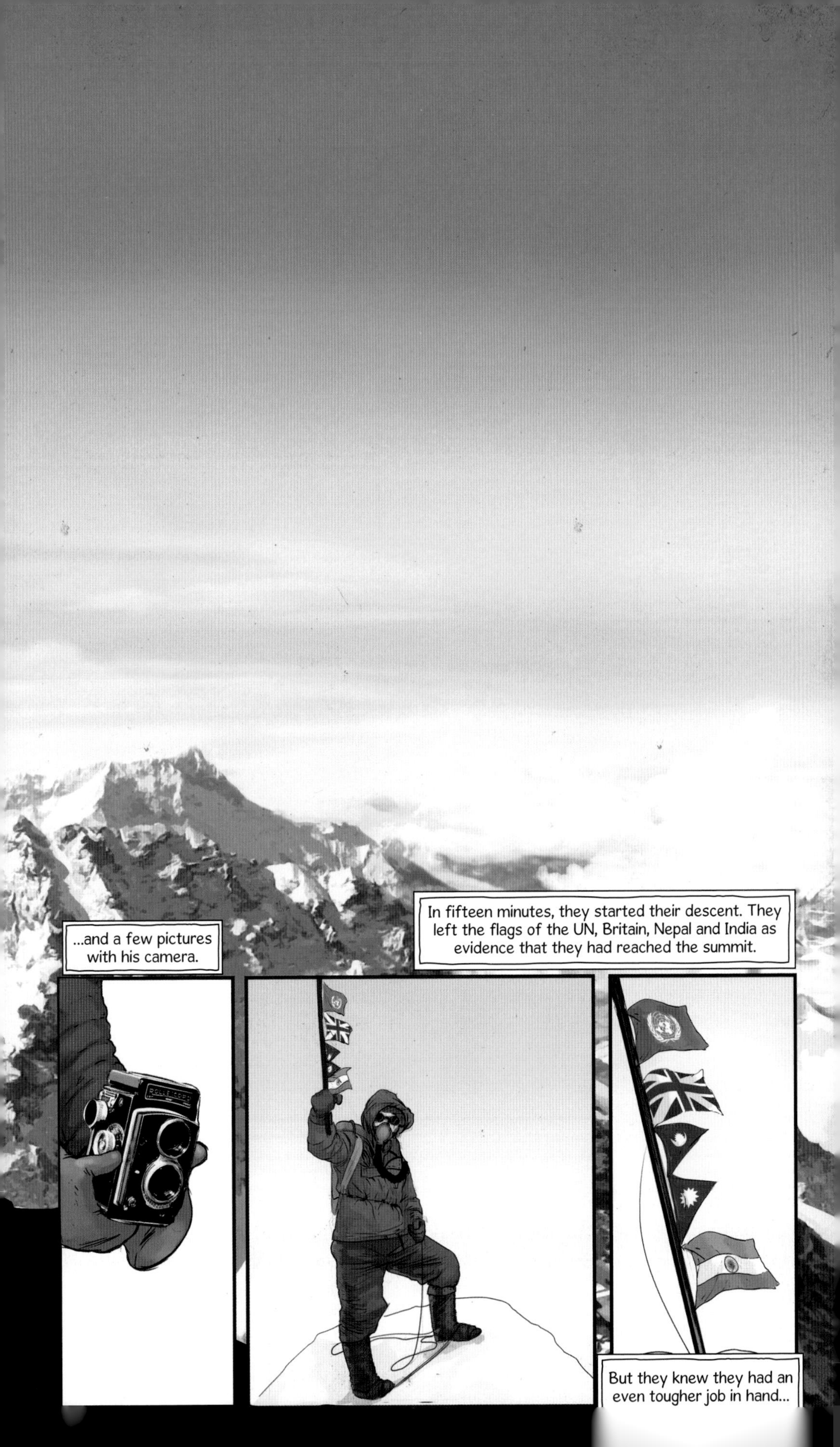
...and a few pictures with his camera.
In fifteen minutes, they started their descent. They left the flags of the UN, Britain, Nepal and India as evidence that they had reached the summit.
But they knew they had an even tougher job in hand...

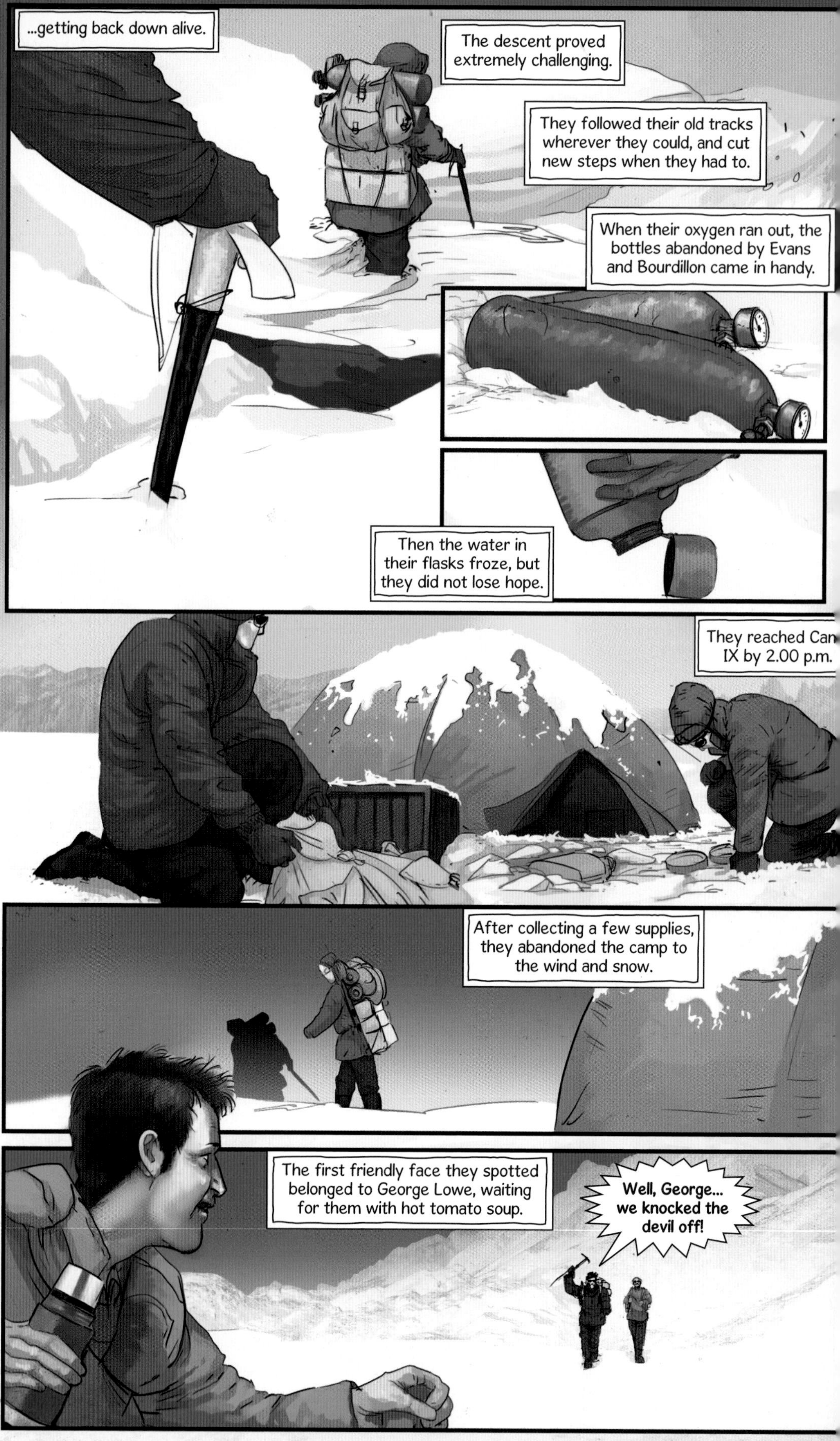
...getting back down alive.
The descent proved extremely challenging.
They followed their old tracks wherever they could, and cut new steps when they had to.
When their oxygen ran out, the bottles abandoned by Evans and Bourdillon came in handy.
Then the water in their flasks froze, but they did not lose hope.
They reached Can IX by 2.00 p.m.
After collecting a few supplies, they abandoned the camp to the wind and snow.
The first friendly face they spotted belonged to George Lowe, waiting for them with hot tomato soup.
Well, George... we knocked the devil off!

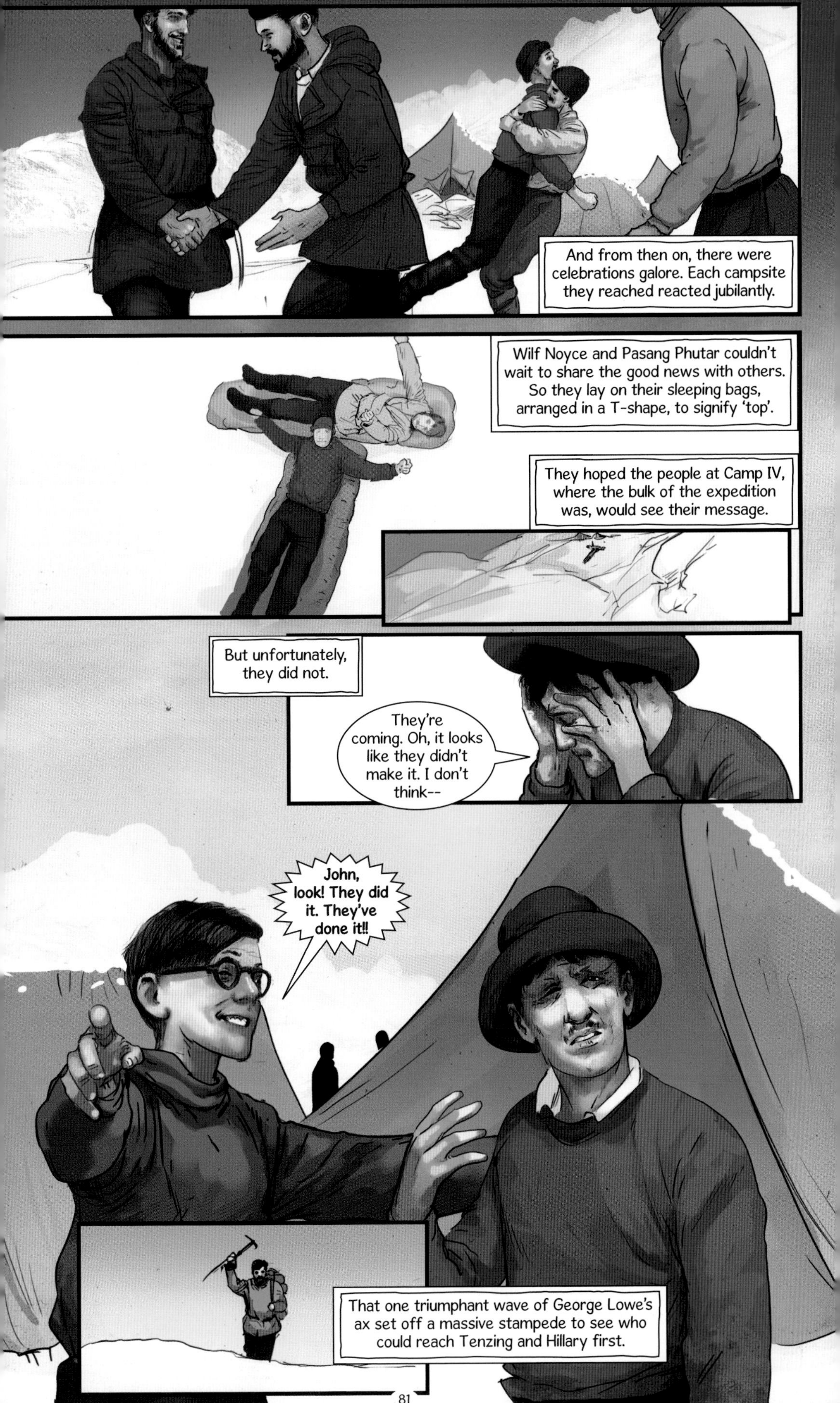

And from then on, there were celebrations galore. Each campsite they reached reacted jubilantly.
Wilf Noyce and Pasang Phutar couldn't wait to share the good news with others. So they lay on their sleeping bags, arranged in a T-shape, to signify 'top'.
They hoped the people at Camp IV, where the bulk of the expedition was, would see their message.
But unfortunately, they did not.
They're coming. Oh, it looks like they didn't make it. I don't think--
John, look! They did it. They've done it!!
That one triumphant wave of George Lowe's ax set off a massive stampede to see who could reach Tenzing and Hillary first.

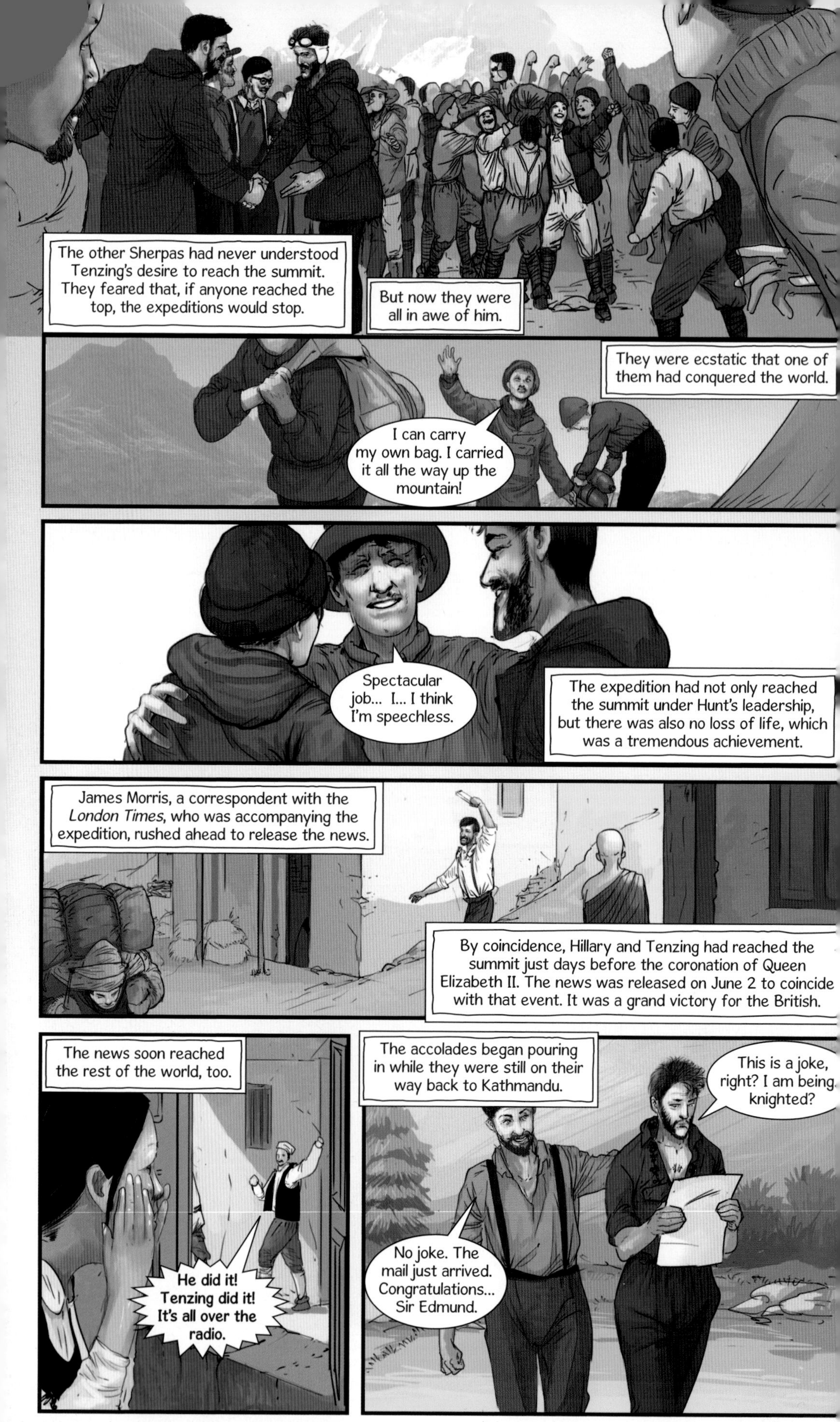
The other Sherpas had never understood Tenzing's desire to reach the summit. They feared that, if anyone reached the top, the expeditions would stop.
But now they were all in awe of him.
They were ecstatic that one of them had conquered the world.
I can carry my own bag. I carried it all the way up the mountain!
Spectacular job... I... I think I'm speechless.
The expedition had not only reached the summit under Hunt's leadership, but there was also no loss of life, which was a tremendous achievement.
James Morris, a correspondent with the *London Times*, who was accompanying the expedition, rushed ahead to release the news.
By coincidence, Hillary and Tenzing had reached the summit just days before the coronation of Queen Elizabeth II. The news was released on June 2 to coincide with that event. It was a grand victory for the British.
The news soon reached the rest of the world, too.
He did it! Tenzing did it! It's all over the radio.
The accolades began pouring in while they were still on their way back to Kathmandu.
This is a joke, right? I am being knighted?
No joke. The mail just arrived. Congratulations... Sir Edmund.

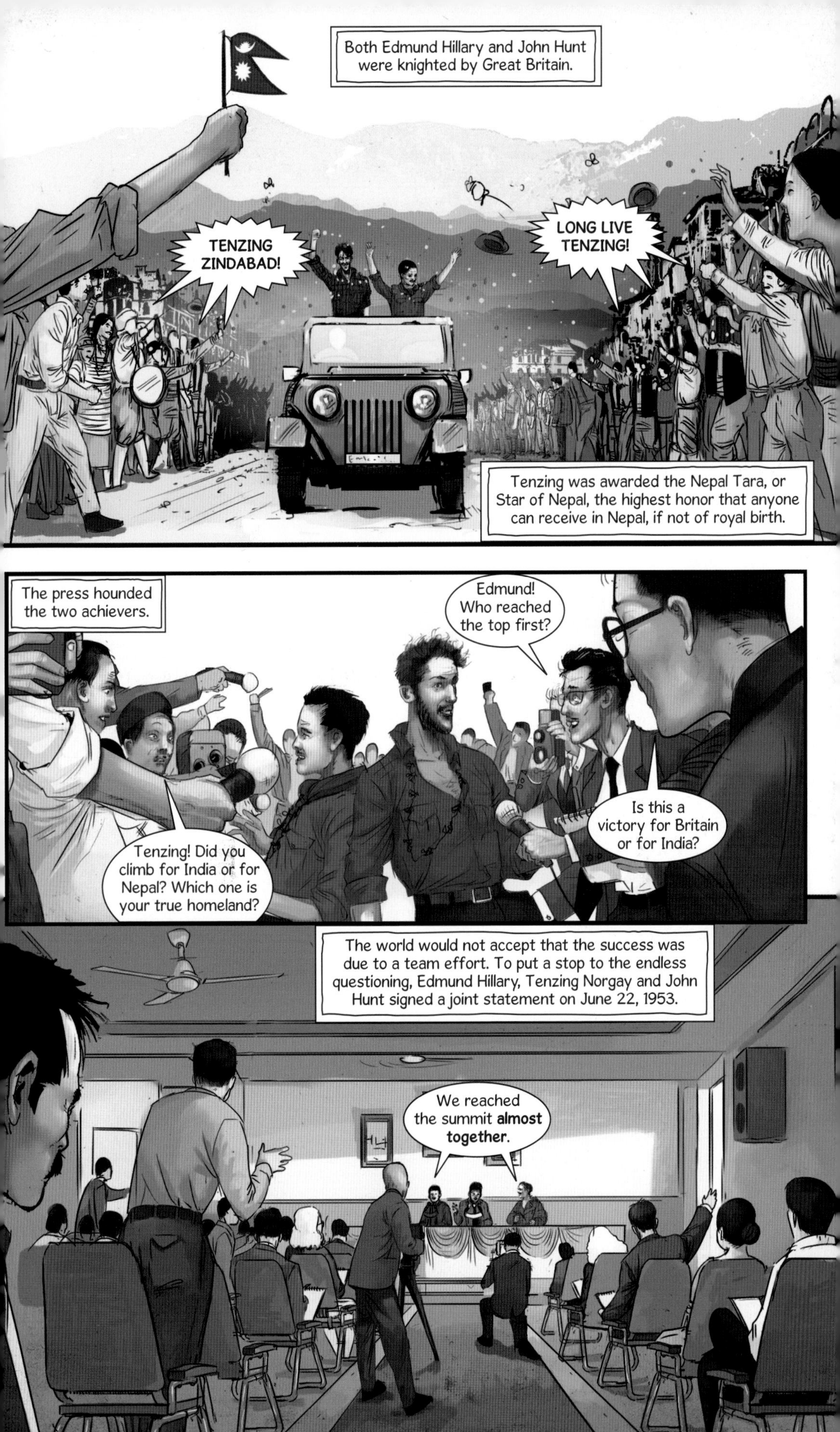
Both Edmund Hillary and John Hunt were knighted by Great Britain.
TENZING ZINDABAD!
LONG LIVE TENZING!
Tenzing was awarded the Nepal Tara, or Star of Nepal, the highest honor that anyone can receive in Nepal, if not of royal birth.
The press hounded the two achievers.
Edmund! Who reached the top first?
Tenzing! Did you climb for India or for Nepal? Which one is your true homeland?
Is this a victory for Britain or for India?
The world would not accept that the success was due to a team effort. To put a stop to the endless questioning, Edmund Hillary, Tenzing Norgay and John Hunt signed a joint statement on June 22, 1953.
We reached the summit **almost together**.

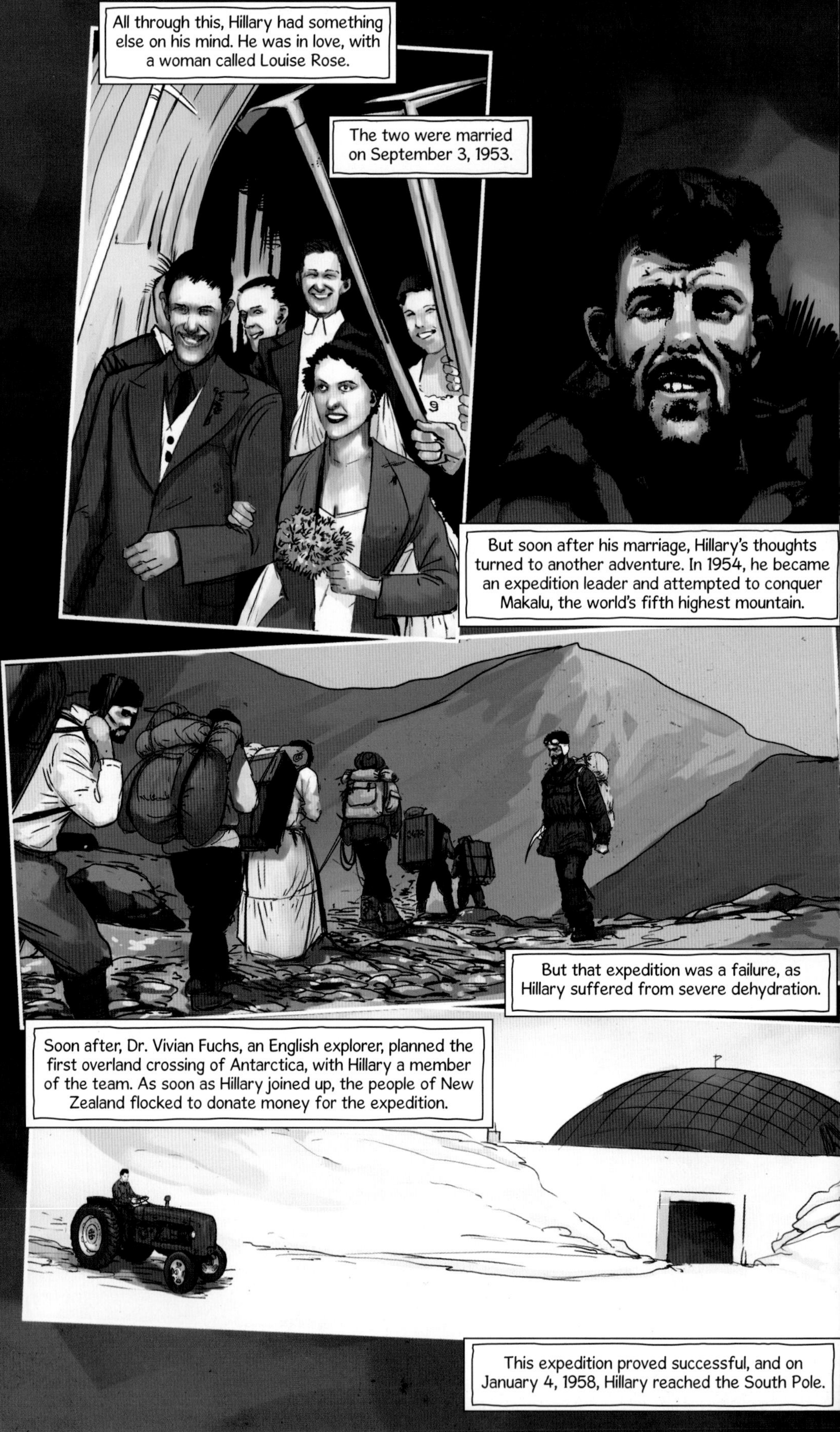
All through this, Hillary had something else on his mind. He was in love, with a woman called Louise Rose.
The two were married on September 3, 1953.
But soon after his marriage, Hillary's thoughts turned to another adventure. In 1954, he became an expedition leader and attempted to conquer Makalu, the world's fifth highest mountain.
But that expedition was a failure, as Hillary suffered from severe dehydration.
Soon after, Dr. Vivian Fuchs, an English explorer, planned the first overland crossing of Antarctica, with Hillary a member of the team. As soon as Hillary joined up, the people of New Zealand flocked to donate money for the expedition.
This expedition proved successful, and on January 4, 1958, Hillary reached the South Pole.

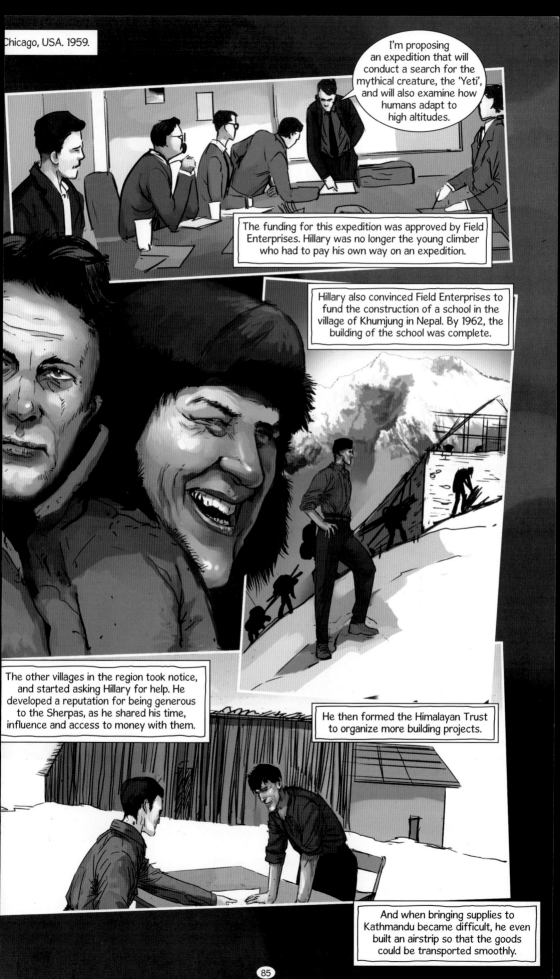

I'm proposing an expedition that will conduct a search for the mythical creature, the 'Yeti', and will also examine how humans adapt to high altitudes.

The funding for this expedition was approved by Field Enterprises. Hillary was no longer the young climber who had to pay his own way on an expedition.

Hillary also convinced Field Enterprises to fund the construction of a school in the village of Khumjung in Nepal. By 1962, the building of the school was complete.

The other villages in the region took notice, and started asking Hillary for help. He developed a reputation for being generous to the Sherpas, as he shared his time, influence and access to money with them.

He then formed the Himalayan Trust to organize more building projects.

And when bringing supplies to Kathmandu became difficult, he even built an airstrip so that the goods could be transported smoothly.

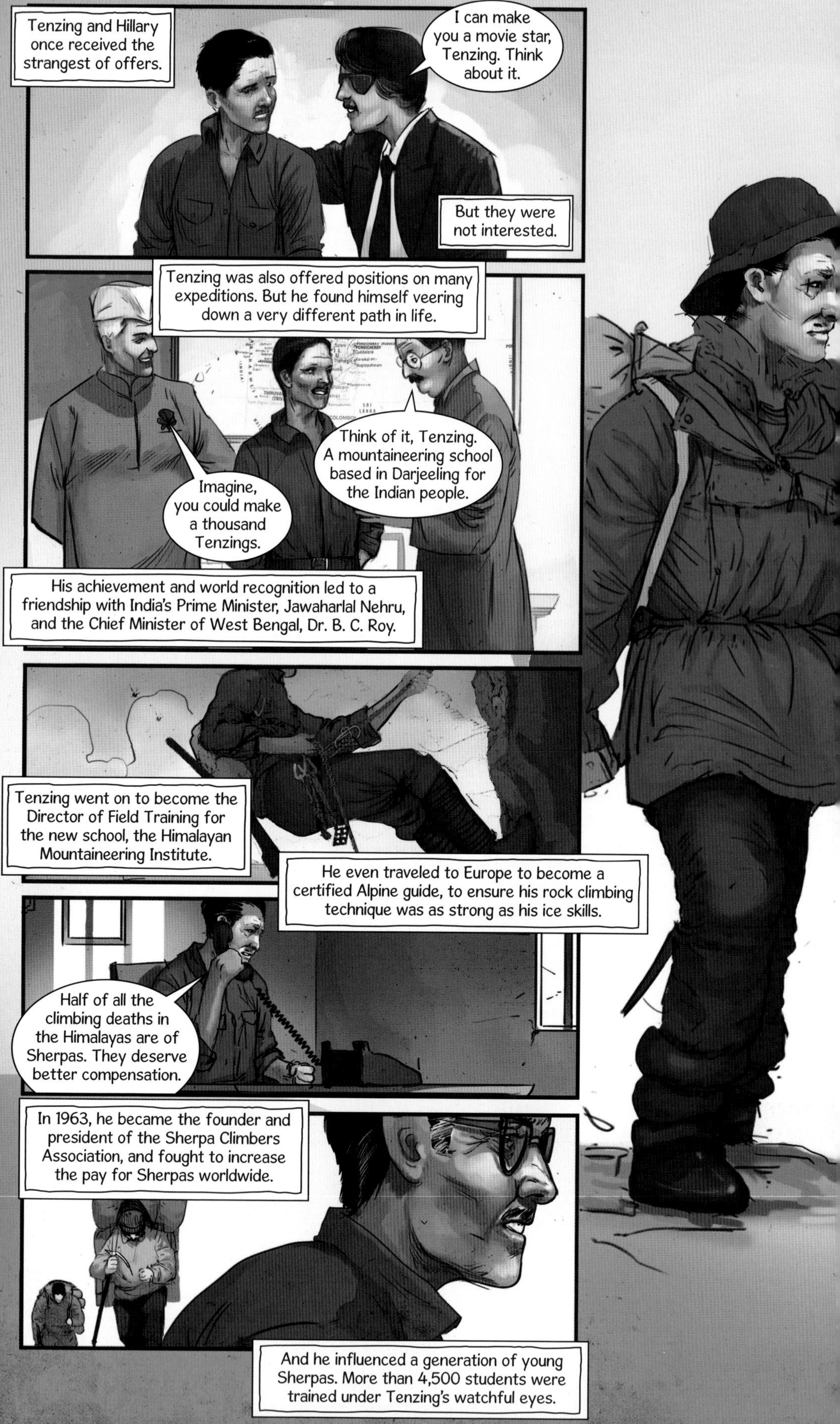

Tenzing and Hillary once received the strangest of offers.
I can make you a movie star, Tenzing. Think about it.
But they were not interested.
Tenzing was also offered positions on many expeditions. But he found himself veering down a very different path in life.
Think of it, Tenzing. A mountaineering school based in Darjeeling for the Indian people.
Imagine, you could make a thousand Tenzings.
His achievement and world recognition led to a friendship with India's Prime Minister, Jawaharlal Nehru, and the Chief Minister of West Bengal, Dr. B. C. Roy.
Tenzing went on to become the Director of Field Training for the new school, the Himalayan Mountaineering Institute.
He even traveled to Europe to become a certified Alpine guide, to ensure his rock climbing technique was as strong as his ice skills.
Half of all the climbing deaths in the Himalayas are of Sherpas. They deserve better compensation.
In 1963, he became the founder and president of the Sherpa Climbers Association, and fought to increase the pay for Sherpas worldwide.
And he influenced a generation of young Sherpas. More than 4,500 students were trained under Tenzing's watchful eyes.

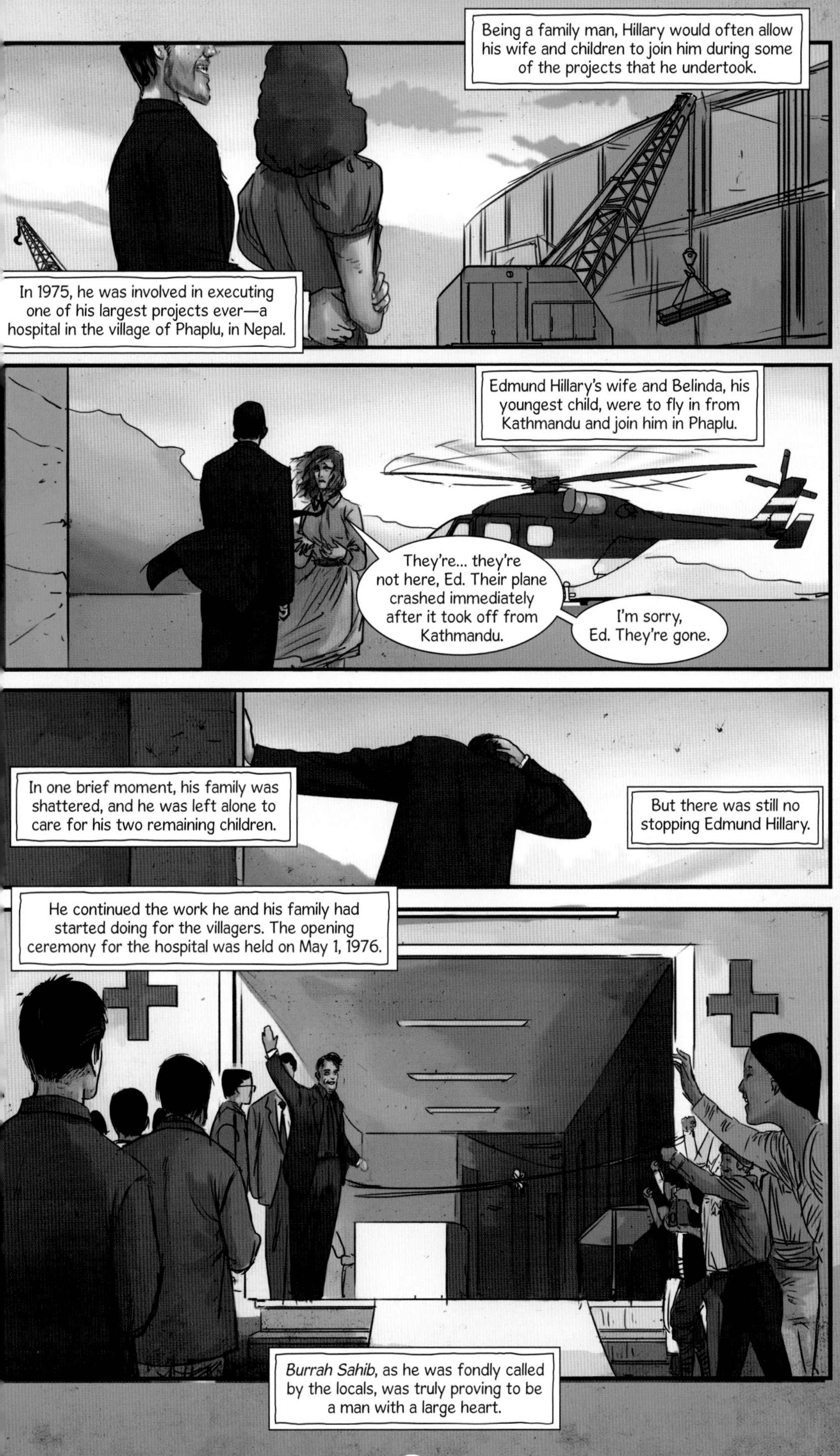

Being a family man, Hillary would often allow his wife and children to join him during some of the projects that he undertook.
In 1975, he was involved in executing one of his largest projects ever—a hospital in the village of Phaplu, in Nepal.
Edmund Hillary's wife and Belinda, his youngest child, were to fly in from Kathmandu and join him in Phaplu.
They're... they're not here, Ed. Their plane crashed immediately after it took off from Kathmandu.
I'm sorry, Ed. They're gone.
In one brief moment, his family was shattered, and he was left alone to care for his two remaining children.
But there was still no stopping Edmund Hillary.
He continued the work he and his family had started doing for the villagers. The opening ceremony for the hospital was held on May 1, 1976.
Burrah Sahib, as he was fondly called by the locals, was truly proving to be a man with a large heart.

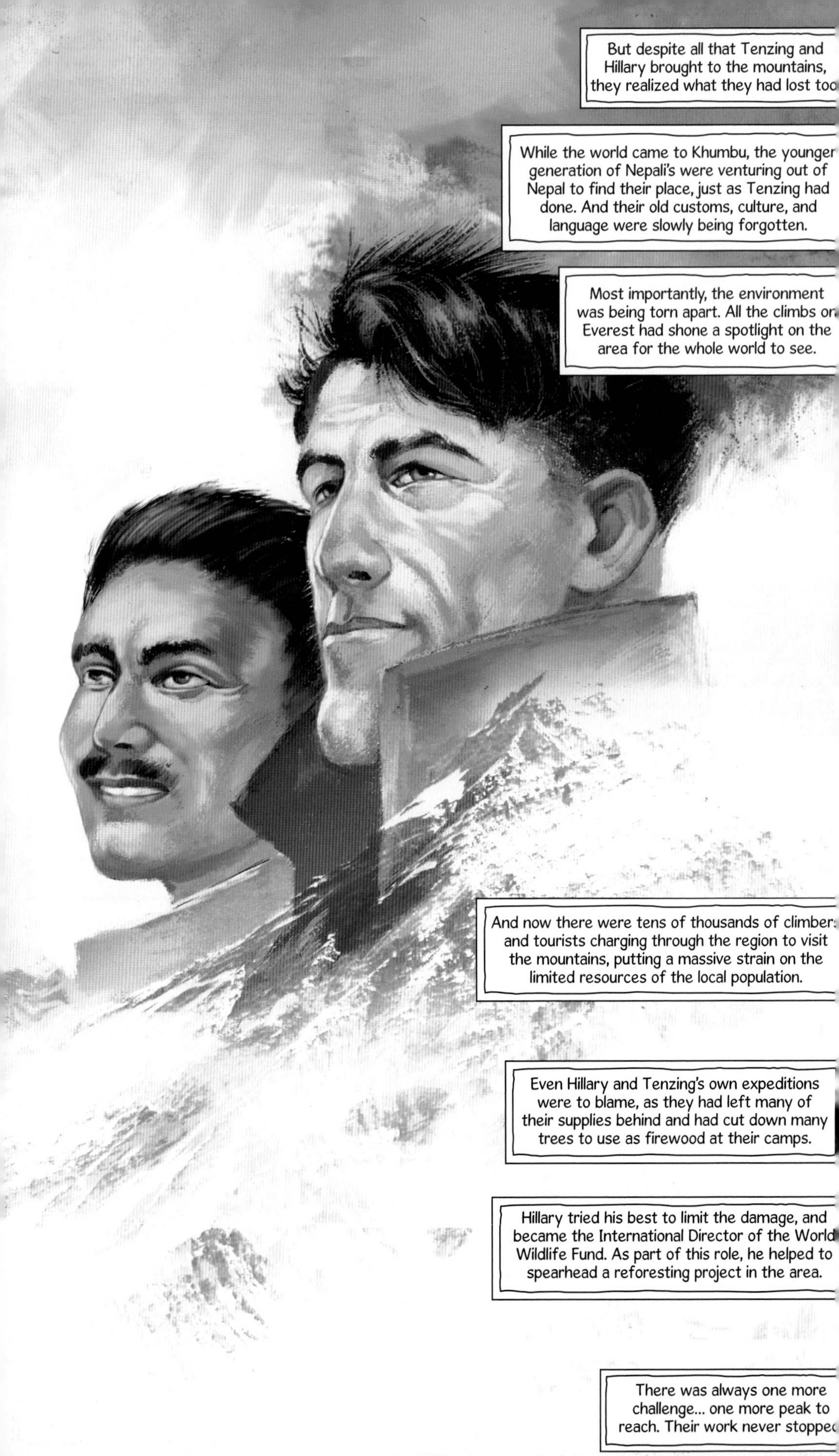
But despite all that Tenzing and Hillary brought to the mountains, they realized what they had lost too
While the world came to Khumbu, the younger generation of Nepali's were venturing out of Nepal to find their place, just as Tenzing had done. And their old customs, culture, and language were slowly being forgotten.
Most importantly, the environment was being torn apart. All the climbs on Everest had shone a spotlight on the area for the whole world to see.
And now there were tens of thousands of climbers and tourists charging through the region to visit the mountains, putting a massive strain on the limited resources of the local population.
Even Hillary and Tenzing's own expeditions were to blame, as they had left many of their supplies behind and had cut down many trees to use as firewood at their camps.
Hillary tried his best to limit the damage, and became the International Director of the World Wildlife Fund. As part of this role, he helped to spearhead a reforesting project in the area.
There was always one more challenge... one more peak to reach. Their work never stopped

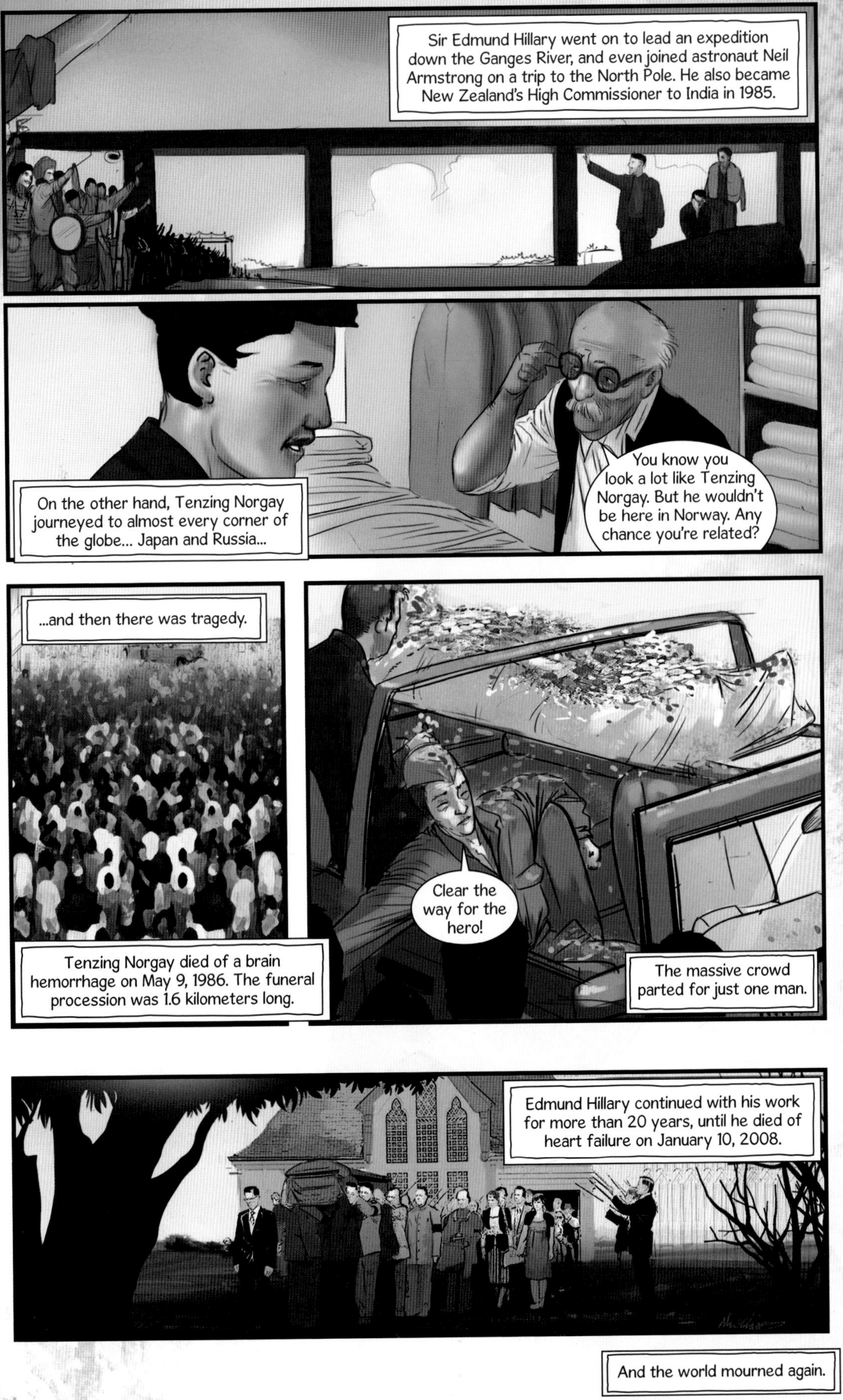
Sir Edmund Hillary went on to lead an expedition down the Ganges River, and even joined astronaut Neil Armstrong on a trip to the North Pole. He also became New Zealand's High Commissioner to India in 1985.
On the other hand, Tenzing Norgay journeyed to almost every corner of the globe... Japan and Russia...
You know you look a lot like Tenzing Norgay. But he wouldn't be here in Norway. Any chance you're related?
...and then there was tragedy.
Tenzing Norgay died of a brain hemorrhage on May 9, 1986. The funeral procession was 1.6 kilometers long.
Clear the way for the hero!
The massive crowd parted for just one man.
Edmund Hillary continued with his work for more than 20 years, until he died of heart failure on January 10, 2008.
And the world mourned again.

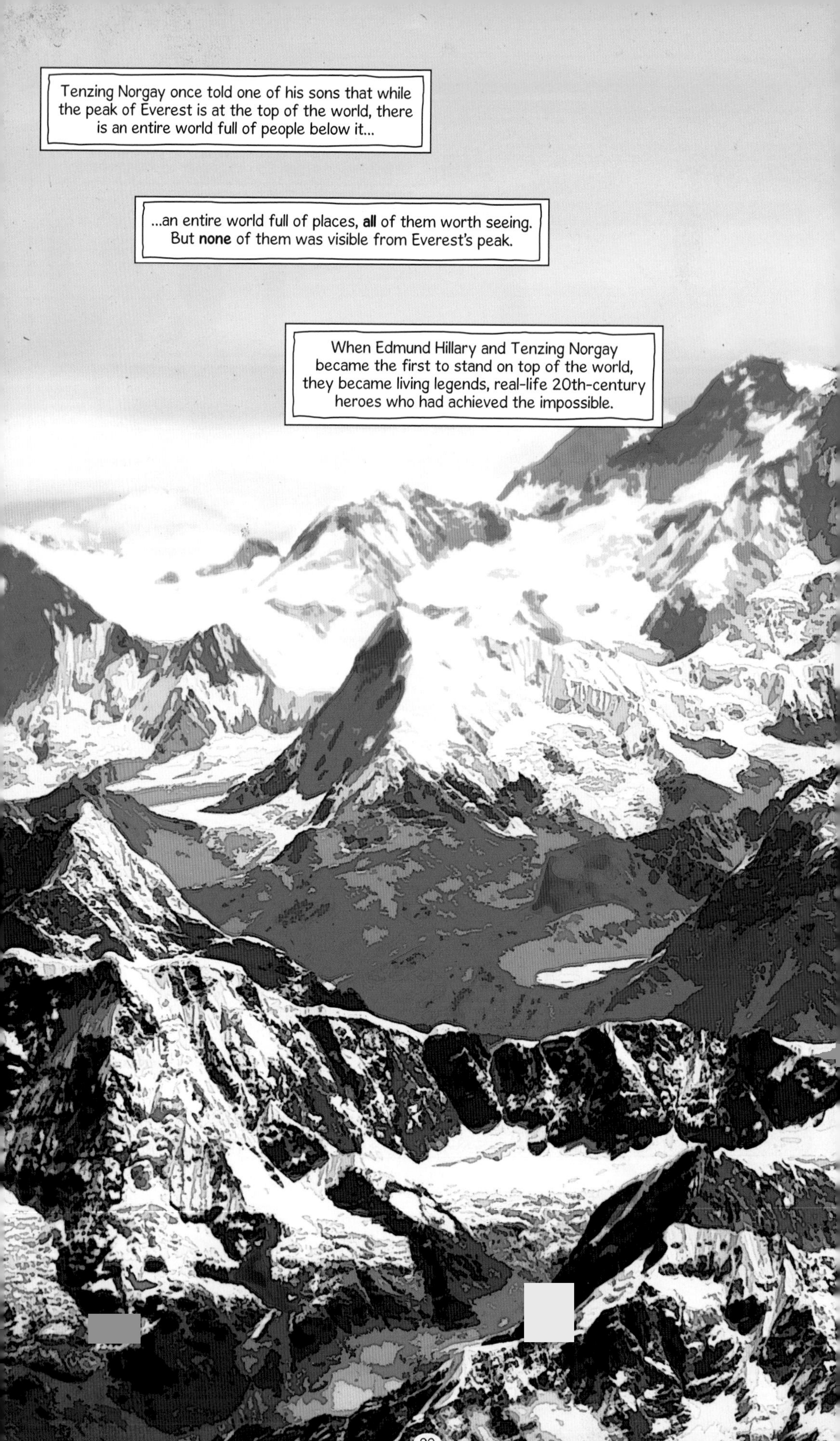
Tenzing Norgay once told one of his sons that while the peak of Everest is at the top of the world, there is an entire world full of people below it...
...an entire world full of places, **all** of them worth seeing. But **none** of them was visible from Everest's peak.
When Edmund Hillary and Tenzing Norgay became the first to stand on top of the world, they became living legends, real-life 20th-century heroes who had achieved the impossible.

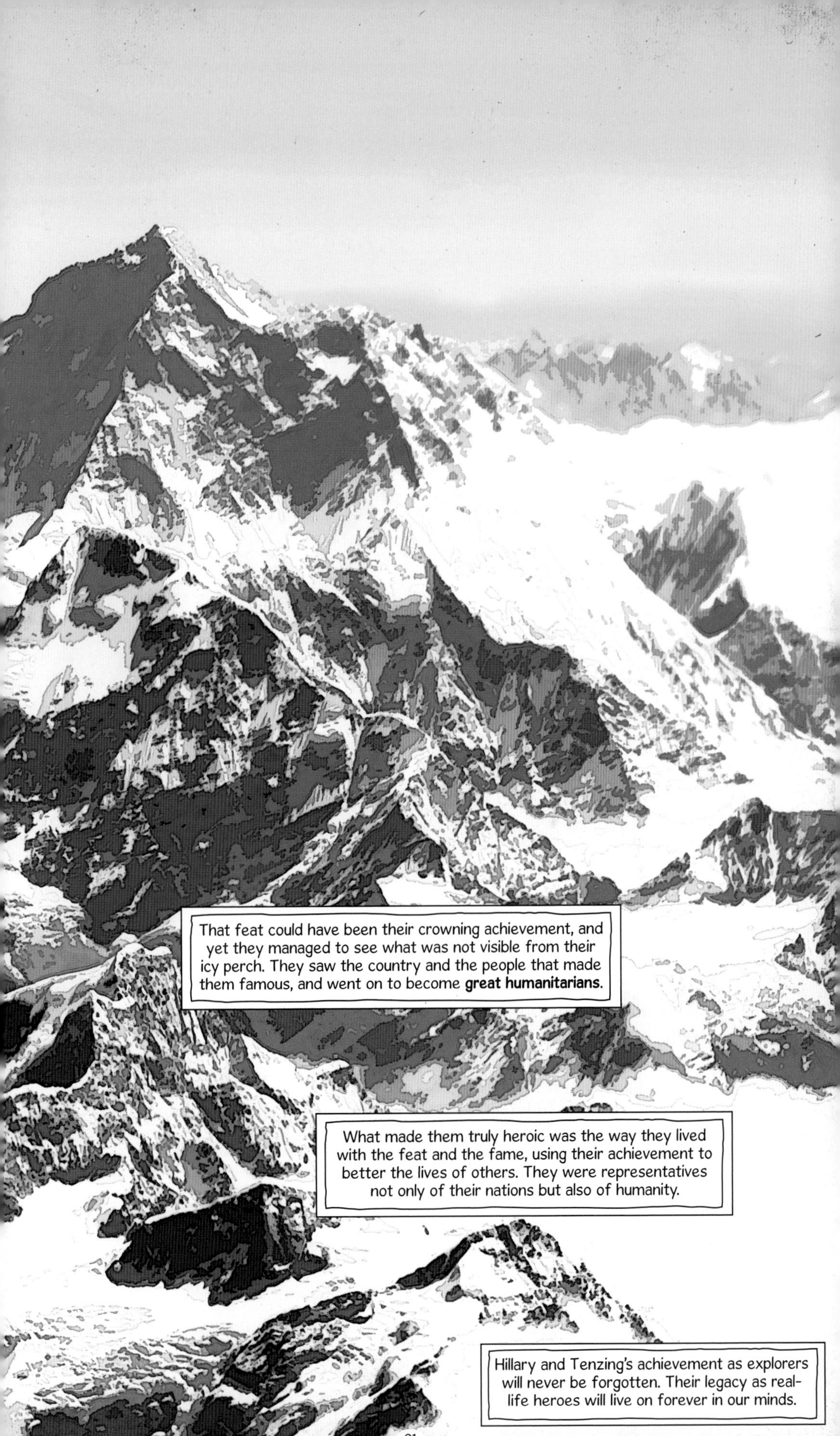
That feat could have been their crowning achievement, and yet they managed to see what was not visible from their icy perch. They saw the country and the people that made them famous, and went on to become **great humanitarians**.
What made them truly heroic was the way they lived with the feat and the fame, using their achievement to better the lives of others. They were representatives not only of their nations but also of humanity.
Hillary and Tenzing's achievement as explorers will never be forgotten. Their legacy as real-life heroes will live on forever in our minds.

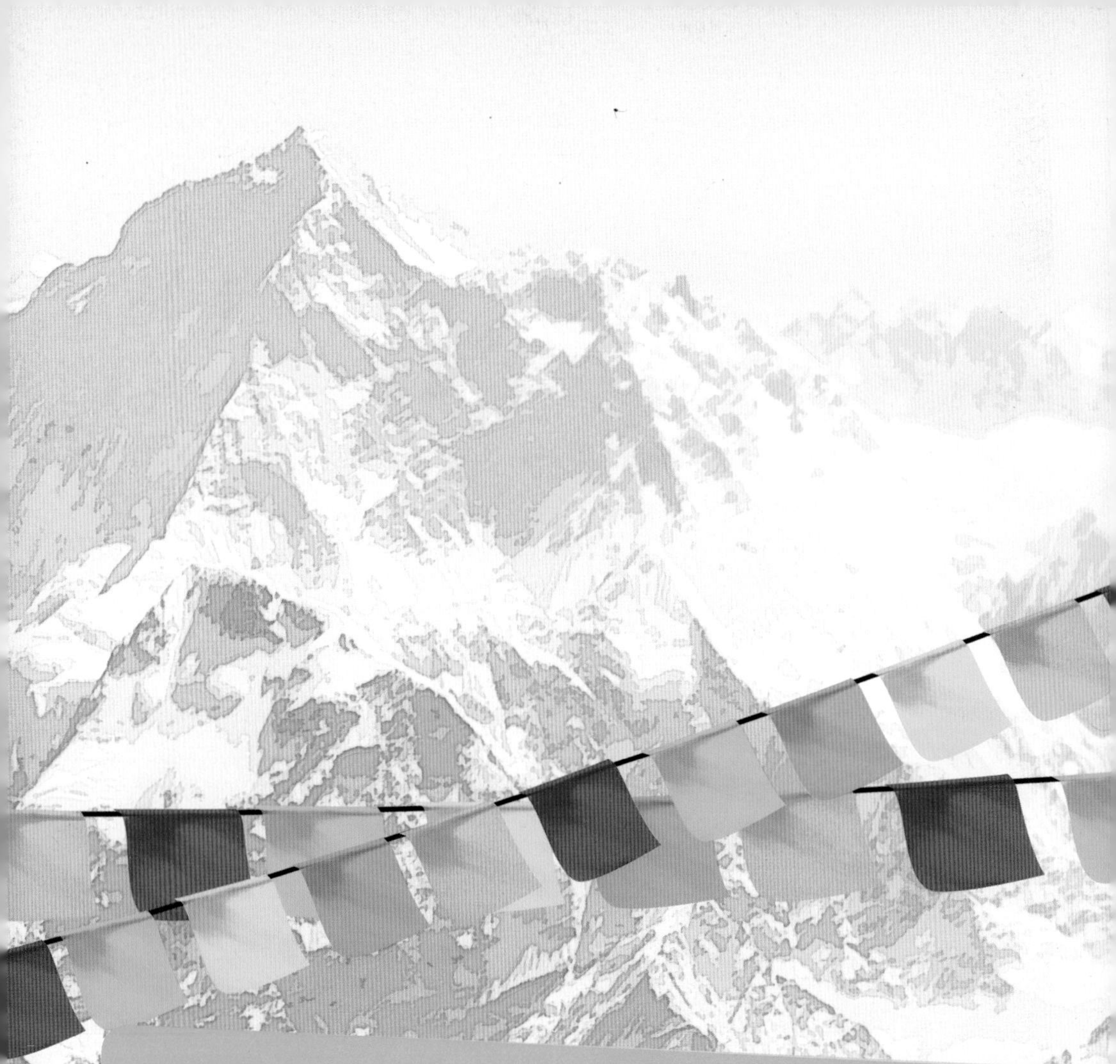

GLOSSARY

Anna: Currency that was formerly used in India, equaling 1/16 of a rupee.

Burrah Sahib: Man of stature.

Himalayan Club: The Indian organization that helped to arrange expeditions.

Icefall: A mass of constantly shifting and flowing ice that can create impossible crevasses or holes.

Lhotse: The world's fourth highest mountain at 8,516 meters.

North Col: The pass connecting Mt. Everest and Chagtse in Tibet.

Sherpas: People originally from Tibet, now settled in Nepal, living high in the Himalayas, who are employed as guides for mountaineering expeditions.

Sirdar: The chief Sherpa in charge of all the Sherpas and porters.

South Col: The path connecting the peak of Lhotse and Mt. Everest, which is taken by explorers to cross over to Everest.

Supply lines: The route over which food and gear are delivered.

Western Cwm (pronounced *coom*): A deep, icy valley leading to Lhotse.

NELSON MANDELA

This is the story of a man who was branded a terrorist, spent twenty-seven years in jail as a political prisoner, and later triumphed to become the father of the Republic of South Africa. This is the story of Nelson Mandela.

As a young man growing up in a small South African village, Nelson Mandela had very simple dreams. He dreamed of being free to choose his own path in life. But being a black man in South Africa—a nation ruled by an oppressive and discriminatory set of laws known as apartheid—even the simple dream of freedom could never become a reality.

Mandela did not give up and took the lead in the fight for the equality of all races. The government of South Africa responded to his pleas for justice by trying to crush him.

Mandela was stripped of his rights, and sent to the harshest prison in all of South Africa to die. But Nelson Mandela's spirit could not be broken. From his tiny prison cell, Nelson Mandela managed to rally the entire world behind his fight for justice. He even taught his oppressors the value of tolerance and compassion, and he brought freedom to an entire nation.

"For to be free is not merely to cast off one's chains, but to live in a way that respects and enhances the freedom of others."

–Nelson Mandela

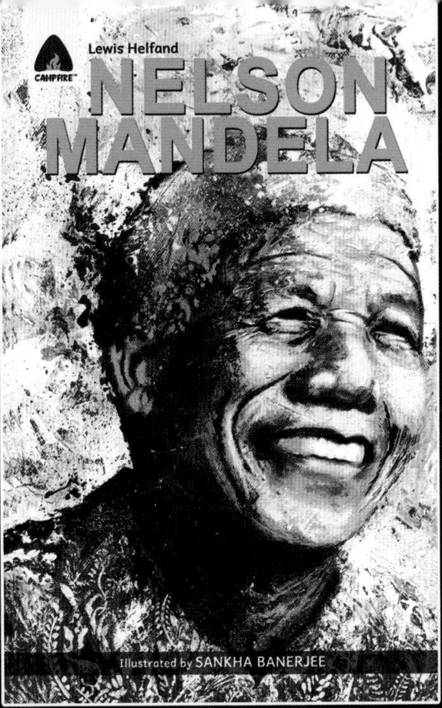

Lewis Helfand
CAMPFIRE
NELSON MANDELA
Illustrated by SANKHA BANERJEE

Written by Lewis Helfand
Illustrated by Sankha Banerjee

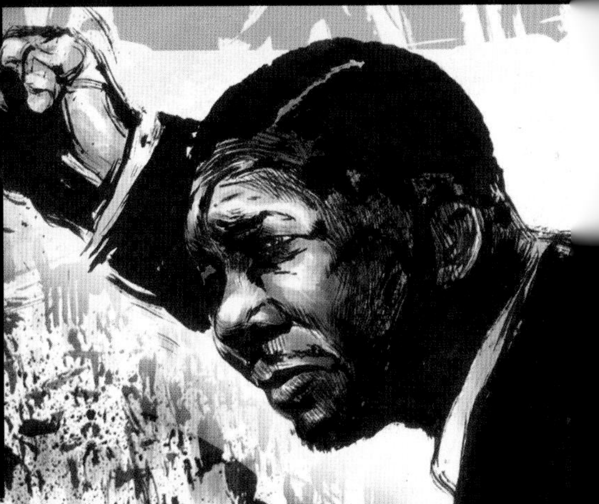
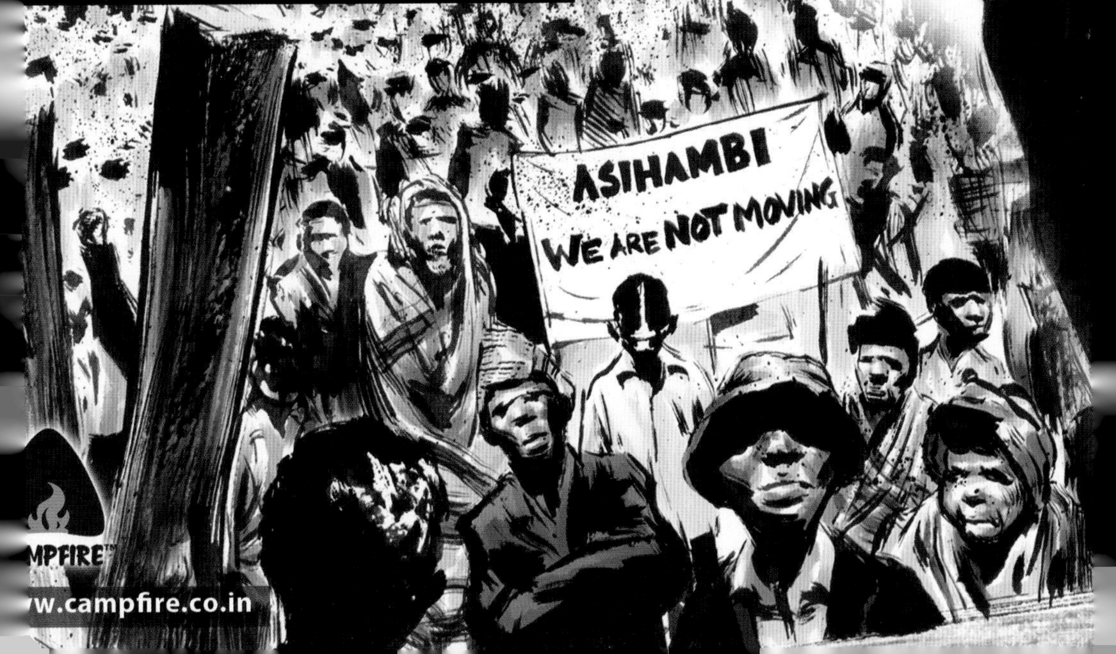

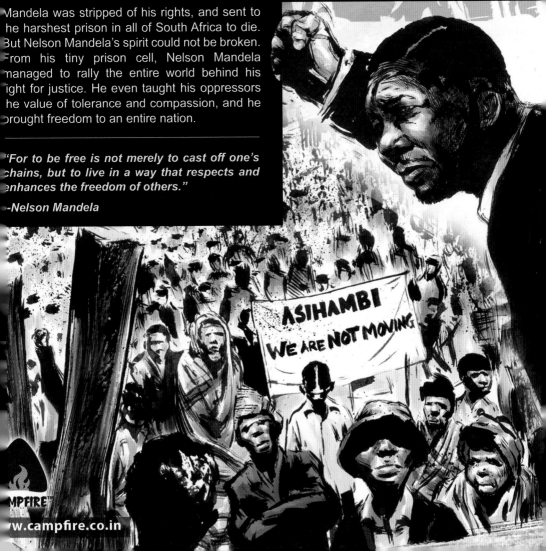

ASIHAMBI
WE ARE NOT MOVING

STANDING ON TOP OF THE WORLD

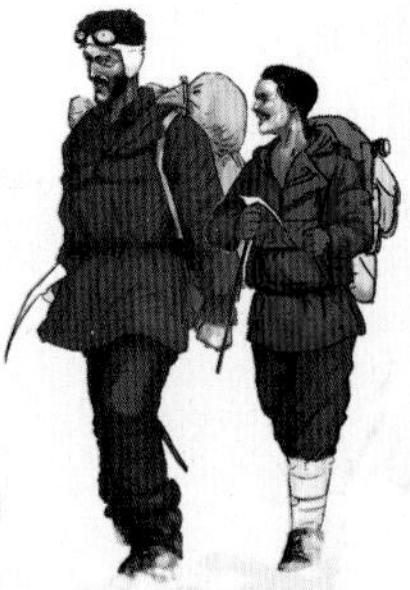

The ultimate test of endurance and one of the most grueling climbs, Mt. Everest, the highest mountain in the world, attracts experienced mountaineers year after year. And some of the people who have been successful in making it to the highest point on Earth, despite all the hazardous conditions, have been teenagers! Let's take a look at some of these young achievers.

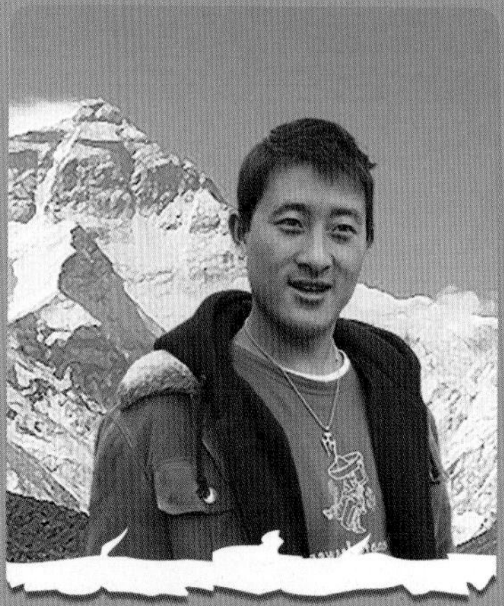

On May 22, 2001, fifteen-year-old Temba Tseri from Nepal became the youngest person to reach the top of Mt. Everest from the Tibetan side. But this feat was not achieved that easily. In June 2000, Temba had made his first attempt to climb Everest, but bad weather conditions had forced him to turn back when he was just 70 feet from the summit! He suffered frostbite on both hands, and five of his fingers had to be amputated. But that did not stop him from giving it another go. In 2001, he tried again, and this time he was successful.

At the age of sixteen, Arjun Vajpai added a new chapter to Indian mountaineering history by becoming the youngest Indian to reach the summit of Mt. Everest. His long-cherished dream of scaling Everest came true on May 22, 2010. An adventure-loving twelfth-grade student, Arjun is also a national taekwondo champion and has a keen interest in sports, especially volleyball and basketball. Arjun's team was led by Apa Sherpa, who broke his own record by becoming the only man to have scaled Everest twenty times!

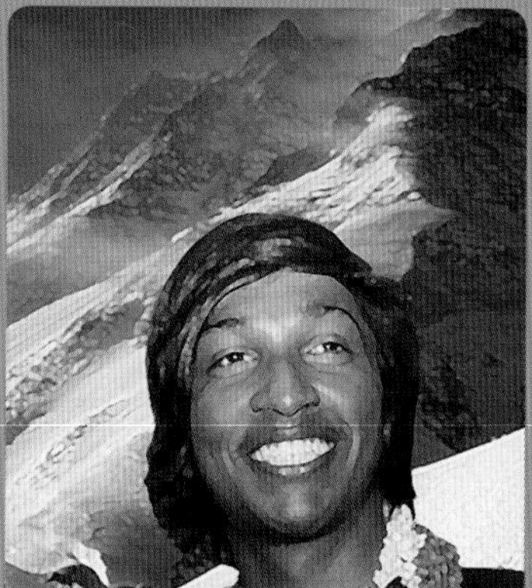

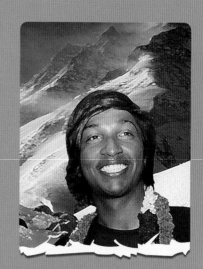

Just a few hours after Arjun Vajpai reached the top of the world, Jordan Romero, a thirteen-year-old boy from Big Bear, California, USA, created history and broke all previous records by becoming the youngest person to have scaled Everest. Jordan's ascent began from Tibet, as the Nepalese authorities do not give climbing permits to anyone under the age of sixteen. His dream is to climb the highest peaks of all the seven continents in the world, out of which he has already scaled six!

SHERPA POWER

Sherpas have always been an integral part of Everest expeditions. Let's find out more about them.

Over 500 years ago, a group of Tibetan Buddhists, known as Sherpas, moved from Tibet to a region near Mt. Everest in Nepal in order to be closer to the mountain they held sacred. The Sherpas are suited to the rigors of high-altitude climbing, and thus play a very important role in Everest climbing expeditions. Today, Sherpas constitute one quarter of the total number of people climbing Mt. Everest.

THE MANY NAMES OF MOUNT EVEREST

- Most people in Nepal call Mt. Everest *Sagarmatha*, which means 'forehead in the sky'.
- Speakers of the Tibetan language call Mt. Everest *Chomolungma*. It means 'Goddess Mother of the world'. In Tibet, it is also known as *Qomolangma*.
- People in Darjeeling, India, call Everest *Deodungha*, which means 'holy mountain'.
- Due to its extremity in terms of height, Mt. Everest is also known as the Third Pole, the other two being the North Pole and the South Pole.

DID YOU KNOW?

- Mt. Everest is approximately sixty million years old!
- Tibet, India and Nepal are the countries visible from the summit.
- Mt. Everest grows one centimeter every year!
- Mt. Everest is home to a very small black jumping spider, of the *Euophrys omnisuperstes* (which means 'standing above everything') species. These spiders lurk in crevices and feed on frozen insects. Their food depends mostly on what is blown by the wind into the area where they reside.